How Economists Think

Many philosophers today take the empiricist or rationalist stance that mainstream economics is self-centered and naïve. For their part too, most economists don't know much formal philosophy.

The purpose of the present book is to help bridge this great divide between philosopher and economist. Arguing for the person-centered mainstream economics over what would be an objects-centered scientific one, it makes a systematic case that the epistemology of the economics used in research and teaching today derives from the philosophy of Immanuel Kant. On these grounds it is shown that understanding modern economics is a matter of becoming familiar with Kant's interpretative forms of perception, judgment, and reason.

It will be vital reading for philosophers, economists, and others interested in these two critical professions.

Steven Buccola is Emeritus Professor in the Department of Applied Economics at Oregon State University, where his research has focused on the economics of science and technology and his teaching on graduate-level microeconomic theory. He is Distinguished Fellow and Past President of the Agricultural and Applied Economics Association, was Editor of the *American Journal of Agricultural Economics*, a Visiting Scholar at Harvard University, a Wade Awardee for Excellence in Teaching at Oregon State University, and a committee member with the National Research Council, National Academies, Washington, D.C., in a review of USDA-funded research.

Routledge Frontiers of Political Economy

The Political Economy of Mediterranean Europe
A Growth Models Perspective
Luis Cárdenas and Javier Arribas

Economics for Humanity
Integrating Well-being, Community, and Practical Philosophy
Mitsuaki Okabe

Sustainable Economic Development
Perspectives from Political Economy and Economics Pluralism
Edited by Giorgos Meramveliotakis and Manolis Manioudis

The Myth of the Global Market
A Marxist Critique of Neoliberalism
Giulio Palermo

Government and Economic Growth in the 21st Century
A Classical Liberal Response
Edited by Juan E. Castañeda

Political Economy in Middle East and North-Africa
Why Institutions, Rents and Power Matter in Economic Reforms
Rachid Mira

How Economists Think
A Kantian Interpretation of Mainstream Economics
Steven Buccola

For more information about this series, please visit: www.routledge.com/Routledge-Frontiers-of-Political-Economy/book-series/SE0345

How Economists Think

A Kantian Interpretation of Mainstream Economics

Steven Buccola

Routledge
Taylor & Francis Group
LONDON AND NEW YORK

First published 2025
by Routledge
4 Park Square, Milton Park, Abingdon, Oxon OX14 4RN

and by Routledge
605 Third Avenue, New York, NY 10158

Routledge is an imprint of the Taylor & Francis Group, an informa business

British Library Cataloguing-in-Publication Data
A catalogue record for this book is available from the British Library

ISBN: 9781032847122 (hbk)
ISBN: 9781032847092 (pbk)
ISBN: 9781003514602 (ebk)

DOI: 10.4324/9781003514602

Typeset in Times New Roman
by Newgen Publishing UK

Contents

Acknowledgment

My great and lasting thanks to J.-C. Spender for his thoughts and support throughout the later parts of this authorship.

Introduction

We hear often of the earthquake in the history of reason that was the downfall of the Middle Ages and dawn of the Enlightenment. Missing in this attractive though monochromatic narrative is that differences quickly developed over what enlightenment would constitute. The differences were wide and deep. The Enlightenment is a house divided. Unsurprisingly then, two fundamentally different views of economics now compete for the world's attention – two contrary notions, in fact, of what economics *is*.

Their common element is that both were sympathetic to science and did their part in founding it. Both recognized, in its own way, that to do modern science was to stand back from the world – in outer space as it were – and view it as an object. A freshman biology instructor once introduced himself by presenting each of us with an odd-looking fish swimming about in an otherwise empty glass bowl. Our assignment was to describe what we saw, using, he emphasized, no prior presumptions, references, or similes, just this one thing before us. We couldn't even say 'fish.' Now here was an effective science instructor.

Every Enlightenment thinker embraced in some circumstances, and still embraces, this objectivity and the general spirit it implies. To some however, the idea that a human person in particular can be viewed as an object was problematic. Can an individual person, insofar *as* a person, stand outside of – resist reduction to – a thing, namely to science? The great rift in today's Enlightenment is a rift over this question. And economics is one of its chief battlegrounds.

The book you are about to read tells the story of the encounter between these two attitudes toward economic reason. Our focus will be as much on intellectual attitude as on particular methods and models. The conflict and complementarity between economic objecthood and personhood is, we will argue, the implied topic of every university lecture, op-ed piece, and opinion blog. As a factor in every economic decision – public and private – the difference between thing and person is uppermost. Yet it is rarely thought about as such. It is usually left between the lines, an uneasy sense of it bubbling below.

We will take a position on the issue, favoring the person-centered contemporary economics over the thing-centered metalogical, metascientific one. A position must, as we will see, be staked. And our understanding will be enhanced when we

DOI: 10.4324/9781003514602-1

do. It is no exaggeration to say that about 90% of books and articles on the *philosophy* of economics today take the empiricist stance that the mainstream view is narrow and simplistic. Yet in instruction, textbooks, and journals – that is in economics itself – it remains the dominant guide to research, meaning, and practice. To avoid the circularity of claiming that most practioners do what is contemporary, I should clarify: most economists teach what Mas-Colell, Whinston, and Green do in virtually all of their graduate text *Microeconomic Theory*. Or to say this differently, in most of today's English-speaking philosophy it is mainstream economics that is heterodox. Yet economic practitioners listen lopsidedly to, well, Mas-Colell, Whinston, and Green.

With the mainstream continuing dominant in economic work and analytics in the assessment of its legitimacy, a correction seems in order. The present book takes a step in this direction. We begin by asking: why do economic practitioners largely disregard their critics in the philosophy profession? By way of anticipating some answers, a few words on what we will mean – and more importantly not mean – by mainstream economics. It isn't individualistic. To the contrary, everyone in it is involved with everyone else. It doesn't operate in 'competitive' or 'perfect information' settings, which are metaphors only, but in ex-ante uncertain ones. It doesn't assume simplistic goals like profit but largely indefinable ones. It isn't airy or abstract despite the equations you see on the whiteboard but conditioned by an individual person's circumstances. How can this be? Because economics doesn't claim to know the world as it 'actually' or 'really' is but only to interpret it, to be a useful decision tool. And finally, and for this reason, it doesn't reduce the world to objects as science must.

The spirit of the scientific is of quite a different order. If the point of economic reason is to face uncertainty, the point of metalogical, empiricist reason is to avoid it. Its objective, as science, is to be certain. Being-certain takes two possible forms. It can be a principle broad or insightful enough that you're confident it is true, in which case anything deduced from it is true as well (rationalism). Or it can be something you measure – taken literally to mean touched, seen, or heard, then correlated (empiricism). Either way, literality of speech, something fully in your head or in your hand, is the sign of these positivist certitudes.

What then would a scientized economics look like? It would immerse itself in principles and definitions or in data and their combinations. It would require no modeling at all or look iteratively for one. It would measure nothing or everything. It would prefer, in general, psychology over risky judgment and in some camps biology over psychology. It would think of uncertainty as ignorance and combat it with more learning. Focus on classes over individuals and breadth over context. It would prefer working with human aggregates, where standard errors of estimate are low. It is mentalist, neuralist, welfarist, and machine language. It is science, literally.

Frank Knight, Fritz Machlup, Lionel Robbins, James Buchanan, Gary Becker, Joseph Schumpeter, and other economists of the early and mid-20th century contributed much to a consistent, rigorous comparison of the economic versus scientific attitude. To do so here is to focus on the principal economic themes and their contemporary vs metalogical interpretations, including scarcity, uncertainty, utility, equilibrium, demand, supply, duality, wealth, and cost. And it is to show their importance for the major economic questions of our day. Said otherwise, this book is a bid to restore to economics the philosophical voice it had at least from the time of J.S. Mill (yes, J.S. Mill!) but in decline since the mid-20th century.

It isn't premature to lay out in simple terms the thesis of this book. It is that contemporary economics, especially in the last century and a half, operates at two levels or spheres of reality. The first and better known is the 'professor': the spokesperson, journalist, or other articulator. The second, more private and less known, is the person herself, the individual decision maker. The professor deals in apparent causes and effects and other apparently literal, mechanical-sounding language. The decision maker he describes on the other hand speaks ultimately in no language whatever – the dimension of judgment, morality, and freedom, which ultimately escape words.

If taken to be speaking literally, the professor could, we will see, have a rather limited amount to say anyway, confined to price and quantity observations that reduce us to inductive logic alone. We therefore must keep this two-tiered setting and its implications for the distinction between literal and metaphorical speech constantly in mind. This we confess may be difficult if you're a mechanically accustomed thinker, for whom truth and articulation are the same. But it will not, we hope, be impossible. What *will* be clear is that a two-tiered, two-leveled economic reason is virtually impossible to grasp without reference to Immanuel Kant, who was, partly thanks to Hume, its virtual discoverer and originator.

Our first two chapters compare the foundational literatures of a mainstream and a scientized economics and the underlying gulf between them. Chapter I focuses on the mainstream's attention to individual persons, to be aggregated with care, in contrast to the positivist's interest in classes and their reduction to measure. Such focus requires examining the nature of judgment, understanding, and decision making. We will find it to be the process in a person of drawing a manifold of appearances up into concepts, expressing thereby the form or possibility of a situation in a way suitable for judgment. Because form is possibility only, an interpretation of a specifically encountered situation, economic cognition is always tentative, never fully defined, only an aid to decision.

Final indefinability is the opening to human freedom and the voice of moral responsibility. Here also will be the distinction between the cause-effect sound of economic theory on the one side and the ultimately free individual on the other, who because she is free, needn't conform to the prof's models and theorems – isn't bound up in cause and effect at all. Today's economics therefore speaks of cause only analogically. In this way it allows human reality to remain itself, and by only pointing to it, releasing any claim to know and control it directly. We examine this symbolical path – and its clarity about what can and cannot be observed – in detail, contrasting it with intents to quantify well-being.

Chapter II examines the positivist alternatives to mainstream economics: the exclusively *a priori* or rationalist and the exclusively empiricist. In both, we show, economic expression must be literal, restricting its reference to classes or groups.

Singular pronouns must be dropped, a feature it shares with the classical economics of the early 1800s. Subjectivity and objectivity each turn out to be an object, where dogmatic claims supersede individuals' fallible judgments. Uncertainty, a matter for persons only, is replaced with the ignorance that can always be engaged-in with more analysis.

Earlier instances of this kind of thought are, on the rationalist side, in the philosopher Gottfried Leibniz and economist David Ricardo. On the empiricist side they are in David Hume – though disputably so, I argue, because Hume didn't always intend his words literally. We will see that rationalism ineluctably finds itself peeking ahead to its empirical outcomes, just as empiricism peaks back at its axioms. We discuss the economic philosophy literature's frequent confusion on these scores, if only in mistaking modern economics' indirect, metaphorical speech for something direct and literal. We find that an economic decision is more an act of openness and judgment than of syllogism or measure, never to be captured in generalized, abstractive language.

The second two chapters peer into economic epistemology more specifically. Chapter III considers economics' epicenter, utility, where your capacity to intuit something is brought together with your capacity to generalize it. Economics, everyone knows, is about goods and services and their various representations – such as money, income, and cost – and about how we assess them by way of supply and demand. All these come together in utility, a symbol of their joint meaning and implication in particular contexts. Every economics student 'gets' that utility has this internal, finally inexpressible character, is nothing like a thing you can see or record. Professors don't need to explain this to any of us. We already know it. Utility quite obviously is never defined, only intuited and meditated upon.

Revealed preference theory was a mid-20th century effort to escape such indefinability by searching for visible consistencies in how people make choices. Inconsistency in a revealed-preference story implies irrationality. This is partly right, but the story has been unable to explain *how* rational decisions are formulated in the first place and why, therefore, reason can never be relegated to just consistency. You will see that mainstream theory addresses rationality too – in the intersection of the Marshallian and Hicksian demand functions, the former expressed in terms of observable prices and quantities and the latter in terms of prices and *un*observable, suprasensible utility. We show how this intersection is an instance of the *synthetic a priori* of Immanuel Kant, a one-to-one mapping between the specificity of a given situation and the articulability of ideas.

One finds that in the uniqueness of the mapping between the Marshall and Hicks demands, the human situation is rescued from abstraction and a person from generality. This rescue in turn explains why, for instance, economists can derive counterfactuals – estimates of how somebody would have behaved had circumstances been otherwise – and how these counterfactuals clarify the distinction between an observation or measure and a judgment or model estimate. We will show how rationalist and empiricist economics are incapable of this kind of interpretation, reducing it instead to a plan that was never followed.

Chapter IV takes these questions further. Economics is about decision making – in fact is the origin and seat of it. And decisions, we all know, involve risk, whether explicitly modeled or not. Efforts such as expected utility and neural decision models to reduce risk or uncertainty to something measurable have a problematic though useful history. We will look at these problematic efforts in depth, underscoring their common theme of trying to reduce the unknown future to something certain. Alas, reductions of the human condition and its ambiguities to abstractions turn out to be futile, a futility evident in what we'll show to be the circular nature of terms like 'well-being.'

We will see the only way out of such circularity is the contemporary (though often hidden) economic theme of completeness and equilibrium, remembering these are symbolic, interpretive expressions only. We can and do estimate them as ways of stabilizing our grasp of a particular situation. But despite their rigorous mathematical formulation they are suggestive notions only, nothing literal. Mainstream theory therefore, as opposed to the rationalist and empiricist goal of reducing economics to directly realized entities, is only an analogical representation of underlying personal reality.

The third set of chapters assesses the influence of the above critique on the major issues of our day. Chapter V focuses on information, strategy, and human capital. Information itself, seeming to transcend persons altogether and constitute a reality of its own, opened a new door to economic thought. Neurological models of rationality began to supersede even the psychological ones, reducing knowledge to synapse and brain function and codified in machine learning and artificial intelligence. The mark of these developments has been their reliance on data and correlation, namely ex-post logic, a reduction to observed facts. We will take a tour through this devolution with a view to its problematic sustainability. We show again that, confined to observed actualities, to facts, unaided analytical reason is deprived of context. Human capital, the integration of subjecthood and objecthood where uncertainties are faced and prepared for, is an answer to the problem.

Finally, Chapter VI asks whether the empiricist view of economics might ever come to agreement with the Kantian. In asking this we return to the role in both schools of counterfacts, the empiricist taking them only as what was planned to happen but didn't and so confining them to measurement. We will walk through the logic of economic inference as empiricism envisages it, a stress on the priority of sufficient causes and so a 'real' world over the necessary causes that give only surety and confidence. In contrast is the uniting of the observable with the unobservable in mainstream economics, bringing the empirical into conjunction with the rational. Prospects for bridging this epistemological gap between empiricist and mainstream are shown to be strongest among Neo-Kantians. Here a synthesis is possible between a moral and logical reason on one side and a cognitive on the other, offering a compromise between a conceptualist and a singularist account of causation that would touch up against mainstream economics.

Main Hypotheses of This Work

Regarding Metaphysical Foundations

Person and Thing are distinct domains of reality.
Person is irreducible to Thing.

Regarding Economic Meaning

Economic meaning is primarily about a person – only derivatively about classes (generalizations, things).

We must therefore, as possibility, anticipate a conclusion's meaning before we derive it, or could never *recognize* it as derivable.

Regarding Economic Inference

No economic conclusion is derived from generalizations (correlations) alone but from possible experience first.

We must therefore, as possibility, anticipate a conclusion's validity before we infer it, or could never *recognize* it as inferable.

Regarding Economic Content

Economics follows a two-tier epistemic framework: *professional* synthetic-a-priori reasoning about how *persons* reason synthetic-a-priori. The professional tier must be articulated, the personal tier need not. Articulation derives from the pure categories of cause and effect. Decision, being free, does not.

No free decision can ever be finally articulated, let alone by someone else. And since professional economics can be privy to no one's particular situation, it can articulate itself only symbolically: analogically, metaphorically.

The seminal categories of economics – cost, scarcity, equilibrium, utility, uncertainty – are references to personal situations. They are transcendental, so only estimated and judged, never directly observed.

DOI: 10.4324/9781003514602-2

Cost relations are pure schemata: mappings between pure intuition and the categories of our understanding. They are not measurable or factual – only estimable and interpretable in given settings.

Thus, economics is also a reflection on possible situations, a looking-ahead, an *ex-ante* relation to time. If a person could be defined economically, it would be as a looking-ahead.

Let's see now how we do in demonstrating these points.

I The Essence of Economics

Economics has a problematic relationship with meaning. It likely is the only quantitative way of thinking to be concerned with a person as such, and the only concern for a person as such to be expressed quantitatively. Most economists for this reason don't think themselves part of any larger category. They just do economics. Like it or not though, economists depend heavily on knowing how they know because they care about what it expresses. One thing for instance economics encounters in tying down one economic term is that it has a frustrating way of involving another. Capital is machines, buildings, and other stable resources. Stable resources are what, in some way, stay put. What then *isn't* capital? Well, whatever is labor. Yet labor – involving, say, skill development – finds itself being a capital. Economic textbooks and journal writers therefore don't even try defining these words in any literal or mechanical fashion.

The notion that they could be defined has its origins in Rene Descartes (1637) and his disciple Gottfried Leibniz (1676), who invented what Charles Taylor (1989) and others have called the disengaged self, one that can turn about and view itself as an object. What it sees is the object that had turned to look. New phenomena can be discovered in the very act of thinking them, as John Harsanyi (1955) did when he realized he could perceive someone's well-being by virtue of a 'sympathetic preference' that said he could. Conception and discovery were identical. A crucial point in recognizing this difficulty was David Hume (1739), who asked how the mere fact of one event (like a thought) could imply another (like a well-being). Was the well-being not something to be observed, an *empirical* phenomenon? How then could it be a consequence, an *intellectual* phenomenon? As we will see, Immanuel Kant took this question much deeper, setting the foundations for the economics that is pursued today.

In brief, we will show in this chapter that contrary to its mathematical appearance, contemporary economics focuses on the personal, concrete aspects of economic reality. Economics is specific to a context. Being quantitative as well though, it can only be an analog to what is personal. It is a concern about, and at the same time an openness to, a person facing a future. The mark of this ex-ante standpoint is that economic theory is a conjunction of the unobservable with the observable, unobservable scarcities joined with observable prices. The alternative

DOI: 10.4324/9781003514602-3

would be to disengage from personal context and fall back on the ex-post – on looking through the rearview mirror, on things that are direct and obvious. This in turn would be what we will call analytical, where concepts are either entirely axiomatic or entirely measured – either way semantic abstractions.

Causality *vs* Freedom in Human Reason

Let's first have a look at the foundation of contemporary economic reason, originating in Immanuel Kant and superseding the earlier one, had there been one, in Gottfried Leibniz. In doing so, we'll also be dwelling on the rationale for our hypotheses at the opening of this book.

Distinguishing between Possibility and Actuality

We start, following Lionel Robbins (1932), with a depiction of economics as a choice of ends or purposes in face of the available means. Economics' concern, Robbins says, is with tradeoffs among 'ends.' But only in a qualified way. "Economics is not concerned at all with any ends as such" but only "with ends insofar as they affect the disposition of means" (30). This disposition is influenced by technology. Technology however is a mere mechanism, to be sharply distinguished from economics. Thus, "economists are not interested in technique as such" either. "They are interested in it solely as one of the influences determining relative scarcity" (38). What then is scarcity? The answer is we don't know what it is *as such*. It is a manifold of impressions you assign to concepts in ways offering the clearest comparisons for decision-making purposes (Kant 1781, B106).

To emphasize economics' non-dogmatic character, Robbins writes, "... it is one of the characteristics of the world as we find it that our ends are various and that most of the scarce means at our disposal are capable of alternative application" (36). Economic decision is a matter of comparing situations that one only mutely senses, then considers in a way that makes them intelligible. This picture Robbins can only be getting from Kant, for whom "appearances are not things in themselves, only representations," as if they weren't, little could explain the possibility of our perceiving them in the first place, a possibility Kant calls "our faculty of intuition" (A109). "... Intuitions in general," Kant writes, "through which objects are given to us, constitute the field, the whole object, of possible experience" (A96, 81). If "this manifold is to be known, the spontaneity of our thought requires that it be gone through in a certain way, taken up, and connected" via concepts (B102, 71). Or as Robbins puts it in economics, "fundamental generalizations are known to us by immediate acquaintance" (105). They aren't, for instance, defined.

Note that Kant's and Robbins' concern here is with possibility, not any actuality (B106). The distinction between possibility and actuality, the former being the transcendental dimension of judgment and understanding, goes back at least to the early Greeks though often pushed aside since. Possibility for Kant involves both intuition and conception. The intuitive part is a capacity to receive. Pure intuition, says Kant, is "nothing but receptivity." The abstractive or categorial elements of understanding on the other hand are what allow us to remain consistent from one intuition to the next (R, 144). In the *Critique of Pure Reason* (1781) these are the pure concepts of quantity (unity, plurality), quality (reality, limitation), relation (causality, community), and modality (possibility, necessity), jointly necessary for any stable human experience (B106, 51). They "combine the manifold [of our intuitions] into one representation," writes Kant, drawing senses together into consistent, stable ideas (84).

Robbins' 'scarcity,' the source of a willingness-to-pay, comes under all four of these pure concepts because an economic valuation is a quality as well as quantity, involving comparisons with other goods in a way a bystander could say they 'caused' you to buy such-and-such (B106, 72). Only five years after the publication of Smith's *Wealth of Nations*, Kant had prefigured the discipline of economics and its circumspective refusal to claim any birds-eye view of reality, but only a fallible judgment of what appears best. Had we a direct vision of the world, focused on looking, correlating, and summarizing as an empiricist economics would do, causality would be next to obvious and precision and rigor at their uppermost, so no real decision would be going on.

The Paradox of Causality and Freedom

This isn't to say Kant's epistemology doesn't involve a necessity of its own. Desmond Hogan (2010) quotes Kant as emphasizing the importance of this necessitation or causality, though only for 'passive substances':

> The proposition: everything which happens has a determining ground, that is, something else which necessitates it, is the principle of the changes of all passive substances.... Reason comprehends [this] when it cognizes it *a priori*, that is through grounds.
>
> (R4338, Hogan 34)

In particular, as Hogan notes, "if something is given under the form of space and time, then it is governed by various mathematical and mechanical constraints..." (37). The 'passive substance' is what both Kant and Walras at the frontispiece of this book call 'things.'

Doesn't economics itself have a freedom problem in its notion of a 'decision' then? The overt language, at least, of economic theory routinely contradicts the possibility of any choice going on. Formal economic thinking is normally couched as optimizing a criterion function subject to constraints, implying force of some kind. And the related newsreel style of economics is couched in the form of one event, an interest rate say, causing another event like a stock selloff. Both speak in terms of one object pushing another. Economics, we've said, can't get along without cause and effect.

What then did the econ professor mean by insisting that this lockstep causation – a computation of optimal goals in the face of constraints, or an income change shifting a demand curve – is a 'decision making,' which must be a matter of freedom instead? Has no bewildered student ever raised his hand on this one? Perhaps the Immanuel Kant who was 'in the air' when academic economics was being conceived in the 19th century had priorly been interpreted as an exclusively pure reason, the necessity, indeed the prior deduction, of effects from causes, with all its suggestion of rigor and science and the prestige attending it.

To the contrary Kant emphasizes, in Hogan's words, "the absolute contingency to all and only free acts of finite rational agents" (34). And herein does Kant's argument that events in space and time are formal and transcendental rather than real or metaphysical have a distinct advantage, as in the absence of this distinction, reality is entirely "governed by various mathematical and mechanical constraints..." (37) and freedom of choice would be impossible. Writes Hogan:

> Kant's denial of the *a priori* knowability of 'first beginnings' can for this reason express his metaphysical claim that such features *lack* determining grounds. (38)

And freedom, synonymous with choice and with a world of entire contingency, is the essential condition of being human. So we have, between rigor and freedom, either a contradiction or a paradox. If a contradiction, one of the two must win, so a person would be either an ultimate robot or under no rational restraints whatever. If a paradox instead of a contradiction, both win: for our *a priori* power to know and its apparent reductions to causes and other determinations are for reasoning purposes only, no claim to know, in the face of freedom, any causes themselves.

Hogan reconstructs the paradox side of this question by showing that Kant locates our awareness of freedom outside of any sensed manifold or deduced category. It is our awareness in ourselves of a demand to act morally. If so, it is a demand that can be satisfied only if we choose to satisfy it. Every choice therefore, even if rendered as an optimization – simply following the math and thus inevitable – would have to be a 'first beginning' of some sort, not inevitable at all. Neither our intuitions nor generalizations – which might have an air of inevitability – would remain to enforce necessity. So the notion of cause and effect, action by necessity, would in economics also be chased out the window by the moral demand. Kant says in this spirit: "[Human] actions are not included under [cause and effect]....I now begin my state as I wish" (R4338, Hogan 34).

Recognizing this difference between cause and choice, Hogan quotes Kant as saying: "the system of the *Critique of Pure Reason* turns on two cardinal points as a system of nature and of freedom...the ideality of space and time and the reality of the concept of freedom" (R 6353, 6344, 6349, 38–39). Every free choice, unlike a passive substance, originates in a first beginning and so has no prior foundation, intuitive or categorical. It is an "*a priori* unknowability and absolute contingency" (39) which, as groundless, is inexplicable. In sum, writes Hogan,

> Kant acknowledges that his doctrine of absolute freedom introduces an essential theoretical unintelligibility into the world. There can be no full explanation as to

> why an absolutely free act is thus and not otherwise – such explanation would have to infer the act from a determining ground that is absent by hypothesis. (35)

Of freedom, a first-beginning at every moment, there can be neither a pure intuition nor a pure concept, which must, in the act of judgment, be linked together.

Note that this doctrine of theoretical unintelligibility is also a doctrine of radical fallibility. As such it is a doctrine of profound uncertainty. This isn't a modern realization. Hannah Arendt (1958) writes of the honor accorded in ancient Greece to those with the courage to speak out in public – surrendering as they did any control of the consequences, namely the later interpretations of their words.

Arendt notes, what could apply to both the classical Greeks and the Kantian Enlightenment, that "it is in the nature of a beginning that something new is started which cannot be expected from whatever happened before.... The new always happens against the overwhelming odds of statistical laws and their probabilities, which for all practical, everyday purposes amount to certainty" (177–178). "Since action acts upon beings who are capable of their own actions, [there will] always [be] a new action that strikes out on its own…" (190). Profound uncertainty then, human indeterminacy or contingency, is the metaphysical price we pay for our inner moral voice.

The causal rigor of any *a priority*, and thus economic, understanding does on the surface seem to contradict the reality of free choice and its risks. Along with others, Hogan acknowledges that "this issue remains a complex and thorny one" (39), particularly to those oriented toward direct speech. Its solution is to look for the specific matters being considered in a decision problem. "Kant's replacement model of *a priori* knowledge," he says, "is not itself fully intelligible unless we give due consideration both to the specific content of the *a priori* knowledge he views as flowing from spatiotemporal form, and to the absolute contingency he upholds consistently from the mid-1760s" (Hogan 40).

In short, we can only reason in terms of cause and effect. But we 'know' – in economics at least, which deals with persons rather than the things of science – that the reality, the matter or metaphysics, is one of freedom. The formal or transcendental then, and its corresponding expression, is indirect and metaphorical rather than direct or literal. The specific matter Hogan is asking into is *persons* and who, able to visualize and reason only in causal *language*, know that reality itself is ultimately indeterminate, addressable only analogically.

Minimizing Metaphysics

Like Hogan, Lanier Anderson (2022) recognizes that Kant's doctrine of the reality of things outside us qualifies him as an empirical realist as well as formal idealist. "Kant himself continues to insist that appearances are 'really given'" (901). "I do not," Anderson quotes Kant, "say that bodies merely seem to exist outside me" (B69), but rather are "a thing outside me and not … the mere representation of a thing outside me" (B275). In general, Kant writes, the word 'object' "should be taken in a twofold meaning, namely as an appearance and as a 'thing in itself.'" The "two ways of representing things" speak, though in a twofold way, of "the very same things" (Bxxvii). It shouldn't escape our attention then, in a theme we'll develop throughout this book, that an economics that would follow Kant must mostly be expressing itself in metaphorical rather than literal terms, as how else would it, speaking *in* and *from* the transcendental (formal) dimension and thus in terms of causality, be pointing *to* the metaphysical (real) dimension and hence in terms of free choices?

Anderson offers a way, complementary to Hogan's, into this causality-vs-decision paradox. He asks how freedom's metaphysical foundation might in the Kantian spirit of critique be *minimized*. For this, Anderson interprets Kant's 'matter' as the 'source' of an empirical sensation – that to which the sensation, and so any consequent decision – is *attributable*. 'Form' correspondingly refers to the way this matter is received by us, judged, and interpreted.

First, however, let's state the problem. Although the appearances inside me refer to "the very same things" that are outside me, we must also satisfy the Kantian insistence that appearances aren't identical *to* the things themselves. Satisfying both these restrictions requires clarifying the nature of the division between the knower and the thing itself. Andrew Chignell (2022) and others have argued that Kant presumed things-themselves to be the ultimate bearer of what is true or correct, while the formal, transcendental, phenomenal dimension is what merely *appears* to someone to be true or correct. Contents, properties of things, can thus drift across the boundary between reality and appearance. If an appearance matches reality, the attribution is correct; otherwise, it isn't. One such content would be freedom, which thereby could be an element of the formal dimension. But if so, that world could never be one of cause and effect (what is unfree) either. We must therefore, with Anderson, reject Chignell's notion of things-in-themselves as bearers of specific truths.

Note Chignell is implicitly supposing reality to be separable in the sense of divisible, so that some elements of it can be shifted back and forth between a thing-itself and merely one's understanding of it, while others can't be. As we will see in detail below then, any distinction between the empiricist attitude, which implicitly assumes this separability, and the Kantian is eliminated.

Suppose, Anderson says, we argue instead that the thing-itself is only the matter or source of an appearance, given or granted *to* empirical intuition. In terms of or insofar as being their source, appearances are now 'real' or mind-independent, although drawn into spatiotemporal formality where they are accessible to judgment and cognition and so to economic model choice and statistical testing. We can then say that the act of economic judgment is attributable *to* that thing-itself, so has metaphysical significance for morality and freedom.

In this manner, Anderson says, Kant effectively conducts the following minimization of metaphysics. It is to hold *simultaneously* (hylomorphically) that:

(i) The (non-spatiotemporal, metaphysical) *matter*, source, or attribution of an empirical appearance is *not* mind dependent, *and*

(ii) The (spatiotemporal, transcendental) *form* of an empirical appearance – ready to be employed in the act of judgment and choice – *is* mind dependent.

A situation's appearances now have both a metaphysical and a formal aspect. What differs between them is the distinction between, in point (i), *that to which I attribute* the sensations or appearances which prompt my understanding, and, in point (ii), *how* it is that I bring these appearances into my judgments. The metaphysical element of a decision – the claim to know what the situation, and so the decisions it motivates, is 'itself' – has been minimized because to *attribute* something *to* is not to say it is *known-from* or *caused-by* it. Attribution, indeed, is distinguished *from* knowledge and cause. Concludes Anderson on Kant's behalf:

> freedom can be saved only by appeal to *something else* (the intelligible [metaphysical] character) which operates as an intelligible ground of the same action, and which, *precisely because it is not identical with my empirical character*, can be treated as a spontaneous cause of the action without violating the causal closure of nature.
>
> (fn 13, 917, my italics)

As he quotes Kant, "for if appearances are things-in-themselves then freedom cannot be saved….[But in fact, appearances] have grounds *that are not appearances* (A536, B564; 917, fn 13).

How in sum can freedom be saved from causality? By attributing *appearances* (empirical intuitions) to the thing itself – to the moral call. Appearances continue to be received into and interpreted through space and time, allocated in the act of judgment to categories and thus causes. Metaphysically, though, the domain in which we defer to or honor something, has been altered in an act of judgment. By virtue of what then has free choice involved a new beginning? In its listening to the moral command, and in this, Hogan and Anderson both say, altering reality. The thing-itself, reality, has intelligibly changed and it is freedom of choice that has changed it. Yet form, and with it empirical understanding, legitimately continue to indicate causality.

Anderson concludes:

> By holding tight to this fundamentally dualistic transcendental theory of experience – realism *and* idealism, common matter and differentiating form – Kant laid down what he hoped would be unbreachable boundaries around the metaphysical pretensions of theoretical reason.
>
> (915)

Anderson says Kant's approach to the metaphysical and its freedom are *by way of* transcendence, which paradoxically are the forms of necessity and causality. The moral individual who holds tight to this paradoxical duality, Kant calls "the person." In particular, he had written, "personality itself is the idea of the moral law and respect which is inseparable from it" (163, *RWLRA*, fn 2). Anderson is asking into the pathway of this freedom – the duality or distinction between the metaphysical and the transcendental – while Kant is asking into its source: the metaphysical, the real itself. But since the former is the 'receptivity' Kant speaks of, they are speaking of the same reality, both taking the hylomorphic view.

Economics as Two-Tiered Expression

Let's first then state this claim as a question. Just *how* can economic optimization, designed to mimic a decision maker's rationality in what appears to be a mechanical or mathematical spirit, be consonant with, help us approach, the freedom comprising a person's economic decisions? Our answer is that, along with the corpus of its earlier thought in Jevons (1871), Walras (1874), Menger (1883), Marshall (1890), and others, economics is Kantian not just in its own reason but in the way it supposes, in two-tiered fashion, that an individual's is too.

Neither Kant nor the Kant literature seems yet to have applied the spirit of critique to such an institutionally two-tiered, overlapping setting, where observations are made and judgments explicitly formed about *how others* make observations and form judgments. The reason presumably is that Kant's more immediate concern in the late 18th century was with science, whose object is 'things.' Things don't, having been observed and judged, turn around and form judgments of their own. It isn't surprising then that only later in his *Practical Reason* does Kant consider the difference between personhood and thinghood as such.

Economics Operates at Two Levels

The outlines, in any event, of this difference – and so of a twofold economic tier – are clear from the paradox of freedom and causality we've just looked at. The economics *discipline* emphasizes, in its propositions and models, the causality and articulability of choice – the one object pushing another that equations always suggest. The professor in other words emphasizes form – the spatiotemporal, mind-dependent aspects of empirical experience –the act of choice considered as an object. These intuitions are in nascent, anticipative form, ready to be matched with categories and associated empirical claims. The *decision maker* on the other hand emphasizes the sense, the gist, of the particular manifold along with the non-spatiotemporal, non-mind-dependent moral duty proximate to that situation. Clearly too, the professor emphasizes anticipations and expectations while decision makers emphasize the choice itself, the 'contents' Hogan points to as the locus of a free decision. We have then in economics an instance of Hogan's and Anderson's division of roles between the *how* or form or phenomena of a decision, which is the province of the professor, and the attribution or *reality* of a decision, which is the province of the decision maker herself.

The merely convenient character of such two-tiered epistemological arrangement is obvious. As Robbins (1932) says, "the concern of the economist is the interpretation of reality" (105). And "Economic Man is only an expository device – a first approximation used very cautiously at one stage of development of arguments…"

(97). For as freedom's moral origins are drawn from Kant's Practical Reason, should it be surprising that the economics discipline has found a practical solution to the causality-vs-freedom difficulty? In this double tier – economics' jointly metaphysical and epistemic dimensions – contingency reigns: contingent yet absolute. Only persons can hear the moral command.

We need to emphasize again here that the reasoning going on in economics – indeed in any field except pure math – isn't, on account of its uncertainty, definitional in any way. We have noted above that economics has no definition of capital or labor. And no wonder that economics doesn't find this embarrassing. Patricia Kitcher (2011) emphasizes the role of the specific 'marks' or characters, the 'partial representations' of an object through which, in the act of judgment, we unite our sense of something under a particular concept (38–39). This piecewise manner of judging, mark by mark, together with the entire difference between a sense and concept, points to the indefiniteness and uncertainty of the judgment process.

The rules or marks used to join intuition with conception are not, Kitcher notes, definitions. "In fact," Kitcher says, "[Kant] thinks that neither empirical concepts nor categories can be defined" (40). Empirical (measurable) concepts are no more definable than transcendental (pure, pre-measured) ones are – as this would imply a certitude, a 'definitiveness' they cannot have – but only serve as aids to a judgment. Kant puts this sharply:

> To define, as the word itself indicates, really only means to present the complete, original concept of a thing within the limits of the concept. If this be our standard, an *empirical* concept cannot be defined at all, but only *made explicit.* For since we find in it only a few characteristics of a certain species of sensible object, it is never certain that we are not using the word, in denoting one and the same object, sometimes to stand for more, and sometimes to stand for fewer characteristics….And indeed, what useful purpose could there be by defining an empirical concept, such as for instance water?...The so-called definition is nothing more than a determining of the word.
>
> (A727/B755 – A729/B757)

To define a word is not to succeed in defining – in making explicit to the mind – any real object. This is why economists, business people, and regulators can be offering valid insights into what capital is, how it is formed, what makes it shrink or grow, without being able to define it, without being scientific.[1]

Economic Knowledge Is Indirect: Definitions Are Questioned

We now then ask, from yet another perspective, what it is to know something economic: the mainstream approach which emphasizes uncertainty versus the positivist approach which emphasizes certitude, the former directed to individual persons and the latter to group generalizations. Either way, the notions of cause and effect will be central.

David Hume was to raise difficulties with these notions when he asked how a second event following a first should make the second one necessary, as this presumably is what a 'cause' entails. The answer, he said, is that we connect the two by way of sense experience, though only insofar as the one event follows another, not in anything about what the events were themselves (77). We can reason tentatively about tradeoffs between capital and labor as if we knew the mechanism enabling the tradeoff. But being at some distance from it, this will always involve some chutzpah. And the closer we come to it, to the conditions in which it took place, the less articulate we must be.

Soon in development despite Hume's warning would be the plastic 'utility' of Jeremy Bentham (1789), a pleasure substance that was addable to someone else's. David Ricardo (1817) would find a slightly more plausible kind of utility in a thing's 'use value.' Modern economics would later ask how use-values translate into price offers. But with the rest of his school, Ricardo simply melts a thing and its price into a Value, which if literally observable, can be reduced to the homogeneous 'toil' we give up to create it. "Toil" would be, as he says, "the foundation of all value, and the relative quantity of labor … almost exclusively determines the relative value of commodities" (11). Utility, price, and labor would be identical, so utility is just as measurable as labor is. An objective science of value was born, though at the cost of conflating utility with price and abstracting personal labor into a one-size-fits-all 'toil and trouble.'[2]

Breaking with Bentham, J.S. Mill (1836) decisively rejected this reduction of value to an object, arguing that, though economics speaks of utility and wealth, it doesn't think them to be observable objects. They are simply a way into analysis, mindful of their myriad "disturbing causes" that can never be fathomed. Economics acts, says Mill, as if it were a science though aware it never will be (42).[3] The thought of wealth in isolation from the family that possesses it, though useful for understanding people's motives, is "purely imaginary" (46). Leon Walras (1874) later developed his theory of general price equilibrium on the same lines: traders express the *rarete* (scarcity) of a good in the relative price they will pay for it. Scarcity is so intimate to the individual that only she can express it, and only in the mute way of a price offer. (145) It can be measured only with the grossest error.

Alfred Marshall (1890, 1920) followed Mill and Walras in these ways. Economics appears to be a science, he implies, and somehow has the feel of one:

> The advantage which economics has over other branches of social science appears … to arise from the fact that its special field of work gives rather larger opportunities for exact methods than any other branch. It concerns itself chiefly with those desires, aspirations, and other affections of human nature, the *outward manifestations* [my emphasis] of which appear as incentives to action in such a form that the force or quantity of the incentives can be estimated and measured with some approach to accuracy.
>
> (15)

Most importantly, and easy to lose sight of,

> the economist does not claim to measure any affection of the mind itself, or directly, but only indirectly through its effect.

Force is a physics term and Marshall's use of it isn't accidental. It offers insight unavailable to other social thinking:

> An opening is made for the methods and tests of science as soon as the force of a person's motives – *not* the motives themselves – can be approximately measured by the sum of money…and desire to pay.
>
> (14)

But a science it is not, because economics doesn't limit itself to "abstract or 'economic' man" (27). It doesn't, that is, "ignore the mental and spiritual side of life" but addresses "man as he is," including a "love of a virtuous life for its own sake" (17). Indeed, it makes no attempt to fathom the spiritual side either – only its outward manifestations. The economist stands essentially therefore in the same position you and I do in ordinary life, because at least with people we don't know well, we're stuck with outward manifestations.

Marshall helped show that rational choice depends more on how much something changes than on its size, and in doing so demonstrated how money can measure the 'force' of our incentives. We don't project some grand vision forward and leap into it wholesale; instead, we examine the cost of each new step (marks), asking whether it is greater or less than the reward. The cost, that is, of our next bit of effort is compared to the value received for it, just as the value of the next bit of service is compared to the price surrendered. Because we're concerned about succeeding, we consider the full cost of both – things internal as well as external. And so we have an interesting result: the money price that the seller receives and the buyer pays – both fully observable – is equated to the cost and value of the service – both *un*observable. The observable has revealed the unobservable, though even here only in its 'moving force,' not in itself.

If economics really is to consider "man as he is" in other words, it must take his standpoint. How else would it be in a position to judge his motives? And because "we cannot measure motives … as they are in themselves," the self-understanding we're speaking of here can't be the quantitative sort. At the core of economic reasoning is a self-projection. "Economic studies call for and develop the faculty of sympathy which enables people to put themselves in the place [of others]" (45). Since furthermore buyers and sellers must, as Marshall says, consider the full costs of their actions, including – at least potentially – their whole world of concern as well as their individual selves, the economist must too. At the source of any insight into a particular economic affair must be an insight into something total.

Here, however, modern economics finds itself in a quandary, as Marshall's readers will be aware. Because the willingness to pay for something differs unobservably from one person to the next and yet everyone may pay the same price for it, we must, in order to use prices to infer benefits, look to everyone who buys it (18). Economics, interested ultimately in *this* person and *her* situation, often relies on groups for the 'forces' it can observe. It isn't accidental then that Marshall often resorts to 'pleasure' to depict these benefits (19). Reduced to the abstractions that group memberships are, he often ascribes banal, abstract motives to them. For banal is what 'pleasure' and 'happiness' are. Like Jevons before him (1871, 1911) and Pareto after (1927), Marshall frequently comes up with mechanical-sounding goals for those integrative, world-connected selves he cares about (33). Economists' very words, demanded by their frequent aggregation to groups, invite them to be misunderstood – even by themselves.[4]

Economic Meaning Is in the Person

It is no irony that one of the chief exponents of Marshall's emphasis on the final ineffability of personal knowledge was Max Weber (1903, 1917), a founder of the sociology that, perhaps because he did take a person's standpoint, has now largely abandoned him. If there indeed is an incommensurability between an aggregate and a person, there is also an incommensurability between an economic *statement* – the 'professor,' which is often about aggregates – and its economic *meaning,* which is directed to persons. The one could never be reduced to, contained in, the other. Any significance we might perceive in a mathematical theorem derives from our prior sense of the *individual* (Weber's italics) concrete situations the theorem points to. Given the economic thinker is interested in the concrete, he must, in the act of knowing, fall back on his own resources, relying on the significance that social phenomena have for *him* and that are internal to *him.* This doesn't mean dreaming up any image he finds appealing. For he is bound up already with those very "significance[s] which the concrete constellations of reality have for him" and which cannot be "revealed to him by any law" (80–81).

The reference here to intuition, to a manifold, is clearly from Kant. It fits also with Kenneth Westphal's (2017) emphasis on Kant's insistence that a valid cognition can only be about a particular. As Westphal notes, Kant shows "determinate cognitive judgments are possible for us only through conjoint spatio-temporal designation of, and predicative ascription of characteristics to, any experienced particular(s)" (1701). That is, only particulars can be intuited or therefore conceived. And, he presumably would add, only an intuition can grasp a particular. This Westphal calls Kant's doctrine of Singular Cognitive Reference. In Westphal's words:

> Terms or phrases have 'meaning', and concepts have classificatory content (intension), as predicates of possible judgments, i.e. as determinables. Yet no proposition has specifically *cognitive* significance unless and until it is incorporated into a candidate cognitive judgment which is [then] referred to some actual particular(s) localized … by the presumptive judge … within space and time.
>
> (1702)

In sum, intuited particulars are assigned to generalizations (concepts) but only in order to apply to particulars again. It is the particulars that both initially and finally matter.

Weber gave, as Lionel Robbins was giving, much attention to the contrary classical, rationalist view: that social and economic principles dawn on us on their own, reinforcing themselves with circular simplicity. Oddly enough, the view in classical economics that principles are self-evident is ultimately indistinguishable from the view that empirical events are self-evident too.[5] The frequent presumption that economic knowledge is deducible from principles is really the presumption that it jumps right out at us from the "facts themselves." "Now in order," Weber writes:

> To arrive at these [deductions] – for they are certain that science should be directed towards these as its highest goal – they take it to be a fact that we always have a direct awareness of the structure of human actions in all their reality. Hence, so they think, science can make human behavior directly intelligible with axiomatic evidentness and accordingly reveal human actions in all their reality.... These abstract theories [then] together must contain the true reality of the object – i.e., whatever is worthwhile knowing about it.
>
> (87)

> This claim fails to observe that in order to be able to reach this result even in the simplest case, the totality of the existing historical reality, including every one of its causal relationships, must be assumed as "given" and presupposed as known. But if this type of knowledge were accessible to the finite mind of man, abstract theory would have no cognitive value whatsoever.
>
> (88)

The classical attitude implicitly supposes it has a total grasp of structural reality. But if it does, why stress ourselves analyzing it further, since the facts are already known by deduction from this total grasp? Yet in Westphal's words, "....their causal descriptions are so vague that they do not suffice even for causal ascription..." (1704). To appear reasonable, all they need do is avoid contradicting themselves. "As Kant noted," Westphal writes, "merely speaking or thinking intelligibly only requires avoiding self-contradiction, whereas cognition or any *claim* to knowledge requires localizing the putatively known individual(s) within space and time..." (1704).

Ironically, the effort to escape this charge of vacuity has been to abstract even more. In Weber's time, especially in Europe, it was the lecturers who were impressed with the sheer generality of their arguments: the circular notion that everything and everyone was, whether it wished to or not, be collapsed into it. Consider Descartes' *Discourse on Method* (1637) and Hegel's *Science of Logic* (1812), to be precise. The case is far different in today's economics journals, which open with three- and four-page introductions laying the model out as a story. Why would they bother? Only if the model's purpose weren't the model itself but the intuition it offers. And this it can offer only if the model bears a certain orthogonal, two-tiered relationship to the decision maker, the model arguing from general to specific, the decision maker standing in a concrete present and facing an even more concrete (precisely because unknown) future.

Economics Is Indefinite Because Ex-Ante

That ex-ante posture was Lionel Robbins' main interest. An important question in the 1930s, and that remains in today's behavioral literature, is whether and how economic reasoning can take psychological factors into account. Given that only an empirical (as opposed to clinical) psychology would try to, this question is a species of the broader one: how and how much should economics restrict itself to what is observable? If utility for instance is to be understood as measured feelings and emotions, it qualifies as a science of things, subject to every new psychological theory coming along. So psychological forms of observability can, in their instability, be only auxiliary to our thinking. A second way that observations could be introduced to economics would be through 'revealed preference': someone's walking out of a store with particular goods we can see and bought at particular prices. If a discipline could be built on prices and quantities of this completely observable kind, a *science* of wealth might at last be possible.

This however, Robbins argues, would be even more difficult than a science of emotions, because it is impossible to form a rationale for the shopper's consequent demands and supplies without appealing to her expectations, namely to "what is going to happen [to her] in the future." Demand for example would depend on

> not merely prices which prevail now, or which might prevail, on present markets, but also as relating to a whole series of prices which people expect to prevail in the future. It is obvious that what people expect to happen in the future is not susceptible of observation by purely behaviorist methods. Yet...it is absolutely essential to take such anticipations into account if we are to understand at all the mechanics of economic change.
>
> (85)

And to come to the point, Robbins asks rhetorically, "How can we observe what a man thinks is going to happen?" To which we would add: especially if he is unsure of what he's thinking on this subject himself.

The futility of just questioning him on the matter is clear. He can't himself observe what he thinks of his future – as if it were an object – because even he doesn't know – other than as possibility – how it will turn out later, so can hardly have a definite view on it. This quandary, the decision maker's inability to quite get his hands around a problem, is what Kant (1788) includes, in terms of a free act in particular, in pure practical reason (59). He is bound to a future, but because it hasn't happened yet, can't know in any literal way what he is bound to. He cannot know it in any literal way, so involves himself the more in it. Aware of this responsibility, he is conversely in an *ex-ante* position – anxious about the future. And as economics is in no better place than he is, it too is in an *ex-ante* posture and finite. Economics therefore must stand in a middle ground: must base itself on the decision maker's practical as well as pure reason. I argue this is the spirit of Mill, Marshall, Weber, Robbins, Knight, and the other expositors of what today can be called the 'mainstream revolution.'

Max Weber in particular appears to have one recent follower in John Dupre (2001), who wonders how phenomena economic could ever fit into the mechanism of science. The idea of a mechanism is that the motion of one part helps move another, Dupre says, and "it appears that economic practice typically assumes that the world it models is somewhat machine-like." However, "in a largely disordered universe there is no a priori guarantee that economics will be possible at all, at least in anything like the form expected of a mathematical science" (326). The error Dupre appears to make here is in thinking economics regards itself *to* be science. Dupre doesn't distinguish between mainstream and a would-be analyticist economics, so doesn't seem to be recognizing that the mainstream makes no claim to know the mechanics of economic thought whatever if you mean literal ones. Its suppositions are mechanism metaphor only, not to be taken literally as science is and must be.

How Subject Is United with Object in Economics

An early demonstration of this specific, forward-looking, uncertain yet unifying theme is the economist Leon Walras' pivotal notion of *rarete* and his equally pivotal approaches to price formation and equilibrium (143–149). Walras makes no claim to observe, define, or derive these concepts. They instead are phenomena – to be recognized only latently: that the value we entertain for goods or situations depends on their rarete, our *sense* of their scarcity relative to desirability.

The greater the *rarete*, Walras points out, the greater the exchange value:

$$Rarete\left(Relative\ \ Scarcity\right)\ \ \Rightarrow\ \ Price \qquad (1a)$$

In his market theory he then does the opposite, showing how rarete is derived from exchange. The greater the quantity to be exchanged, the lower the rarete because, after all, the "intensity of the last want satisfied" (marginal utility) would go to zero if enough more of it, via supply, were available:

$$Quantity \Rightarrow Rarete\ (Marginal\ Utility) \qquad (1b)$$

In sum, while rarete as scarcity explains price, quantity explains rarete as marginal utility. It is *as if* rarete were marginal utility. And as such, it is marginal utility that brings the measurable price and measurable quantity together, *the indefinable and unmeasurable mediating the two definables and measurables.* That is,

$$Quantity \Rightarrow Rarete \Rightarrow Price \qquad (2)$$

Walras' translator wisely leaves rarete in French, only occasionally translating it to its English equivalent and so allowing him – by juxtaposing its intuitive (relative scarcity) meaning with its mathematical (marginal utility) meaning – to retain the joint sense of the two. For though in equation (1a) here it is a buyer's or seller's intuitive grasp that determines market value, this grasp is inarticulable; while the manner in which quantity affects scarcity in (1b) can be represented as a marginal utility function, *as if* it is something that can be graphed. Walras writes: "The rarete [defined in exchange theory] of the intensity of the last want satisfied is precisely the same thing as the scarcity…in terms of the twin conditions of utility and limitation in quantity" (145).

Economic Demand Links Subjectivity with Objectivity

We see in this treatment that the foundation of microeconomics – the relation between marginal utility and price – is a relation between pure intuition and empirical observation. At the tangency of the quasi-convex utility indifference curve to the linear budget line in Figure 1, purely intuited (nonmeasurable) scarcity conforms to the observed prices, while the measured quantity yields the representation (marginal utility) of the scarcity.[6] In what comprises the consumption framework of economic textbooks, measured (actual) quantity and price are being mediated here by the unmeasured (pure, nonempirical) scarcity. I will now formally prove that this Walrasian tangency, and with it the foundation of demand (and as we will see below, supply) is an instance of Kant's schemata of pure reason, uniquely linking the unmeasurable with the measurable and so preserving the human person.

First consider that the price ratio constituting the slope of Walras' budget line in Figure 1 is, by equation (1a), determined solely by unobserved and unobservable rarete. And the mathematical representation of this rarete – observable on a utility graph but *not in itself* – is the ratio of the corresponding marginal utilities.[7] Thus, we can write the demand or valuation process as the formal, transcendental, phenomenological one of proceeding from unobserved space to observed space:

$$\text{Relative Scarcity} \Rightarrow \frac{mu_1}{mu_2} \Rightarrow \frac{p_1}{p_2} \qquad (1a')$$

Second, consider that the relative availability of these two goods, which for Walras leads the consumer toward the sense of what she most wants or needs (*rarete*), is the observed slope of the budget line (CB) in Figure 1 and therefore of the indifference curve at the resulting point A, being of course the ratio of the marginal utilities. We therefore have, for what here is a supply (availability) effect, a progress from the measurable to the unmeasurable:

$$\frac{\partial q_2}{\partial q_1} \Rightarrow \frac{mu_1}{mu_2} \qquad (1b')$$

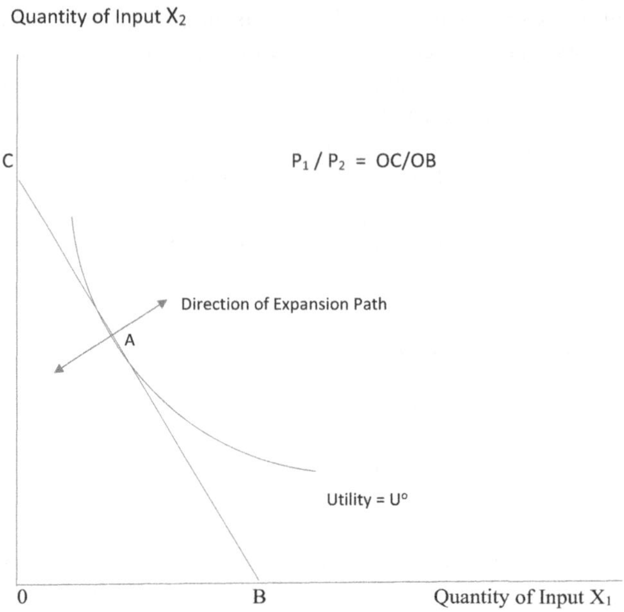

Figure 1 Cost Allocation (Equilibrium) in Mainstream Economics.

Drawing (1a') and (1b') together gives, for Walras, the conditions for consumer optimization:

$$\frac{\partial q_2}{\partial q_1} = \frac{mu_1(q_1)}{mu_2(q_2)} = \frac{p_1}{p_2} \tag{2'}$$

The two empiricals – prices and quantities – are here united by way of the nonempirical possibilities represented by the marginal utility functions, where the budget line is the empirical (because prices and quantities are observable) and the utility indifference curve is the unobservable but form-building, interpreted possibility. The empirical, that is, is explained by way of the transcendental. Crucially, the linkage embodied in this tangency is unique because it is specific to *this* person in *this* situation. *QED*

Walras also interprets the unique linkage in equation (2') – and so the tangency in Figure 1 – as a uniting of subjectivity with objectivity: "*Rarete* is personal and subjective; value in exchange is real and objective" (146). 'Real' here is improper; he means to say, or should say, impersonal or 'thing.' But his use of 'subjective' and 'objective' is correct and, in fact, demonstrates something of profound importance to the economic theory of rationality: in a free act of exchange, subjectivity and objectivity are brought integrally together and so become nonseparable, though remaining heterogeneous (Berofsky 2017, Anderson 2022, Tegtmeyer 2022). Equation (1a') is our pure, nonempirical formation or possibility of the empirical signals, not as data but as the joint possibility of economic value. Equation (1b') is the data which prompt and draw our attention to such possibility (which following Kant, Walras calls pure reason), expressed in the abstract form of an indifference curve but only in a metaphorical, 'as-if' sense of a 'curve.'[8]

Budget line / indifference curve tangencies at given price ratios in Figure 1 therefore are Kantian schemata, representations of the heterogeneity yet jointness between intuition and generalization in human understanding. The unobservable interprets the observable – but only because the unobservable can remain itself, so can *be* the meaning of what we observe. This heterogeneity between the pure and the empirical is what J.S. Mill (42) refers to when speaking of the "disturbing causes" of things that cannot be fathomed, and what Marshall means by the economist who doesn't presume to measure "any affection of the mind itself" (15). Paradoxically, and contrary to the generalized groups of strictly empirical reasoning, the economic interpreter is united with the interpreted – is capable of interpreting it – only by respecting at the same time the incommensurability between she and it. She is unassailably she and it is unassailably it. In her capacity to infer and interpret, a person in contemporary economics is a kind of being radically different from the things or objects that science deals with, including any groups of persons except those they voluntarily choose.

The Economic Unity of Sense and Concept Needs Metaphorical Language

As Kant would have said had economics been there in his time, at the heart of a good's utility are the situations it entails. This applies both to the path *from* one's sense of utility *to* the price to be paid for it (demand 1a) and *back* from its availability *to* this utility sense (supply 1b). Economic supply in other words is just as dependent on receptivity – on pure intuition – as economic demand is. Take note that the terms here aren't definable as they are to be in any positivist economics, either rationalist or empiricist. Walras' language is, as it must be, couched in metaphor. Utility, scarcity, and value aren't objects or entities despite superficially looking that way. They don't constitute a 'system' other than a proxy for one – can never, outside the forecaster or classroom, be observed or parameterized by anybody, including the decision maker.

Why then would Walras use causal, abstract terms? Because he must. Most articulation involves generalities (concepts) along with empirical referencing, namely direct, literal language. But this is inadequate for a person as a person, who, as a free agent, is engaged in a new beginning at every moment. Everyone senses that personal reality is deeper than words go, and only analogy and metaphor can convey this. Richard Moran (1997) writes that a fundamental quality of metaphor is its very "indefiniteness and open-ended character"(251), the 'open end' being a pointing to what is ineffable. Open ends don't imply sloppiness or indeterminacy. To the contrary, "when a content or thought is held to be ineffable, not simply indeterminate, … one may have a perfectly definite content in mind." "It [simply] cannot be fully expressed in words." Indeed "in various contexts the sense of the indescribability is a response to the highly determinate character, the *utter specificity,* of what one has in mind" (257, 263; my italics).

Economic value and utility then are neither generalities nor observables. Walras essentially says this. It is the nonconceptual and nonempirical in his work that is providing the meaning of the empirical. "The pure theory of economics ought to take over from experience certain ... concepts like those of exchange, supply, ... and capital," and "from these real-type concepts the pure science of economics should then abstract and define ideal-type concepts in terms of which it carries on its reasoning" (71). As we shall see more, we are squarely in the domain of Kant's critiques of pure and practical reason. The foundation of economic market analysis is an intuitive sense, drawn unobservably from one's immediate experience. One then abstracts this sense by the analogy or metaphor of a 'marginal utility' to help make the point. The abstractions are analogies only.

> *We should never, though, allow an economic model's abstract appearance to imply that the underlying reality is abstract.*

It is only *as if* it were abstract since, quite the contrary, economic reality is the ultimate of concretions – some *one's* sense of something. Walras' term 'pure' here is taken directly from Kant (1781). Market model (1) – (2) we have just shown is an instance of Kantian schemata, in which someone's pure intuition of a situation is judged to come under certain categories to form a conceptual whole (108–114).

In this we cannot forget, and are continually reminded, that economic thought takes place at two tiers or levels: of reasoning and theory which is cause-and-effect (but only metaphorically so), and of human choice which is aware of its freedom. To be free is to accept or reject the moral call, inseparable from being a person. Privacy of situation – yet an openness to the world – is finally what mainstream economics is.

Summary Points of Chapter I

1. Mainstream economics is an evaluation of ends given the means, not of the end itself but relative to other ends. Scarcity is this judged relative value, based on an intuition of a situation that is the value's ground.
2. Economics therefore is not, as would appear to many, a reduction of an individual's wants and efforts to quantitative measure.
3. Insofar as formal or transcendental, ends are rather a matter of judgment – expressible in some manner. Insofar as metaphysical, moral, or logical, they are free – hardly expressible at all.
4. Economic rationality therefore must be two-tiered: on the one side in the form of cause and effect (theory, teaching, model-building), on the other as personal decision-making (free).
5. Because decisions are ultimately free, and to which theory then can never be privy, the economic theory of decision is expressible only analogically, an 'as-if.'

6. Economic decision, in short, is judgment – a uniting of unobservable scarcity with observable prices that constrain and thereby illuminate one another (nonseparability).
7. As confined to reason alone, rationalist economics instead is finally a reduction to generalization, just as, confined to measure, empiricist economics is finally a reduction to correlation. Both positivisms are abstractions.
8. In this respect the rationalist presumption that economic thought can be deduced from principles becomes ultimately equivalent to the empiricist presumption that it can be known from observations.
9. Two economic attitudes thus emerge, reflecting the two metaphysical realities: things or generalizations the locus of the rationalist and empiricist, and persons the locus of the mainstream.
10. To be confined to things, entities, or objects that is – the *ex-post* attitude – is to do rationalist or empiricist economics. To be a person, the *ex-ante* attitude, is to do mainstream economics.

Notes

1 Very recent literature has been further confirming and developing the hylomorphic character of Kant's thought. (*a*) In his review of the Heilmann and Reiss edited *Routledge Handbook of Philosophy of Economics* (2022), and on Verreault-Julien's and Jhun's chapters in particular, Wade Hands notes the "extremely difficult and contentious, but also important, question about the exact and/or proper relationship between idealized economic models [what I'm calling the 'professor'] and their associated explanatory targets [the actual decision makers]." (*b*) In his paper "Classical Compatibilism," Bernard Berofsky (2017) examines the question of whether, in a given decision, "the agent could have decided (or acted) otherwise," and asks "where then do Hume and Mill stand on the relation of [such] power to freedom or liberty," and quotes J.S. Mill (1874, 550) saying, "a person feels morally free who feels that his habits or his temptations are not his masters, but he theirs; who even in yielding to them knows he can resist." (*c*) It is Paul Guyer's argument in *Kant on Freedom and Spontaneity* (2018, 269–294), also discussed in Saunders, that "there is always a gulf between nature and freedom for Kant, but not an unbridgeable one,"(1180) in other words Kant takes the same hylomorphic position these others, such as Hogan and Anderson, have taken. And (*d*) Maximilian Tegtmeyer (2022) takes Stephen Engstrom's (21) account of Kant's hylomorphism to be an argument that "Kant characterizes the distinction between understanding and sensibility as one between form and matter," the matter being "the determinable in general" and the form being "its determination." The hylomorphism buttressing my own account of a two-tiered economics here derives, that is, from a common Kantian view.

2 The seeds of Marx's subsequent labor theory of value, in his view also a science, are obvious.

3 In even less mistakable terms, he says, "Not that any political economist was ever so absurd as to suppose that mankind are really … constituted [as thinking their money to be objects], but because this is the mode in which science necessarily must proceed." (42) J.S. Mill is hailed as a pioneer of scientific objectivity more than of modern economics. This misinterpretation tells us much about the importance of keeping context in mind,, of which we will have much to say later.

4 I'm not implying these writers didn't hold self-contrary views on many questions and change their minds in the course of their careers. Robbins (see Wicksteed 1933, xvii) notes that the early Marshall retained for quite a while the classical argument that a good's value is 'natural' and absolute rather than relative to other goods and your utility.
5 An instance of this rationalist logic is Murray Rothbard's (1957) paper, "In Defense of Extreme Apriorism."
6 The utility is emphatically of some *one*. It is to be satisfied, says Walras, "as far *as he is concerned*." (144) [my italics]
7 Walras says, "Values in exchange [measurable prices] are proportional to the *raretes*," and "if indeed *rarete* and value in exchange are concomitant and proportional phenomena, it is equally certain that *rarete* is the cause of the value of exchange." (145) We shall discuss extensively below how this term 'cause' is to be interpreted.
8 McCloskey (1985) has discussed the metaphorical *as-if* character of economic language from an especially rhetorical standpoint. He writes, "A literary man with advanced training in mathematics and statistics stumbling into *Econometrica* would be astonished at the metaphors surrounding him, lost in a land of allegory. Allegory is merely long-winded metaphor, and all such figures are analogies. Analogies can be arrayed in terms of explicitness, with simile ("as if") the most explicit and symbol ("the demand curve") the least explicit; and they can be arrayed by extent, from analogy to allegory." (78)

References

Anderson, R. Lanier. "Transcendental Idealism as Formal Realism." *European Journal of Philosophy,* Vol. 30, 2022, 899–923.
Arendt, Hannah. *The Human Condition.* Chicago: University of Chicago Press, 1958, 1998.
Bentham, Jeremy. *An Introduction to the Principles of Morals and Legislation.* J.H. Burns and H.L.A. Hart (eds.). New York: Oxford University Press, 1970. First published in 1789.
Berofsky, Bernard. "Classical Compatibilism." In: Kevin Timpe, Meghan Griffith, and Neil Levy (eds.), *The Routledge Companion to Free Will.* London and New York: Routledge, Taylor and Francis, 2017.
Chignell, Andrew. "Mind-Independent Physical Properties and the Mind-Dependent Moral Properties." In: K. Schafer and N. Stang (eds.), *The Intelligible and Sensible Worlds.* Oxford: Oxford University Press, 2022.
Descartes, Rene. "Discourse on Method." In: Norman Kemp Smith (Trans.), *Descartes Philosophical Writings*. New York: Random House, 1958. First published in 1637.
Dupre, John. "Economics Without Mechanism." In: Uskali Maki (ed.), *The Economic World View: Studies in the Ontology of Economics.* Cambridge: Cambridge University Press, 2001.
Engstrom, Stephen. "Understanding and Sensibility." *Inquiry* 40 (1), 2–25.
Guyer, Paul. "Nature and Freedom in Kant's Practical Philosophy." In: Kate A. Moran (ed.), *Kant on Freedom and Spontaneity.* Cambridge: Cambridge University Press, 2018.
Hands, D. Wade. "Review of Conrad Heilmann and Julian Reiss" (eds.), *The Routledge Handbook of Philosophy of Economics.* In: *Erasmus Journal for Philosophy and Economics* 16 (1), 2023.
Harsanyi, John C. "Cardinal Welfare, Individualistic Ethics, and Interpersonal Comparisons of Well-Being." *Journal of Political Economy* 63, 309–321, 1955.
Hegel, George Friedrich. *The Science of Logic.* George di Giovanni (Trans.). Cambridge: Cambridge University Press, 2010. First published in 1812.

Heidegger, Martin. *Being and Time.* Trans. John Macquarrie and Edward Robinson. New York: Harper-Collins, 1962. First published in 1927.
Heilmann, Conrad and Julian Reiss (eds.). *The Routledge Handbook of Philosophy of Economics* (2022). New York: Routledge, 2022.
Hogan, Desmond. "Kant's Copernican Turn and the Rationalist Tradition." In: Paul Guyer (ed.), *The Cambridge Companion to Kant's Critique of Pure* Reason. Cambridge: Cambridge University Press, 2010.
Hume, David. *A Treatise of Human Nature. Book I, Of the Understanding.* L.A. Selby-Bigge (ed.). Oxford: Clarendon Press, 1893. First published in 1739.
Jevons, W.S. *The Theory of Political Economy*, 4th ed. London: Macmillan, 1911. First edition 1871.
Jhun, Jennifer S. "Modeling the Possible to Modeling the Actual." In: Conrad Heilmann and Julian Reiss (eds.), *The Routledge Handbook of Philosophy of Economics*, New York and London: Routledge, 2022.
Kant, Immanuel. *Critique of Practical Reason.* Lewis White Beck (Trans.). Chicago: University of Chicago Press, 1949. First published in 1788.
Kant, Immanuel. *Critique of Pure Reason*, 1st and 2nd eds. Norman Kemp Smith (Trans.). New York: Random House (Modern Library), 1958. First published in 1781; revised in 1787.
Kitcher, Patricia. "Kant's Spontaneous Thinker and (More) Spontaneous Agent." Keynote essay in: *Cultivating Personhood, Book One*. Steven Palmquist (ed.). New York: Walter de Gruyter, 2011.
Leibniz, Gottfried von. "Theory of Knowledge and Metaphysics." In: Philip Wiener (ed.), *Selections*. New York: Scribner & Sons, 1951. First published in 1676.
Marshall, Alfred. *Principles of Economics*. New York: Macmillan and Co., 1890, 1920.
Marx, Karl. "Capital, Vol 1." In: Robert C. Tucker (ed.), *The Marx-Engels Reader*, 2nd ed. New York: W.W. Norton & Co., 1978. First published in 1849.
Mas-Colell, A., M.D. Whinston, and J.R. Green. *Microeconomic Theory*. New York: Oxford University Press, 1995.
McCloskey, Dierdre. *The Rhetoric of Economics*. Madison, WI: University of Wisconsin Press, 1985.
Menger, Carl. *Investigations into the Method of the Social Sciences with Special Reference to Economics*. Louis Schneider (ed.). New York: New York University Press, 1985. First published in 1883.
Mill, John Stuart. "On the Definition and Method of Political Economy." In: D. M. Hausman (ed.), *The Philosophy of Economics*, 3rd ed. Cambridge: Cambridge University Press, 2008. First published in 1836.
Moran, Richard. "Metaphor." In: Bob Hale and Crispin Wright (eds.), *A Companion to the Philosophy of Language*. Oxford: Blackwell Publishers, 1997.
Pareto, Vilfredo. Manual of Political Economy. Ann S. Schwier (Trans.). New York: Augustus Kelley, 1971. From 1927 French edition.
Ricardo, David. The Principles of Political Economy and Taxation. Mineola: Dover Publications, 2004. First published in 1817.
Robbins, Lionel. An Essay on the Nature and Significance of Economic Science. London: Macmillan, 1st ed. 1932.
Saunders, Joe. "Recent Work on Freedom in Kant." *British Journal for the History of Philosophy* 29 (6), 1177–1189, London: Routledge, 2021.
Smith, Adam. *The Wealth of Nations*. 1776. New York: Modern Library, 1937.
Taylor, Charles. *Sources of the Self.* Cambridge: Harvard University Press. 1989.

Tegtmeyer, Maximilian. "Overcoming Compositionalism by Appreciating Kant's Insight." *Synthese* 200 (1), Springer, February 2022.

Verreault-Julien, Phillippe. "Explanation in Economics." In: Conrad Heilmann and Julian Reiss (eds.), *The Routledge Handbook of Philosophy of Economics*. London: Routledge, 2022.

Walras, Leon. Elements of Pure Economics, 4th ed. William Jaffe (Trans.). Homewood, IL: Richard D. Irwin, Inc., 1954. 1st edition 1874, 4th edition 1900, definitive edition 1926.

Weber, Max. The Methodology of the Social Sciences. E. Shils and H. Finch (Trans.). New York: Macmillan, 1949. First published 1903 and 1917.

Westphal, Kenneth R. "How Kant Justifies Freedom of Agency (*without* Transcendental Idealism)." *European Journal of Philosophy* 25 (4), 2017, 1695–1717.

Wicksteed, Philip H. The Common Sense of Political Economy. *Introduction by Lionel Robbins*. London: Routledge and Sons, 1933. First published in 1910.

II Economics of Persons versus Things

In our summary of Walras' thought above, the arrows in expressions (2) and (2') indicating a reputed 'causality' between observable quantities and prices are being mediated by an unobservable utility or preference. They cannot therefore, given that preferences reflect a person's freedom as well as intuition, be causation. There certainly is an appearance of cause. And it is useful to discuss it as cause because any variations in preferences may be disappearing into the model's error terms.

You'll also notice that Walras speaks strictly of an individual person. Group actions and preferences are to be computed only by carefully aggregating the individuals and in that way only a proxy for those individuals. Note as well the metaphorical tone in the word 'utility,' which being a preference, speaks to more than the mere usefulness that 'utility' seems to. It speaks also, like *rarete*, of the future. If indeed contemporary economics uses such ex-ante, metaphorical expression, the positivist alternative must be to drop the unobservable terms altogether, so (1a), (1b), and (2') in Chapter I reduce to observable quantities, and prices alone and to the involuntary groups – the 'things' – that this strict observability implies.[1] Measurement opportunities now proliferate in all their asserted definiteness that an automatically aggregated group would always suggest.

Immanuel Kant and the Enlightenment revolt he pioneered would point instead to the transcendental (pure, phenomenological) dimension of reality that accepts the empirical into itself. The way to what is now mainstream economics, sensed by Adam Smith around the same time, was fully opened up. We will show in the present chapter that in economics, equations and propositions are in service of something more fundamental than the math: your sense and intuition of a situation. They are your ability to be consistent with and articulate yourself. You can articulate something only when you are grounded in it. This essential relation between outer articulation and inner sense, we will see, is the core of economic thought. Economics' role is to help us judge and interpret. It is a receptivity or openness in which a decision maker stands out in a possible world, success and failure brought together in a single view. In other words, it is an intuition of, and so a receptivity to, an uncertain future.

If so, economic data and generalities can only be epistemic aids to personal decision-making, an external frame one looks to as guidepost, though never in a

DOI: 10.4324/9781003514602-4

rote way. Economic modeling therefore can only have this suggestive quality, can never be a view of the 'real' world. Economics' groundedness in particular situations is a reminder of the anti-mechanical, jointly subjective and objective nature of human choice – the uniqueness, finally, of every situation and deliberation and for which general categories are for consistency and emphasis only. A decision is an intuition of a 'this' together with a generalization of a 'that': a union of the possible and actual.

Your sense of a given situation, then, is organized under the categories that render it reliable and expressible. This organized-under, in what Kant calls transcendental schemata, is itself an act of intuition. Abstractions can now represent what is common to each particular in the whole without losing sight of what is special to that particular – namely without infringing on what that particular is. A category *does nothing but receive and interpret* what is under it. For if and only if such an identity-preserving view is maintained can each particular in the group remain itself, even if later reinterpreted under another category. Switching your ideas about something doesn't change what it is. This stability of identity is especially important in economics, where it is a person's choices that are being categorized. To have any continuous experience of one's world and self, they must be invariant to the way others group them.[2]

All this would be of no concern to an economics reasoning down from first principles only, because the role of a principle is to preaggregate individuals in this very way, defining for us which groups are to matter more to us and which less. It is the threat of this interchangeability – this casual rearrangement of personal identity and focus – that the Kantian schemata rule out, and they do so because the intuition at their center is *this person's,* e.g. this customer's or this supplier's. Obviously the only way for someone to remain a person is to transcend, remain incommensurable with, merely empirical aggregations.

In short, the possibility or interpretation of someone's situation must be sharply distinguished from any actual or observed object associated with her. As Kant puts it in the *Prolegomena* (1783), "reason by all it's *a priori* principles never teaches us anything more than objects of possible experience..." (110). Reason isn't, in theory or daily life, about actualities but possibilities – despite when, as in economic counterfactuals, they are compared *to* earlier actual outcomes. Were this not so, we would have no way of grasping what any eventual outcome would signify. I will call this situation an incommensurability, yet hylomorphism and mutual need, between a person's transcendental and metaphysical dimensions – the essentiality of *leaving a decision maker to her self and situation* – the ontological invariance principle in economics and argue that the spirit of economic theory is its chief representative in the social disciplines.

Intuition as the Source of Reason (So of Economic Demand and Supply)

The only way to maintain this principle is to question the Cartesian presupposition that reality is preeminently an idea in someone's mind. David Hume does question it, and with simplicity and persistence. In his *Treatise of Human Nature* (1739) published in his late 20s, he challenges the implied notion of earlier Enlightenment writers that our ideas pop self-evidently into our heads as true. They arise instead, he says, from sense impressions, and the real truth in us is this vividness of our immediate impressions of things. Only from vividness do ideas come forth.

Hume Flees from His Literal Words

On the other hand, Hume seems often to say ideas are nothing *but* these sense impressions as they lapse into a sort of dotage. "All ideas are derived from impressions, and are nothing but copies and representations of them" (19). They in turn beget even more remote secondary ideas, "images of the primary" (8). Successive ideation or generalization, that is, draws us away from the individual objects that constitute primary reality (19). We now become prey to our imaginations, our unruly urge to create any ideas we fancy, ungrounded in sense (6).

For the sake of lucidity, we're forced to create an abstract notion called 'cause.' In this forced construction, Hume says, we have logic on our side. We can selectively homogenize our lazy phantasmagoria of postures into certain groups of 'like' ones and argue, in a rule we assert to ourselves, that Category A causes Category B if a happening in the A group makes necessary, is sufficient for, a happening in the B group (73–79, 87). Unfortunately these rules are hopelessly vague because our groupings are hopelessly homogenized to start with. Our impish imaginations can now easily suggest that Category C caused B instead, and it is useless to argue otherwise: "Accordingly, we shall find upon examination that every demonstration, that has been produced for the necessity of a cause, is fallacious and sophistical" (80). It is immediate experience where authentic life is to be found (253).

This self-disparaging message is all one can draw from most of Hume's literal words. Is he really, though, in such despair? Has he really conceded that the only path to what is reasonable, to ideas, is to flee from what is real? His undertone suggests nothing of the sort and indeed leaves clues otherwise. One such clue is buried in the most allegorical of his expressions, the theatre metaphor. Each passing scene, he says, is a "situation," which, far from just an A bumping into a B, implies interrelationship – something fraught with possibility, of a whole picture in front of us. Even the impressions, he says, that are all we have of the world, could never have been actual had they lacked a wholeness and possibility in the first place. What remains is to examine the conditions of such possibility.

Inner Intuition (Anticipation) Is the Source of Reason

Not ten pages into Hume's opus, this father of empiricism and our reliance on our sensations of repetitive events to understand anything, has pointed twice toward the integral character of human understanding. The first signal is one we may have missed: his very argument that "ideas are regularized impressions" – his claim in other words to the validity of inductive proofs – is *itself* neither inductive nor syllogistic. It is a 'don't you get what I'm saying' argument. And a 'don't you get it' argument is an appeal to our inner intuition or experience, not our surface impressions. The second signal is that no sooner than proclaim his famous "no ideas are innate" (7), he promptly retracts it in favor of a 'nature' as "pointing out to everyone those simple ideas, which are most proper to be united into a complex one" (10–11). Unity in complexity! What else could these be but something inner?

Hume's dissatisfaction with either self-evident abstractions (rationalism) or atomistic regularities (empiricism) – what Immanuel Kant (1783) a half-century later said "woke me from my dogmatic slumber" – becomes even more evident in later parts of Hume's treatise. "To explain [our thinking] perfectly we must take the matter pretty deep," Hume says (253). Taking it deep he suggests, in an insight presaging Kant's (1781), would be *via* a 'quality' that associates one idea with another. 'Purpose' inevitably enters the picture: there is a "reference of parts to each other, and a combination of some end or purpose." Mutual dependence and sympathy would be among them: "This is still more remarkable, when we add a sympathy of parts to their common end…" (255–257) what Walras later argues is the undefinable *rarete* or scarcity of a good underlying our demands for it. Their point is that if the empirical dimension of reality were all there were, no one could ever understand it. Objectivity must be joined with subjectivity.

Hume's ultimate contribution was to help show – what he himself was only beginning to see – that this getting-to-know a reality's empirical dimension is a receptivity to it. The difference for Hume between sense impression and imagination is that impressions are an *inner receptivity to an outer reality*. Sense receives the object or event in the form of a situation, one that conveys an overall look and mood of the scene before us. In this way, Hume was a beginning of today's mainstream economic attitude – the first Enlightenment thinker to detect the priority of receptive over self-productive understanding that would soon emerge, in an economic context, in Adam Smith.

Supply Too Links Subject with Object

James Buchanan has, more than most since Jevons (1871), Walras (1874), and Menger (1883), been aware of the ongoing contention in economics between subjectivity and objectivity. Over in the subjectivist corner he puts the Austrian school. Especially, he says, "for Hayek (1974) and Mises (1949), [this school] amounts to an explicit denial of the objectivity of the data that informs economic choice" (1969, 25). What he calls neoclassical orthodoxy falls in comparison somewhere between the subjectivist and objectivist. In it, "the dependence of price (value) on marginal utility, subjectively determined, can be fully recognized, while an essentially objective theory of cost is retained." By cost Buchanan is referring to the theory of supply, which usually is expressed – on the surface – as a hard currency in contrast to demand theory's subjective utility. And he seems to imply the mainstream either doesn't understand or care about this inconsistency between subject and object:

> The difference between … objectivist and subjectivist … is profound but it continues to be slurred over in the neoclassical concentration on the idealized market interaction process in which all individuals behave economically.
>
> (1969, 25)

I wonder, however, whether such a slur could be credible. As how could a completely subjective consumer be willing to buy something from a completely anti-subjective producer? Doesn't she know he'll turn around and spend most of his producer gains as a consumer himself? And mustn't she as a consumer pay for it by producing something *her*self? And since both parties know so, wouldn't they quickly settle down to regarding each other as subjective *and* objective, in their own actions as well as their expectations of the other? And finally, doesn't the standard theory of partial equilibrium say precisely this? Buchanan does seem partly to glimpse so:

> In Jevons' famous statement, marginal utility depends on supply which, in its turn depends on cost of production. As stated, this theory is wholly objectivist in character, although, of course, the valuation of buyers and sellers is incorporated as part of the objective data.
>
> (1969, 24)

Representationally in other words there is no inconsistency here at all. Buyers are incorporating objectivity when they observe prices, which are objects. And given that in their subjective behaviors buyers are affecting these prices, price must reflect that subjectivity, in turn influencing supply. This is what partial equilibrium means. For what else besides supply could determine the objectively observed value that prices are? Answer: demand. And what drives demand? Marginal utility, a subjectivity.

In his "Methods and Morals in Economics" several years later, Buchanan's 'slurring' charge has in fact vanished. "The task of economic theory," he says, "is not that of predicting specific patterns of behavior; it is that of providing *structural understanding* of the processes within which divergent behavioral plans of persons are integrated and reconciled" (127, my italics). It is structural understanding too that is the pure, transcendental dimension of knowledge in Kant's epistemology, the dimension of the form or structure of a judgment. Buchanan says therefore "economic theory does not relinquish its explanatory role if its central predictive hypotheses fail to be corroborated empirically. This principal, the heart of eighteenth century wisdom, remains untouched by modern empirical testing…" (127–128). I would refine Buchanan's comment as follows. Because structure is only formality, to be distinguished from the *matter* of what is being structured, economic language – including homo economicus – can only be figures of speech. Transcendental language, the language of economic models, is the form because it cannot be the matter. The matter is finally your decision. The rest of us then can speak of it only metaphorically. Indeed, even you and I can speak of ourselves only metaphorically.

The Metalogical as a Constructing, the Kantian as a Receiving

A useful fixture of present-day economic textbooks is what they call the Ricardian model of rent, in his case land. Interestingly, what you read in these books is the modern interpretation of Ricardo rather than Ricardo himself. The modern rendition is that a tenant working the land to produce some good seeks utility by driving expected marginal production costs up to the good's output price, so that as the prices vary the tenant's marginal costs do too, tracing out, and so identifying, the cost function. The tenant's profit goes to zero if competition is strong enough, so any net rewards go to the owner of the scarce resource, which is the land. Ricardo's own reasoning to the contrary doesn't suggest any such optimization. It lacks any rigor in this intentionality or human sense of the word.

Ricardo's Tautological Distribution of Taxes

In particular, there is nothing in Ricardo's account for a tenant to 'drive up.' A good's price for Ricardo is identically the labor expended to produce it, which, as a substitute for improving the land itself and so its long-run value, rises automatically (becomes variable) as the tenant works harder on crop production alone. By *definition* then, "the value of corn is regulated by the quantity of labor bestowed on its production on that quality of land ..." (38). Corn's consumer price is determined by its variable costs only – not because tenant-producers maximize utility by (when producers have market power) driving marginal cost up to equal marginal revenue but because total value or revenue is defined to *be* labor quantity. We have here pure deduction from observable first principles, where, exactly as in balance-sheet accounting, conclusions are transparently already there in the premises.[3] This is classical, rationalist economics.

We can see it too in Ricardo's assessment, almost touching in its self-conscious syllogy, of land taxes. Adam Smith (1776) had asked whether any tax connected to land – in Ricardo's words to "the land itself" – or its *products* could under long-run tenant competition be borne by anyone but the landowner. Smith had concluded, consistent, if land is the only fixed input, with current reasoning, that it will indeed be a debit to the landowner. Ricardo disagrees, and here we have a classical economist commenting in 1817 on the reasoning of someone 40 years before him who held what is largely today's view. Ricardo's disagreement is on the grounds that if the tax is on products, it is the tenant – because he is the producer – who will be charged. This was to forget his own acknowledgment that tenants will, if output prices are inadequate to cover the tax, deduct it from their rent payments to the landowner. 117

He mightn't have been forgetful this way had he a notion of length-of-run, since he then would recognize that expectations and scarcity would have pushed variable profit toward zero, leaving the tax to be borne by the owner of the scarce resource. Or maybe it was the other way around: his inadequate notion of expectations and scarcity impaired his sense of a length-of-run. Regardless, neither time nor producer anticipations enter in any essential way into Ricardo's thinking. Though he may speak of prices, incomes, and production, Ricardo hails from a discipline entirely different from J.S. Mill's. And it is Mill's that, heavily dependent on Adam Smith, is the older of the two. One thing we have seen here is that the distinction between mainstream and classical/positivist economics is not, as you might casually assume, even close to being a chronological one.

The forerunner of Ricardo's confusing term 'land itself,' with its presumption of having everything literally in your head, seems to have been Gottfried Leibniz, who in his *Theory of Knowledge and Metaphysics* (1676) says it is "the nature of an individual substance or complete being to have a concept so complete that it is sufficient to make us understand and deduce from it *all the predicates of the subject* [my italics] to which the concept is attached." The completeness of a thing – what makes it a thing – is the completeness of its core concept, which as containing by deduction all the thing's properties, must essentially *be* the thing. This circularity is implicit too in Whitehead and Russell's demonstration in *Principia Mathematica* (1920) that the logical foundation of mathematics is the $A = A$ identity.[4] The collapse of everything into everything else that is the spirit of circularity explains why it's so easily supposed that utility can be added across persons, reducing them to a concept, which is a homogeneity, in turn a circularity.[5] But then it cannot be a ground after all, which is to be a starting and resting point. We can summarize this as follows: *Direct literal speech, free of any metaphor and so groundless in the sense of untied to any particularity or context – is a circling around an identity: a tautology.*[6]

The Cartesian "I think" – that since I know I *am* because I think, my thinking must be who I am – is, formally speaking, this same tautology. But like any circularity it is substantive too: in expressing an attitude. Ricardo's continual slippage into circularity isn't for dearth of sincerity, intelligence, or skill. Quite the contrary. It is rather, following Descartes and Leibniz, that they presume an idea in their mind to be a complete grasp of the thing they are thinking. It must therefore be a sharply defined thing because ambiguity and indefiniteness are, literally speaking, unthinkable. Ricardo has this pronounceably rationalist habit of reasoning literally, its way of relying on sharp deductions from sharply defined principles and categories. They *define* themselves into thinking their thoughts are clear and definite.

Defining One's World

Note the implication. It implies our thoughts are productive in the literal sense.[7] Cartesian coordinates fix our ideas in space; our ideas must, therefore, conform to mathematical coordinates. Ricardo's own concern was who would bear the tax cost – the landowner, the producer, or the customer – in any case a simplified version of the social welfare orderings of today and consistent with Kirzner's (1960) remark that Ricardo cared for the distribution rather than the production of wealth. It may explain Ricardo's insistence that we stand still and be counted and his consequent failure to follow his reasoning over into related issues, to a total cost and not just its distribution. It also is consistent with the consensus among scholars that classical economics presumes resources to be largely immobile, that it has no concept of equilibration.

This is no little technical failing. It is a grand attitudinal one. For any presumption, implicit or otherwise, of resource immobility implies discretion over where – at which collateral agent – the mobility will stop, and which, being immobile by assumption, will effectively be the cost-bearer. The presumption of resource immobility introduces the quizzical logic of mercantilism, the notion that someone must be better off when his neighbor is worse off. Here is a certain intellectual corruption because the thinker not only defines his world but decides who will pay for it.

It would be helpful to reflect for a moment on rationalist (infallible) thought itself and its sharp contradiction to the discursive (discrete, fallible, tentative) thought of Immanuel Kant underlying modern economics. The spirit of this rationalism was to draw all of reason into itself except perhaps fiction and poetry. Its mark was a supposed intuition, so sharp as to pierce through to underlying reality. Economics would be a special case of this new, perfect way of reason. And though it failed at this, it did help prompt or initiate the quantification of economic theory. Derek Parfit (2011) crystallizes the rationalist position by emphasizing its traditional distinction between objectivity and subjectivity, and which, as presumed to be separable from each other, has no place in economic or Kantian thought. Parfit argues the objectivity school is the more rational of the two because more fundamental. Objective rationality for him is science itself – the conduct of it and the conclusions it draws. Science is reason and reason is science; and given this is so, it is the only form of rationality.

Brian Hedden (2015) argues instead that since rationality would have to be in a particular person, the subjectivity form, namely in being one's own self, is the truer one. And since at the same time reason can't contradict science, it would have to be the self that science sees us to be. It follows then that to be subjectively rational for Hedden is draw the syllogistically correct conclusions for oneself *from* science. Thus, his subjectivity hasn't gotten Hedden anywhere beyond Parfit's objectivity. No sign of personhood has emerged in either.

Personhood gone, we can return with a cleansed mind to the rationality that in the behavioral disciplines has been called the view from nowhere (Nagel, 1986). As Hedden concludes, "given a total body of evidence, there is a unique set of preferences that it is rational to have." 149 Here we have the beliefs-vs-desires standpoint reduced to its nutshell. The total body of evidence is the sum of the scientific information at hand which, as the correct beliefs, determines our collective desires and actions. The burden of rationality thus rests on the syllogistic reasoning used to derive the correct behavioral implications.

Both the objective and subjective sides of rationalism have turned out to be *thought processes*. Total reason thenceforth would be to adopt scientific principles and, in an inexorable syllogistic advance, derive their implications for your desires and actions. Because syllogism is always perfectly articulable, the positivist attitude leads inescapably to the conclusion that if you can't explain why you're doing something, you aren't rational. Rationality, both in your outer and inner self, becomes your articulability – your ability to conceptualize.[8] This view had been perfected in the late 19th and early 20th centuries under Alfred Whitehead and Bertrand Russell (1920, then Rudolph Carnap (1935), Moritz Schlick (1936), A.J. Ayer (1936), W.V. Quine (1953), and others.

Moritz Schlick had set the tone: "To see that primitive experience is not first-person experience seems to me to be one of the most important steps which philosophy must take towards the clarification of its deepest problems" (44). By first-person here Schlick had meant the first-person singular. He thus would rule out the second- and third-person singular too because singular you's, he's, and she's are equally persons, who precisely are what he is ruling out. He must then be proposing to reduce human experience to something plural, as in the recent syntactic reduction in our language of she and he to 'they.' That too is nothing new, anticipated nearly a century ago when Heidegger (1927) characterized the penchant for escaping personal responsibility as "the They" (126–130).

The homogeneous 'they' does solve what Schlick said has been philosophy's greatest obstacle, the irreducibility – the unthinkability as it were – of the person. 'They' and only 'they' satisfies the three criteria sufficient for opening the person to positive inspection: (*i*) a separability of 'facts' (syntheticals) from any logical reasoning about them (analyticals) (5, 6); (*ii*) a reduction of reality to these two – fact and logic; and (*iii*) a consequent exclusion of any activity but a watching, measuring, and consistent categorizing. This we will largely be calling metalogical or empiricist in this book, the two 'isms' that rely on one another.

Necessity and Sufficiency as Principles of Logic

Fact and logic then are at the epicenter of the positive, metalogical world. In David Lewis (1973) we have both fact and logic in the conditions or correspondence rules between things that are possible and those that are necessary. It is worthwhile paying attention to them. Lewis suggests that: "Possibility is truth at some accessible world," in which "the accessibility restriction imposed depends on the sort of possibility under consideration" (5). His appeal here is to the *if – then* connection in a syllogistic sentence, the 'if' being the presence of an accessible world. To say that "if *x* happens, *y* will happen" is to say the world of the *x* is not only accessible to but occupied by the world of the *y*. Equivalently then *x* is *sufficient* for *y*, so we can call this possibility condition the *sufficiency* one. Sufficiency therefore in Lewis's world is a power to create or make-be in that *if* this power is present, the event in question *must* happen. Thus, the *if* aspect of a statement is the possibility or sufficiency side of a causal relation.

Note also, as Lewis does, that such a condition lacks a certain strictness because it appeals to the vagaries of the worlds which, by happening to happen, step forward to supply possibility seemingly at random. 'Possible' isn't a very comforting word. Only under certain unknown conditions is a 'possible' operative. These conditions, Lewis says, philosophers have sought to specify, and I would add, economists have sought as well.

Let's summarize this inexactness by way of the equivalency relation (and in it a definition) of *sufficiency*. Possibility (sufficiency, in Lewis's vocabulary), is the 'if,' the sometimes, the would be – an indeterminacy and thus, in my words rather than his, an uncertainty (3). The sense here is of a tentativeness and dependency, of a mere means – which, as opposed to ends, are ever questionable, a preliminary or mere path-toward. These transient worlds, Lewis says almost humorously, contain "more things than actually exist" (86). 'World' therefore is neither more nor less than a situation someone is in. In his getting-ready-to-leave example, packing the previous evening would have been sufficient for departing in the morning only *if* all other events had either conduced to that end or managed to change in some complementary way. So there isn't any 'need' or necessity going on here.

Sufficiency then is a world in which if you pack now, you will leave Tuesday. Suppose there is another encounterable world though, comprising conditions that are *always* there on Monday when you manage to leave on Tuesday. This world would be a necessary condition for getting out Tuesday. Concerned with events or empirics as he is, Lewis wants to minimize the number and variety of possible conditions required on Monday for safely reaching the actuality of a Tuesday departure. Despite its emphasis on events therefore, Lewis's inquiry here is a metaphysical one. It is as Kant likely would say, an inquiry into necessity itself. Lewis says, "necessity is truth at *all* accessible worlds" (13).

Now to arrive at this necessity, this 'only-if' side of an 'if-and-only-if' proposition, Lewis says we must emphasize the contrast between the possible 'if' and the necessary 'only-if.' The necessity side he calls the *strict conditional*, the stable, ever reliable presence at any such-and-such kind of event. Since this is so, necessity could never – speaking literally at least – be a counterfact. To the contrary it *must* be, and so the ever-predictable fact, in order for the outcome to be. For this reason, however, it cannot be the event-in-question's proximate mover either. Rather, by virtue of its stability, it is present in every world where the event is present, plus generally in others.

The necessary therefore can be regarded as a collection of many facts common to a variety of worlds. It and its associated accessibility might for instance be modeled, as they are in economics, in the form of a constraint set of a choice problem, where *in*accessibility comprises the case in which the constraints to the economic objective function are being violated. But there seems to be no formal or explicit objective function in Lewis's thinking – no explicit trying-to-achieve as there is in economics. In any event the strict, all-encompassing character of his necessity conditions, and so their essentiality, require that they be posited by the analyst even when not completely evident. We then can summarize all these considerations by saying that necessity is the world of the *strict, the only if, the always.*

The 'Only' having been satisfied here along with the 'If,' we can be confident of encountering causality wherever we go. Our success at finding the absolute minimum requirement is rewarded in the permission it gives us to impute these very causes. If strictness then is what affords analysis – the imputation of causality – our work will only be to identify *how* strict we legitimately can become in doing so. Lewis regards this identification issue to also be a metaphysical, and a difficult metaphysical, problem. The key to imputing causality, our ultimate goal, is to face the situation or presence involving as little strictness (necessity) as possible. This goal is to be pursued only to the point that going any further would involve complete *vacuity* – one's demands on the world so small that there isn't much to look at (13).

Vacuity then is a certain emptiness. But that is only because it takes so little to capture everything. And the point at which, while moving in vacuity's direction, we wish to stop, says Lewis, varies according to the type of causality sought for. "We call these worlds accessible, meaning thereby simply that they satisfy the restriction associated with the *sort of necessity* under consideration…" (5). This necessity checklist depends on the type of entity we are involved with, as he writes:

> Thus the logical strict conditional is stricter than any other; the material conditional is the least strict of all the conditionals that obey the constraint that every world is self-accessible; and the physical [physics] strict conditional, for instance, falls in between. The vacuous strict conditional is the least strict conditional of all.
>
> (8)

As with everything else, Lewis appears to be taking the word 'necessity' here literally. At least he makes no effort to explain the various types of being he has in mind, suggesting only that they're readily observed to be different from one another. And if the typological boundary between, say, what is a matter of logic and what is a matter of materials or morality is unclear, also unclear will be the question of how we should be gauging any degree-of-strictness.

Indeterminacy as Unreason

Franz Dietrich and Christian List (2016) reach, in their self-conscious loyalty to a metalogical rationality, near the summit of Lewis's thinking and for economic applications in particular. A visit is paid to a leader of positivist thought, W.V. Quine (1948), who defines in what seems to be a linguistic confusion what he calls a theory's ontological commitments. To represent these commitments, suppose say Dietrich and List that what is common to a theory or set of models is a large circle containing the conditions *necessary* for the theory:

> We have a defined theory as a set of sentences, endowed with a set of admissible models. By considering all these models, we can ask which kinds of objects, properties, and relations are present in *all* of them. These can be seen as the objects, properties, and relations that the theory is – in a logical sense – minimally committed to. We call these the theory's ontological commitments.
>
> (263)

Within this larger 'commitment' circle of a theory's necessary conditions is found, as in Lewis, a smaller one comprising the empirical *evidence* for the theory, namely for it to be realized in action. Outside it, we have a "case of indeterminacy," where models fail to be both necessary *and* sufficient so are not yet fully determinative. As partly underdetermined, decision makers are walking about freely, unpredictable by us thinkers.

As you may have guessed, this is supposed to be a bad sign. Along with Quine, D&L regard indeterminacy to be an interim failure. Successful economic models they say are those that fully *determine* economic actions, constituting therefore both the outcome's necessary *and* sufficient conditions. And how do we achieve such determinacy? By reaching further into science for the conditions requiring these actions be taken, either as laws (nomological) or as specifically required decisions (reductions), even if this requires, as they admit, some "creative" (273) work in finding the additional conditions. These new factors, like the older ones, will be *conceptualizations* for Dietrich and List, not the *intuitions* (anticipations, expectations) they would be in mainstream economics. Necessarily then they apply only to physical mechanics. Say D&L, "any non-physical explanations – such as psychological or social explanations – are at best provisional and reflect a lack of understanding of underlying mechanisms" (274).

That Dietrich and List are excluding moral law and its freedoms (which, they argue, are resistances to logic), but in mainstream economics are part of reality, gives an idea of the divide between the two. A great deal of economic phenomena are out there that cannot be predicted or therefore understood or recognized by empirical science. We have then, say D&L, choice behavior that "routinely underdetermines its theoretical explanation" (273), inadequate data on, or witnesses of, economic activity, "real" phenomena such as electro-magnetic fields (250). That is, there is a great deal more rational economic behavior out there waiting for science to discover. But this would be, mainstream economics and I argue contra D&L, because it isn't scientifically discoverable at all.

Though many professional philosophers may find it surprising, the logico-empiricist attitude here brings classical economics closely to mind. Ricardo's observed land-tax incidences were being derived from their deducible public *purposes*, remindful of Dietrich and List's corresponding suggestion to *watch out* for logical sequences, or as some have said of positivism that it similarly "deduces its observations." Behaviors are the facts (empirics, syntheticals), and principles their logic (analyticals). And the reasoning goes the other way too. For just as the maxim is to found oneself on observed facts from which conclusions are to be derived, so are economic conclusions, as founded on logic, to be the ones we will observe.

In our own spirit of critique, we should note that empiricist reason's sharp distinction between mathematical conclusions (as analytic) and 'facts' (as synthetic) falls immediately apart. For to call something a fact is to assign it an empirical category in order to speak of it, and such assignments themselves are quantitative, abstract therefore in the way any measurement demands. The facts (synthetics), that is, are being interpreted measurably, and measurable terms are precisely what qualify as its categories (analytics). Thus, by way of this inference of their mutual derivability, there finally is no distinction for them between analytic and synthetic in the metalogical senses of these words. All is logical analysis, presumed observable.

It is easy then to see how, if science is ever to pull economics into its orbit, it must do so under the subjective-*vs*-objective, beliefs-*vs*-desires framework, that is the bedrock of any scientific reasoning about human choices. Yet you will never see these distinctions mentioned in economics textbooks, and for the simple reason that they don't exist in economics. Whether then it quite grasps it or not, and Dietrich and List do appear to grasp it, analyticist (scientific) philosophy is on a mission to submerge economics into a special case of itself.

The problem is in its supposition that economics thinks it can know what is literally 'true,' 'actual,' or 'causal.' Hypotheses lose support in economics not when they fail to demonstrate underlying 'causes,' because that is finally hidden in the depths of personal decisions, but when they cease predicting the counterfactuals well enough that we will find them useful – in other words when the demand for economics as we know it falls away. The failure or success of economics is a matter of the economic supply and demand for its own self. Economics is itself then an economic phenomenon.

In short, it is the attitude that is finally important. It is the reduction of reality to the general and empirical, to empirical mechanics – to a reality comprising only manipulable objects – that I argue is the alternative to the contemporary economic standpoint. And it is this reduction that I want now to explore further.

'Thing' as Actuality, 'Person' as Possibility

Let's first characterize the anti-reductive approach to economic reason, one necessary for connecting up with a human person. A place to begin is Marshall's commentary in *Principles* (1920, 8th ed.) on the two ways in which the economic attitude to reason differs from others. First, its outlook and method are, in Heidegger's phrase, primarily noncategorial. It doesn't start with broad principles and subdivide them into narrower ones, as the situations it deals with cannot, except in superficial ways, be forced into a hierarchy. And this is because economic decisions are ultimately, and thus basically, acts of integration rather than categorization. Not even in looking back, let alone in looking forward, can we categorize ourselves except in tentative, indefinite ways. This Heidegger also says of There-Being, a person out in a world, as economics depicts her as well.

Second and for the same reason, Marshall says, the motives economics is concerned with cannot be captured in generalized, abstract language, as we otherwise would be content to categorize them. For Mill and Weber too, mainstream economics is simply lucky. In the medium of money, it has found a measurable quasi-correspondence to unmeasurable human phenomena, *as if* they were measurable. In this reference to metaphorical language, they are in line with Hume's tentative, and Kant's confirmed, insight into the transcendental (interpretive) character of human understanding.[9]

Persons *vs* Things: The Possible *vs* the Observed

About this, they are insistent and unmistakable. On the first count, says Marshall, economics "studies mental states rather through their manifestations than in themselves" (16). It "reaches [its] provisional conclusions by observations of men in general under given conditions without attempting to fathom the mental and spiritual characteristics of individuals" (16). "No one can compare and measure accurately against one another even his own mental states at different times: and no one can measure the mental states of another at all except indirectly and conjecturally through their effects....by the incentives they afford to action" (15–16). Consequently, and in case we miss his point, and keeping in mind morality's metaphysical status:

> the greater part of those actions, which are due to a feeling of duty and love of one's neighbor, cannot be classed, reduced to law, and measured.... so that the machinery of economics cannot be brought to bear on them.
>
> (24)

Science in contrast is driven by categories:

> in the physical sciences indeed, whenever it is seen that a group of things have a certain set of qualities in common, ... they are formed into a class with a special name ... and a new technical term is invented to represent it.
>
> (51)

Economics however has no wish for such factory-like views because, unlike science, its own standpoints "call for and develop the faculty of sympathy," a connectivity of self to world.

Precisely for the sake of this connectivity, which can be achieved by way of will, intuition, and judgment only, economics cannot in its own abstractions claim to know the world's underlying motives and incentives. "It is then not the want of will but the want of power, that prevents economists from reckoning in the motives of action ..." (24). We can only speak as if we had that power: "We speak of the measurement of desire only by the action to which it forms the incentive..." (20).

Economics cares about things only because persons do, and even then, only as seen through persons. This is a burden to the profession because persons are more profound, not just more complex, than things are. But it also is an advantage because, being persons themselves, economists can as Marshall says have a certain sympathy for their subject. They can stand symbolically in their subject's shoes, a privilege accorded to few or no other systematic disciplines. They simply cannot, being outside of her, know the person herself.

What I hear as common to the modern founders is that only by drawing a distinction between possible (indefinite) and actual (definite) reality can you find meaning in – provide any interpretation for – actual events. Precisely then because you are operating in the domain of possibility, of decision and not of actuality or 'outcome,' you must surrender any pretense of knowing many actualities themselves, that your words somehow envelop and dominate their object, *make* the object as it were. For this is precisely what rationalism does by requiring that the structure of a decision be divided into a separately observed belief (objective) part and preference (subjective) part, instead of merely noting that in any decision the two must be joined inextricably together.

The Engaged *(*Mainstream Economic*)* View

Let's then give some instances of what we mean, with Marshall, that economics takes a point of view, namely where experience is immediate and possibility is unified. We then can be more precise about what we mean by interpretative, phenomenological concepts, how, despite the difficulty of articulating them, they represent the sharpest of concretions and are the only real human condition.

In his depiction in *Being and Nothingness* (1943) of the "the body" (401–470), Jean-Paul Sartre takes this question from what in the present context we could call the consumer side of economics. Van den Berg (1962) exemplifies it as a hiker beginning an arduous mountain assent.

> The evening before, he examines his gear, tries it on, notes its advantages and flaws, regards his arms, wrists, ankles. Off the next morning, he 'forgets' the gear, forgets himself in fact. There is now only the mountain: he is absorbed in its structure....The size of his foot is measured by the measurements of the projecting points which serve as footholds....The fatigue of his body shows itself in the first instance in the too-steep parts of the way presaging the top, [then] in the changed aspect of the landscape, as the changed physiognomy of the objects....The vulnerability of his body becomes clear to him a long time before he falls, in the dangerous incline or the movable objects under his feet."
>
> (107–108)

We approach a road intersection the same way, absorbed in the entire structure of what it might signify. Concentrating on particulars would distract our attention from the whole, and conflating the whole would submerge the important particulars. Any laziness in the guise of averaging the difference between two distinct objects would miss their potential relationship, and that invites accidents. The true picture of the intersection is one in which each opportunity and danger is brought together into a whole of possible significance, before any particular outcome, distinguishable as good or a bad, can be recognized. Sense and concept, success and failure, are integral to one another here as part of an openness to an entire 'scene.' To slightly rework Thomas Hora's remark, the risk-taker "stands out in her own future and invites herself into it."

Something similar is taking place on the producer side. A new restaurant is opening. The entrepreneur looks about her the evening before, a successful dining experience 'present' to her in look and feel, in the orientation of the decor, the cleverness of the seating arrangements, the preparedness of the waitstaff. How could she revel in this way unless, in the same moment, she sensed it collapsing as well, the empty tables, the obtrusive silence, the triumph forsaking her? In a unity we can with Heidegger call Concern, her perception of her risk joins indissolubly with her willingness to bear it. Possibilities for every other aspect of her life, her other career chances, her child's school performance, opinions of friends and critics, obviously cannot be separated from this concern, nor it from them. As Heidegger (1927) puts it,

> By Others we do not mean…those over against whom the 'I' stands out. They are rather those for whom, for the most part, one does not distinguish oneself. (118))

Every human dimension – biological, psychological, intellectual – is involved in this joint possibility, a bond dissevered only for theoretical simplification. And the good economic theoretician, who speaks *as though* it is dissevered, knows this.

The economics of the person constituting modern economics must therefore, as its founders emphasize, be of someone in a possible, uncertain world. Uncertainty and its concerns are precisely an indefiniteness, but for the same reason 'focus the mind' and in that way highly concrete. Possibility is the height of concretion *because* it is the future's final unknowability. As Frank Knight wrote, "we do not react to the past stimulus, but to the 'image' of a future state of affairs," to what is "forward-looking" (201). Suppose now we were to call this image – pure intuition, unmeasurable in itself but constituting the meaning of what we do measure – 'utility' or 'risk bearing.' Then all we would mean by them, and fully what we would mean, is the hiker's and restaurateur's own particular situations. This in any event is where the modern economic founders were pointing: away from the They and toward the Person.

It is to utility then we now turn.

Summary Points of Chapter II

1. Just as *observations* in mainstream economics are mediated by what is not observable, *estimates* are mediated by what is not estimable. In each case Kantian pure intuition is the mediator.
2. Your mediation is your sense of a situation, your openness to your world, expressed in the *synthetic a priori* act of assigning sense impressions to judged-appropriate concepts.
3. Economic understanding, that is, is an act of integration. Our first view of this integrality derives, despite his popular reputation, from Hume and his dissatisfaction with what earlier in history had been regarded as self-evident: concepts and causes.
4. What we find is that fully conceptual *or* fully measurable expression – in either case fully literal – is circular, a failure of structure. It is the task of mainstream economics to re-integrate this structureless circularity.
5. To reintegrate it means to think no longer syllogistically alone nor inductively alone, but as an inner receptivity to an outer reality, a pointing of parts toward a whole.
6. In particular, classical (rationalist) economics is an excellent guide to what mainstream economics is *not*: a reliance on literal language. That a tax on a farmer's products means the farmer will pay the tax is a misconception triggered by taking "a farmer's products" literally.
7. Similar confusions appear in the words 'objective' and 'subjective,' the one a belief, the other a wish, which taken literally can be connected only mechanically.

8. Twentieth century empiricism sought to strengthen such reasoning by reducing reality to facts and logic. A fact would be that Event 1 has caused Event 2. The logic would be that Event 1's *sufficiency* for Event 2 was preferred over Event 3's *necessity* for it, which would restrict the scope of science.
9. Following this lead, positivistl models stressed sufficient conditions that would be realized in action, backed therefore by data and so determinative. Both the facts (synthetics) and the categories (analytics) would be measured, converging on and so reduced to each other.
10. The mainstream stressed the final nonseparability of the intuitive and conceptual dimensions instead, a receptivity to a possible world, success and failure brought together in a single view.

Notes

1 As we can see, positivist economics has nothing to do with the word 'positive' in normative vs positive. The distinction between normative and positive collapses anyway when we realize that optimization itself is a normative event, which when data are applied to it becomes positive as well. That is, if the 'positive' in 'normative vs positive' really referred to positivism, there could be no distinction at all between positivist and contemporary economics.

2 In Kant this is the distinction between a 'thing-itself' and one's understanding of it. This Kant explores in his Transcendental Deduction and Schematism. See Lanier Anderson (2022) for an excellent discussion of this issue as one of *containment* or *analyticity* versus syntheticity in conceptual reasoning.

3 Ricardo does allow for capital inputs, though not any that might influence this relation between value and labor.

4 It is an aspect for them of the category of primitive ideas as consisting of elementary propositions and their associated elementary propositional functions, whose foundational role is to be perfectly general. (91–94)

5 John Updike (1960) may have had such Leibnizian circularity in mind when he had a writer, gazing out to sea, pose himself the following conundrum: "Let us posit a world of two halves: the ego and the external object ... a kind of biform Parliament, where two members sit, and speak for all parties. Tell me what I must do. Or rather, give me my excuse, for my vote is fore-ordained. It must be in opposition, and our Parliament will be stalemated until one of us dies." (160) A tautologous world would be a depressing experience.

6 Leibniz thought his intuition so powerful as to peer through to underlying truth, so his deductions from it contained the same truth, a 'thing-in-itself.' See for instance Allison's (13, 28, 156, 160–167) and Gardner's (95–96, 200–203) discussion of this. We will revisit it more below.

7 I borrow from Heidegger (e.g. 1927, 50) on this, in particular his distinction between 'Being-In' and 'Being-Next-To.'

8 This meaning of metaphysics applies also to most post-Socratic philosophy through to the medieval scholastics, for whom our grasp of the universe was supposed to be direct. As Kant says (1783, 106), echoed by Heidegger, Sartre, and much of depth psychology, we escape this dogmatism by accepting that "I do not hereby know [it] as it is in itself but as it is for me, that is, in relation to the world of which I am a part."

9 The recognition in the modern world that the interpretive dimension of understanding is the dimension of possibility seems to have first been emphasized by Soren Kierkegaard,

writing in the 1840s when the contemporary economic spirit was only beginning to flower. In *Concluding Unscientific Postscript* (1846) he says (320): "Existential [as opposed to empirical] reality is incommunicable....When reality is apprehended by an outsider it can be apprehended only as possibility. Everyone who makes a communication, insofar as he becomes conscious of this fact, will therefore become careful to give his existential communication the form of a possibility...." The economics founders all essentially say this of economic communication.

References

Allison, Henry E. *Kant's Transcendental Idealism: An Interpretation and Defense.* New Haven: Yale University Press, 1983, 2004.

Anderson, R. Lanier. "Transcendental Idealism as Formal Realism." *European Journal of Philosophy,* Vol. 30, 2022, 899–923.

Ayer, Alfred J. *Language, Truth, and Logic*. London: Victor Gollancz, 1936. Esp. in "The Function of Philosophy." 2nd ed., NY: Dover, 1952.

Buchanan, James. *Cost and Choice: An Inquiry in Economic Theory*. Chicago: Markham Publishing, 1969. Republished in: The *Collected Works of James Buchanan*, Vol. 6. Indianapolis: Liberty Fund, 1999.

Buchanan, James. "Methods and Morals in Economics." In: Science and Ceremony: The Institutional Economics of C.E. Ayres. William Bright and William Patton Culbertson (eds.). Austin: University of Texas Press, 1976.

Carnap, Rudolph. *Philosophy and Logical Syntax.* London: Psyche Miniatures, 1935.

Dietrich, Franz and Christian List. "Mentalism vs Behaviorism in Economics: A Philosophy of Science Perspective." *Economics and Philosophy* 32, 2016, 249–281.

Eliot, T.S. "Little Giddings." *Four Quartets*. Harvest Book, Harcourt, Inc., 1943.

Gardner, Sebastian. *Kant and the Critique of Pure Reason.* New York: Routledge, Taylor and Francis, 1999.

Hayek, Friedrich A. von. "The Pretence of Knowledge." Nobel Memorial Lecture, December 11, 1974. Reprinted in *American Economic Review* 79, No. 6, December 1989.

Hedden, Brian. *Reasons Without Persons: Rationality, Identity, and Time*. Oxford: Oxford University Press, 2015.

Heidegger, Martin. *Being and Time*. John Macquarrie and Edward Robinson (Trans.). New York: Harper-Collins, 1962. First published in 1927.

Heidegger, Martin. *Kant and the Problem of Metaphysics.* James S. Churchill (Trans.). Bloomington, IN: Indiana University Press, 1962. First published in 1929.

Hora, Thomas. "Psychotherapy, Existence, and Religion." In: Hendrik Ruitenbeek (ed.), *Psychoanalysis and Existential Philosophy*. NY: E.P. Dutton, 1962.

Hume, David. *A Treatise of Human Nature. Book I, Of the Understanding*. L.A. Selby-Bigge (ed.). Oxford: Clarendon Press, 1893. First published in 1739.

Jevons, W.S. *The Theory of Political Economy*, 4th ed. London: Macmillan, 1911. First edition 1871.

Kant, Immanuel. *Prolegomena to Any Future Metaphysics*. Lewis White Beck (Trans.). New York: Bobbs-Merril, 1950. First published in 1783.

Kant, Immanuel. *Critique of Pure Reason*, 1st and 2nd eds. Norman Kemp Smith (Trans.). New York: Random House (Modern Library), 1958. First published 1781; revised 1787.

Kierkegaard, Soren. *Concluding Unscientific Postscript*. D.F. Swenson and W. Lowrie (Trans.). Princeton: Princeton University Press, 1941. First published in 1846.

Kirzner, Israel M. *The Economic Point of View*. 1960, 1976. Institute for Humane Studies, Menlo Park. Also Sheed and Ward, 1976.

Knight, Frank H. *On the History and Method of Economics*. Especially "The Ricardian Theory of Production and Distribution" and "What is Truth in Economics?" Chicago: University of Chicago Press, 1956.

Leibniz, Gottfried von. "Theory of Knowledge and Metaphysics." In: Philip Wiener (ed.), Selections. New York: Scribner & Sons, 1951. First published in 1676.

Lewis, David K. *Counterfactuals*. Cambridge: Harvard University Press, 1973.

Lewis, David K. *Philosophical Papers, Vol. 1*. Oxford: Oxford University Press, 1983.

Marshall, Alfred. *Principles of Economics*. New York: Macmillan and Co., 1890, 1920, 1930.

Mill, John Stuart. "*On the Definition and Method of Political Economy*." In: D. Hausman (ed.), *The Philosophy of Economics*, 3rd ed. Cambridge: Cambridge University Press, 2008. First published in 1836.

Minski, Marvin. *The Society of Mind*. NY: Simon and Schuster, 1986.

Mises, Ludwig von. *Human Action: A Treatise on Economics*, 3rd ed. Chicago: Henry Regnery Co., 1966. First published in 1949 by Yale University Press.

Nagel, Thomas. *The View From Nowhere*. Oxford: Oxford University Press, 1986.

Parfit, Derek. *On What Matters (Volume One)*. Oxford: Oxford University Press, 2011.

Quine, W.V. "On What There Is." *Review of Metaphysics* 2 (21–38), 1948.

Quine, W.V. *From a Logical Point of View* (especially "Two Dogmas of Empiricism"). Cambridge: Harvard University Press, 1953.

Ricardo, David. *The Principles of Political Economy and Taxation*. Mineola: Dover Publications, 2004. First published in 1817.

Rilke, Rainer. "Duino Elegies." In: Edward Snow (Trans.), *The Poetry of Rilke*. New York: Farrar, Straus, and Giroux, 2009. First published in 1923.

Sartre, Jean-Paul. *Being and Nothingness*. Trans. Hazel E. Barnes, Washington Square Press of Simon & Schuster, 1956. First published in French by Gallimard, 1943.

Schlick, Moritz. "Meaning and Verification." *The Philosophical Review* 45, 1936. Reprinted in W.P. Alston and G. Nakhnikian, *Readings in Twentieth Century Philosophy*. London: Collier-Macmillan, 1964.

Smith, Adam. *The Wealth of Nations*. 1776. New York: Modern Library, 1937.

Van den Berg, J.H. "The Human Body and the Significance of Human Movement." In: Hendrik Ruitenbeek (ed.), *Psychoanalysis and Existential Philosophy*. New York: E.P. Dutton and Co., 1962.

Weber, Max. *The Theory of Social and Economic Organization*. A.M. Henderson and T. Parsons (Trans.). NY: Oxford University Press, 1947. First published in 1922.

Whitehead, Alfred N. and Bertrand Russell. *Principia Mathematica*. Cambridge: Cambridge University Press, 1920.

III The Centrality of Utility

The point of the positivist message of Auguste Comte (1830, 1842), presaged no doubt by Descartes but of which Comte remains the fountainhead, is that all reality, so all human reality, is ultimately reducible to – essentially becomes – mathematics. Math indeed, being the logic of science, was to be superior to anything discovered by way of it. Math and mathematized language, a quintessentially literal one, had burst through its earlier limits as something occasionally useful. It had come to *be* reality. We can think of mainstream economics as a resistance to this reduction, to a corralling into any technical corner. Economics is best approached by first knowing what it isn't: it isn't reductive.

In the notion of utility we come to the heart of this anti-reductive message. Utility is a symbol, the central one, of the inviolability, the entire unmeasurability and unmanipulability of a human person as person. 'Black box' is a code word for proposals to attempt a reduction, itself a symbol or call to relegate ourselves (or more usually others) to mere objects of interest. At the same time, and shockingly, utility is the foundation of some subtle mathematics and which are prerequisite to understanding what economics is engaged in: *synthetic a priori* reasoning in the sense of Immanuel Kant – or duality as economists call it – in which, as we've seen, contemporary economics is fundamentally situated. *How* fundamentally is what we will see in this chapter, inasmuch as in its absence, modern economics collapses into the reductivity of positivist thought.

Among the more important conclusions we will draw: because positivist economics reduces to classification, it is resigned to regarding subjectivity and objectivity as opposites, despite that they are unified in every human person. The way to avoid this conflict is to recognize that economic reason is primarily discursive (judged, tentative, risky) on account of the singularity or particularity of each situation. Economics' discursive reason explains why cost, profit, demand, and supply can only be estimated, never observed. At the same time, it is the only path to a counterfactual, to possible reality, and so to any true policy analysis.

DOI: 10.4324/9781003514602-5

Decisions Considered as Free, Their Expressions as Metaphor

The usual taxonomy that confines modern economics to one that allows resources to be mobile has its virtues, especially in being easy to spot. The conventional (and accurate) story is that if production inputs are fixed and can't be shifted, we have classical economics; if they can be, we have mainstream economics. But this is also superficial because it considers itself to be answering a 'what' question only. *What* are modern economics' analytic frames? What do they imply for value? What sorts of policies are they inclined to favor? In this 'what' emphasis, it unconsciously tips its hand in favor of the positivist, especially empiricist, attitude. For suppose the whole point of the revolt that is phenomenology, its skeptical view of easy abstractions, was to defer the 'what' question until the 'how' is answered? *How* is the analytical frame to be derived, how will it express itself, how will its applications be restricted, how will it make sense as a whole? The classical, rationalist view we see in Ricardo (1817) and Sen (1979) and the more recently empiricist one in Lewis (1976), Parfit (2011), and others points us away from asking these how questions. It thinks it already knows how to know and just wants to get on with it.[1]

If we want to use the 'how-versus-what' to distinguish the phenomenological from these, we must recognize it to be part of the deeper question of being human, for a person is more a how than a what. In asking this question, it is natural to suppose the positivist arose jointly with the phenomenal rather than fruits of distinct eras, because attitudes toward humanity haven't changed in the past half-millennium. One way then of expressing the distinction between a how and a what is to argue, as we shall below, that while mainstream economics acknowledges a phenomenal or interpretative dimension of understanding, the positivist in particular does not. It doesn't allow for any interpretative dimension as such. Knowing isn't an explicit issue for it. It simply looks, classifies, correlates, and knows.

This hyper-simplification is so great we can appreciate Kant's insight into our proclivity for bare generalizations, our presumption that we can know what the world is in itself. Kant says,

> There is indeed something seductive in our pure concepts of the understanding [oftensatisfying itself] with nothing but beings of thought, without [recognizing] it has transgressed, with its otherwise legitimate concepts, the bounds of their use.
>
> (1783, 62)

Kant is referring here to the specifically rationalist abuse of generalizations: the notion that everything of importance can be deduced from them. But as he shows in the Antinomy of Pure Reason, the opposite empiricist error falls under the same critique: the notion that we can know everything of importance by simply looking at it and measuring it, innocent of any prior capacity to grasp it in its uniqueness and immediacy (1781, 211–268). And as we've said, both these are fallacies – whether it be depriving our rationale of evidence or our evidence of rationale.[2]

Either way they lack a certain self-awareness: that we spend our days making judgments that involve both thought *and* observation. This isn't to say they're being haphazard. Amartya Sen's (1979) abstractive social welfare functions are a model of diligence. It only means he never considered the problem of knowledge itself and incorporated it formally into his thinking. Like Parfit and Hedden, he shows respect for the truth but little regard for the problem of how we come to know it.

As every bald generalization is a mechanism – lacking in any particularity of situation or context – rationalist or empiricist reason is mechanical either way it turns. On the one side it is lost in the generality of its ideas and on the other side its measures. They are equally abstract. It is precisely because mainstream theory regards personal decision makers as unique, involved in a situation to which the professional economist and policy maker can never be privy, that it expresses itself with such simplicity. It doesn't pretend – as rationalism and empiricism indeed must pretend – to know particular situations. Only decision makers know them.

Kant's task rather was to show that a situation is grasped only intuitively – in the first place an empirical intuition and in the second place a pure one – and which along with conceptualization or theory constitute understanding. But the understanding then is the person's own, not economic theory's, which is a visualizing and consistency-enhancing device only. Only the user can supply the pure intuition that both anticipates and constitutes the act of understanding we call contemporary economics. What you see on the white board, in the textbook, in the journal article is nonliteral, phenomenal, metaphorical, symbolical – the dimension of the *as-if*. Only the decision maker can 'get' the situation. The distant analyst, the textbook author, the article writer, the regulator, cannot.[3]

And what of the empirical, measurable, literal dimension? I'm glad you asked.

Pure versus Empirical Economic Concepts

As the modern economic seed began germinating in the late 18th century and flourishing in the 19th through the present, the classical – positivist – attitude that Heidegger says originated in Descartes never faltered. It began in fact to cast itself as overseer and articulator of its neoclassical opponent, of utility in particular. It was this claim to the articulator role that prompted 20th century expositors like Lionel Robbins to redouble their efforts to explain utility's nonliteral sense, despite that Adam Smith had grasped it175 years earlier. Robbins' task in the much critiqued and influential *Nature and Significance of Economic Science* (1932) we saw in Chapter I was to explore a certain way, a human way, of understanding economic reality. He was acutely aware his effort would invite misrepresentation and spends as much time explaining what economic modernity isn't as what it is.

Economics Is More Sense Than Concept

Most prominently, he rejects the idea that economics is something classificatory in the sense of dividing up a pie. The classifications Robbins rejects are the empirical sort, those successively generalized and particularized by a chosen logical rule. In the scientific attitude – perfectly legitimate in its place – you know a thing when you've worked your way down to it from something more general, then observed it, or the reverse. Thought hierarchies like these are inadequate however for understanding humanity *as* human. Economics approaches the person, Robbins says, as a certain orientation or stance, marked by a mood of concern (16–17). Concern comes with, and only with, freedom. "Where independent initiative ... is permitted the individual, there economic analysis comes into its own" (19). The difference between economics as a 'what' and as an attitude is the same we are making here between a thing and a person, for a thing is best approached as a 'what' while a person is best approached as a 'how' or an attitude.[4]

It applies as well to economics' own unifying categories: utility and uncertainty. To treat either as a thing is to consider it an entity. Then it wouldn't be economics. "The habit," says Robbins, "prevalent among certain groups of economists discussing economic satisfactions, is alien to the central intention of economic analysis. A satisfaction [they think] is to be conceived as an end-product of activity," an observable or empirical category (25). "Economics," however, "can neither detect nor is necessarily interested in the multitude and mutual relationships of somebody's ends," which like the means to achieve them fluctuate in ways no one, even the decision maker, can track. Had they been empirical objects, they certainly might have been tracked, but economics would then have devolved into a branch of technology. "One of the main dangers to civilisation arises from the inability of minds trained in the natural sciences to perceive the difference between the economic and the technical" (34).

How then does economics represent human motivation in a way that doesn't devolve, like a 'satisfaction,' into an end-in-itself? Economics' answer is to deploy a theme or symbol in place of the object, a utility *u* whose meaning is a sense of scarcity and concern rather than any psychological feeling. If we're to proceed both systematically *and* imaginatively, we must treat this sense as a physical shape, while never taking that literally. Because a decision isn't real until you are pushed into some kind of corner, *u* must bear a concave relation to goods, bending inward to what is feasible rather than outward to an illusion of magic. The more therefore of this symbolic *u* that you have, the less in general you want it to grow. Concavity fits with this scarcity theme because even if supply were unlimited, your capacity to consume it wouldn't be. Or as Robbins put it in his Richard T. Ely Lecture at the 1980 American Economic Association meetings, "the generalizations which emerge [from the propositions of economics] are statements of existence or possibility" only, and the finite character of this possibility is precisely what decreasing marginal utility points to.[5]

Note that it is only a pointing-to. Possibility as such! As Heidegger (187) notes, we aren't speaking here of actual possibilities like job offers, but your gist of the situation allowing you to choose among them meaningfully. The law of diminishing marginal *u* doesn't mean anyone knows whether your or my *u* curve, if we actually had one – and we don't – is convex or concave at any point in the day (137, c141). Why for instance wouldn't young parents watching their income grow not see in it even wider opportunities for their children, steepening rather than flattening their utility line? And it could work the other way: "there may be an opportunity cost of internal arbitrage," says Robbins. Time constraints imply a certain decreasing marginal utility for "bothering about marginal utility" (92). Resource limits mean nothing if not the infeasibility of constantly focusing oneself on being rational. There is no thing or black box here to observe and divide into parts.

And notice, we wouldn't be seeing all this if it weren't for economic theory. Much of its value is to show, to point to, what we cannot know itself.

Is There a 'Natural' Price?

This hasn't, in a tone deafness to the distinction between pure and empirical categories, fazed many of economics' critics. It will be useful to consider for a moment one of the many views of Robbins taken recently from the analyticist side. Brown and Spencer's (2012) is particularly interesting because they regard Robbins as a philosophical ally rather than opponent, a conscientious though crude harbinger of the more advanced science to come. Unlike other neoclassicists they say, Robbins didn't think his "abstract theory of value" and "perfect rationality" to be "indubitable postulates," but temporary simplifications to be later upgraded to the true "underlying processes."[6]

Their own upgrade is to propose dropping the current assumption of the relativity of prices, and so the freedom to judge and choose, and in an obvious gesture to physics replace it with the "natural property of the relevant commodity." Individual value judgments will be substituted with boards of experts who will identify these natural properties. Curiously, this quasi-religious belief in a yet-unknown but scientifically discoverable underlying process takes us not forward but back to Bentham, indeed to the 13th century notion of a just price, the 'actual' value that the distant planner – theologian then and scientist now – espies. This is the cognitive disengagement Robbins had called pseudo-scientific bravado (121), so he wouldn't be in much of a mood, if he were here today, to return Brown and Spencer's compliments.

It is the error of supposing economics to be a mere forerunner of the reduction of reason to IQ that we need to reflect on. In doing so, it seems to me, we must acknowledge the difficulty of understanding any alien viewpoint without first standing in a sympathy to it. Remaining sympathetic is crucial. The distinction between unanchored abstractions and personal sense is obvious to everyone, mainstream and positivist alike, from their ordinary experience. It is just that, when they put on their professional thinking caps, you'd never know this. For the Leibnizian or Comtean view of reality, in which generalizations have epistemological priority and your intuitions are mere private fancies, is entirely incommensurate with an ordinary person's view that intuition is what is central and generalization is only for consistency.[7] Important for our purposes here is that the economics of a person contains no 'theory of value' as Brown and Spencer think it does if they mean we can know what a value is in itself – in its 'nature' – by abstract reasoning. And perfect rationality isn't a modern postulate of economics, let alone 'indubitable.'[8]

Only a disengaged viewer could think it were because personal situations, being particular and risky, could never be part of any claim to know an 'underlying process.' That would be perfection, and the perfect is rather in the dimension of fancy and imagination than of human estimation and judgment.

To avoid this disengagement ourselves, we must hypothetically adopt the attitude of those we critique. Contemporary economics does so. It is aware that its estimates lie under a penumbra of uncertainty, just as a consumer and producer do. Indeed, economics' risk stems from the buyers' and sellers' risks. Estimates are only questionably predictive because traders predict themselves questionably – or at least, the world they live in questionably. Let's then look in more detail at the 'how' of understanding in contemporary economics. We will first scrutinize its most prominent interpretive category – utility – so that we don't allow it to slip by us as something either conceptual *or* empirical. We will pay particular attention to the intuitive grasp of one's total, unified possibility that constitutes the interpretive dimension of reality, distinguishing it from the actual – observable and measurable – phenomena it interprets. As we do, we will see that utility's superficially literal meaning quickly dissolves, even as its significance grows. We will then move on in Chapter IV to the closely related interpretive categories of uncertainty, completeness, and equilibrium.

The Suprasensibility of Utility

Let's then reconstruct the contemporary understanding of utility. For if any economic notion could encompass the entirety of human meaning we have described, oriented toward a future whose indefiniteness is the motive and focus of every decision, it would be embodied in this concept.

Yes, Utility Sounds Ambiguous

Even among those sharing Mill's view that it is merely a "bracket for motives," including "self-abnegation and beatification," utility has a problematic history. Having just reminded us that it doesn't reflect any "affection in the mind itself" (15), so is never psychologically measurable, Marshall (1890) says something like the opposite. It is correlative to Desire or Want, he says, "the total utility of a thing" being "the total pleasure or other benefit it yields." This total rises "with every increase in his stock of [goods]," a gain which, following Jevons, Menger, and Walras, he calls marginal utility and uses, "on a plan now coming into familiar use," to construct and articulate the demand function (93).[9]

John Hicks devotes the prominent early pages of his *Value and Capital* (1946) to disposing of any credibility to the claim that utility can be measured, concluding that "we have now to undertake a purge, rejecting all concepts which are tainted by quantitative utility" (19). But Hicks is now the name of the compensation necessary to restore a consumer to the same utility he'd had before some price rise, requiring that we know how much utility he'd ended up with and, consequently, how much it had changed. First they say in no uncertain terms that utility can't be measured, then explain economic concepts in ways that seem to require it to be. First they say they can't, then suggest – on the surface of things – that they can.

In defense of my sharp manner of putting this, consider Vilfredo Pareto's innovation of the continuous indifference curve. If a consumer can simply list the bundles equally acceptable to her, we might be free of any further messing with her 'utility.' Suppose in particular we can find two bundles x_1 and x_2 such that, in her opinion, small switches dx from one to the other would be equally 'costly' (i.e., $p_1\, dx_1 = p_2\, dx_2$). Since she finds bundle changes dx_1 and dx_2 equally acceptable, she essentially is saying she is satisfied staying where she is. We've found her demand for the median bundle to be a function of its own and the alternative bundle's price. Better yet we can forget the indifference curve altogether, merely pointing to a bundle she can afford and asking whether it is suitable. If it isn't, we point to another, and so forth until she stops saying no. The dream of banishing those utility-things has been realized. She simply doesn't care to move any further. The basis of economic decision, that is, has been shown to be essentially inarticulate. As Frank Knight (1956) put it, "it is typical of all value that men want it without concretely knowing what it is, but as the solution to a problem, and especially desired *because* it is a value" (132).

And Has Indeed Been Continuized

This alone of course offers no conceptual insight into the inner workings of a person's decision, and it was Slutsky who developed, and Hicks who helped explicate, a way to decompose the demand effect of a price change into the above-mentioned Hicksian or compensated (substitution) effect and corresponding income effect, showing how the changed real income consequent on the price rise has also affected demand. Unfortunately that entire income effect is restricted to a mere constant unless real income $v(p, m) = \max_x u(x)$, where p is the vector of prices and m the minimum total expenditure, be a positively sloped, strictly concave function of m so that its inverse, the expenditure function $e = e(p, u)$, be positively sloped and strictly convex in u.[10] As derivatives are employed in this decomposition, we in turn require that ordinal utility u be real-valued and continuous rather than the discrete ordering it was originally to have connoted.[11]

Importantly, once u becomes continuous in this way, permitting $e(p, u)$ to be a real-valued function – in particular the least expenditure that, at fixed prices p, can provide utility u – this u itself simultaneously loses its ordinality, in which a situation with any higher utility number is preferred to one with any lower number. Any continuity is now lost. Yet something more important is gained. For function indicator e too now is symbolic, as indeed it must be, given that the meaning of one's expenditures is nothing more than the utility it offers, so must be as nonempirical (even to the customer) as utility is. Relation $e(p, u)$ is now restored to its original meaning: as something estimable only, never observed. In happiness and justice indexes such as Partha Dasgupta's (1993) they are taken as literal instead. I argue most economists consider expenditure data therefore, and so income data, to have only latent, unobservable meaning.[12]

Utility became 'continuous' in economics by way of its symbolic power. An elegant theory of choice became possible as a joint mapping or duality between a consumer's expenditure choice and bundle choices, each yielding the other. An apparent thing-utility can be very elegant, and microeconomic theory has indeed become very elegant. The rate of change of utility $v(p, m)$ with respect to price change dp, divided by the negative of its rate of change with respect to expenditure or income $e = m$, gives the demand $x(p, m)$ for bundle x provided u is continuous, locally nonsatiated, convex, and differentiable (Roy's lemma). This is easily shown as an instance of the more generic envelope theorem in mathematics, in which the rate of change with respect to parameter p of the support of a nonempty closed convex set equals p's coefficient x. Generality however comes at a cost: the lemma holds equally well if u is replaced with some arbitrary ex-post variable, some ϕ, provided it be continuously measurable, locally nonsatiated, and convex. Yet few of us, given that it is entirely abstract, care in the least bit about ϕ. The reason we begin caring when u is involved is that we 'get' that it represents a person, not in any tangible way but in the ex-ante way that a person is, namely the way *we* are. The a-literal, metaphorical meaning of Roy's lemma – that it is a declaration of the human condition and so of human rationality – is precisely what draws us to it.

But Remains Suprasensible

Recovering this meaning requires backing the real utility out of it. That means finally letting go (though it provided insight in the meantime) of the pseudo-cardinality of a continuized ordinal measure. For if choice really is a question of continuous measurement, then economics would be the ex-post science of constructing utility indifference curves, observing where they are tangent to the budget line, and looking down on the abscissa to see how much to buy. Anything like risk would be lost, even if a risk model were brought in to claim otherwise. In its depth then, utility must somehow be discrete. Only when it is, can the decision maker have a sense of what troubles him: that despite his satisfaction with the prospective sizes of certain efforts, he cannot finally make himself comfortable with any of them. And obversely, he cannot recognize this puzzlement in himself until he views the problem as discrete. What ultimately is important in a production or consumption decision, in other words, once its scale has been pinpointed, is whether to take it up at all. What is important isn't finally how much to do but whether to do it, whether to cross the intersection.[13]

If so, retrieving the real utility means letting go of its literal continuity. That means letting go of its measurability too because metrics aren't adequate to 'whether' questions. They can bring us to decision's door but never open it. This nonliteral, *ex-ante* character of utility and decision making is so basic and universal in us that a capacity to 'get' the overall look and feel of a situation is already strong in our childhood. The evidence is our capacity – our predilection even – for innuendo, irony, paradox, frustration, anxiety, humor, and boredom, testifying to the discontinuity between our formal language and our reality, namely that we are always facing a future. Economics shares these predilections because it too has a kind of utility. Its continual drive to express itself more effectively, its dissatisfactions with itself when doing so, its recognition of a finite capacity for saying what it really means, are manifest in the tentative, model-building attitude it brings to everything it does, in contrast to the confident generalizations, arbitrary groups, and abstractive identities of classical, and the now proposed empiricist, economics.

Utility in short fulfils all the requirements of a phenomenal or transcendental category: unmeasurable because indefinite, anxious because forward-looking, irreducible to literal language, unified with the decision maker's other concerns because ultimately indistinguishable from them. It is an aspect of finite human possibility. In this, it seems to me, continuous-space modelling – economics' ontic or measurable dimension – has an essential place. For just as it is the experience of decision making that provides theory with its meaning, it is the consistency and imaginability of theory that helps us make better decisions. It is abstraction's completeness and symmetry that brings the unity of reason to our conscious minds, allowing us to talk about it. Yet even in its most abstractive and continuized modes, economics is *ex-ante* in intention: it has the person's *ex-ante* situation at the back of its mind.

Mill, Walras, Marshall, Weber, Robbins, and Knight for example, conversant at least implicitly with Enlightenment philosophy, would I think agree with me in this, though they don't often make it explicit. One thing we need to make clear about 'making explicit what is implicit' is that it always involves asserting something literal, then reminding ourselves we don't mean it that way.[14] To most economists, a utility function remains an essential aspect of reason, despite that no one, including the decision maker, can see it. It answers a certain kind of 'why.' If you want to know explicitly why an observable indifference curve is convex, there can be only one answer: the unobservable utility function is concave. This 'why' writers like Hausman insist on. And they have an important point in their favor as long as they promptly backpedal. Utility maximization is "a definition or model" of what is rational, Hausman says. Then, questioning his own empiricist orientations elsewhere, withdraws it: "All it does is connect preference and choice" in the sense that, if preferences are rational and the person is too, so is choice (18). The converse reasoning therefore also applies. To wit, there is no literal sequence at work here. Yet utility is its critical link, so when Pareto proposes replacing it with an indifference curve, someone will ask him where this new curve comes from, and utility will be right back in the picture again.[15]

The revealed preference theory Paul Samuelson (1947) and his colleagues developed in the 1940s at MIT was a further effort to stop us from asking this 'why' question. An economist meets a shopper as she leaves a store on Week 1, notes that she bought item x, and that her budget could have afforded y also. If on Week 2 her budget is still big enough to buy both of them and she now buys y as well, she had better be buying x too. That is, if x has been shown at least as good as y, it should never be shown worse than y (Weak Axiom of Revealed Preference, WARP). On this theme of logical consistency, significant aspects of the theory of demand, including its decomposition into a substitution and income effect, can be built up. And all those u's on the page that had been tempting us to regard them as 'things' will no longer be there to tempt us. This perhaps was Samuelson's hope. Others say he was trying to convert economics into a science (see below). But he also never claims to observe anyone's inner self, as science would.

The difficulty with his story, as persuasive as it is in the parking lot, is that it fails to walk us through the implications for any additional transactions possible with that same budget. We haven't checked further, in other words, to see whether y is revealed preferred to some z, and so forth, across any other bundle she may come in touch with. So, no full concatenation has been established for her preferences (the completeness axiom), allowing a complete picture of all her possible, mutually connected demands. Given that economics drives itself toward a marketplace, where these complete individual demands are aggregated up, WARP alone is inadequate.

Demand and Supply as *Synthetic a Priori*

Hausman says revealed preference theory prevents any consideration of this completeness problem (1992, 20–22; 2023, 39–41). But it seems at least to have encouraged one. In a 1950 article, Hendrik Houtthaker proposed a strong axiom of revealed preference specifying the necessary and sufficient conditions under which, if x is revealed preferred to y, y to z, and z to n in a chain across all possible bundles, that x will be revealed preferred to n, providing the concatenation missing in WARP. Crucially, these necessary and sufficient conditions (and as we will show in Chapter IV for equilibrium also) turn out to be the very preference completeness and transitivity assumed for u. The u's in the duality between demands $x[p, e(p, u)]$ and $x(p, m)$ in a decision neighborhood are nothing therefore but signals of the completeness and transitivity – the rationality – of preferences. Revealed preference has, it turns out, helped reveal preferences: $h(p, u) = x[p, e(p, u)]$ and $x(p, m)$ together reveal u which, though unobservable, is the underlying phenomenon (source of intuition) of these estimates.[16]

Hicksian Demand Is the Interpreter, Marshallian Demand Is the Interpreted

In particular, demands $x(p, m)$ and $x[p, e(p, u)]$ are dual to each other in the sense that – via $e(p, u)$ – any rise in m in the first boosts u in the second by allowing more x to be purchased. And because in a cost-minimizing decision maker, $e = m$ at the decision base point, this of course means the two functions uniquely imply one another. I assume this mutual implication is what Mas-Colell, Whinston, and Green have in mind in calling Marshallian demand $x(p, m)$ "an ordinal concept" despite the absence of any utility on its right-hand side (73).[17] If so, it is an unusually paradoxical statement for a graduate textbook to make because x can be estimated and u cannot be. How do we get hold of this paradox? It seems to me there is only one way, and that is to distinguish between a demand's empirical and phenomenological dimensions. That is to say, it is to cast the notion of demand, and hence its derivation, in an explicitly Kantian framework.

Note, in doing so, that the Hicks demands $h(p, u)$ are distinctively phenomenological– expressive of the individual's immediate situation and possibility and hence unmeasurable – while the Marshallian demands $x(p, m)$ are empirical insofar as estimated from observed data.[18] We can in fact call $h(p, u)$ the Kantian relation, after the first thinker to depict the phenomenal dimension in any explicit way, and $x(p, m)$ the Humean one, after the first thinker to address the empirical dimension in all the nakedness and directness he insisted upon. Certainly, without both there would be no contemporary economics as we know it. Let's then think about this duality, i.e. this correspondence and unity, between the Kantian and Humean more closely.

Before doing so in detail, it is well to step back a moment and review and deepen our Chapter II discussion of Kant, which has been much illumined by Heidegger's interpretation in *Being and Time* (1927) and his later *Kant and the Problem of Metaphysics* (1929). A schema for Kant, as we discussed earlier, is the act of uniting the intuition of an object with corresponding general concepts, so the generality will have a mood or sense that fixes and enlivens it. We then have a "sensible (intuitive) concept," says Heidegger, and "the formation of schemata is the sensibilization of concepts" (1929, 94–113). Conversely, the concept can 'determine' the intuition by assuring it will be applied consistently to empirical problems, giving us an empirical – measured and so conceptualized – intuition. Adjective and noun will have successfully been reversed. We have a unique correspondence between a certain generalization and a certain concretion, so that the thinker doesn't shunt either of them off to alien contexts or concepts.

Only in this unique correspondence, as Allison puts it in his *Kant's Transcendental Idealism*, "can a concept itself come into relation to an object and thereby gain objective reality" (1983, 182), for only then is the knower both sensible and consistent with himself. Kant shows these schema to be *a priori* because they conform to the pure categories of our understanding, and *synthetic* because they are referred, compared, and applied to empirical data. We can't, as we have shown – and in contradiction to many of economics' own staunch defenders – see, hear, or count any market demand. It isn't empirical, to be identified by just looking at it. Measurement and estimation are not the same order of phenomenon.[19] But as phenomenal, it *can* be estimated and compared with, say, balance sheets and inventory statements.

Kant says our pure intuition takes two expressly different forms. The first (transcendental aesthetic) is, in the form of time, "the form of inner sense … the intuition of ourselves and our inner state" (B50). Given that time is a locus of uncertainty too – the decision maker's concern for her possible world – this form is consonant with Heidegger's, Knight's (1921), and others' depictions of risk bearing, and that I've been including in the u in the Hicks-Kant demands. The succeeding form of pure intuition is our grasp of this very schemata, in which pure intuition and pure categorization are united in the act of understanding. Learning something is a matter of "providing an image for a concept" says Kant, and

> the schemata of the pure concepts of understanding are thus the true and sole conditions under which these concepts obtain relation to objects and so possess *significance*.
>
> (A146, B185)

An awareness or sense of the latter kind is what I've been characterizing as the duality in economics between the Hicks-Kant and Marshall-Hume demands, the correspondence or complementarity between the unobserved and observed, the conjunction of our intuition of the future with our capacity to generalize and articulate it (A138–A147, B177–B187).

Economic Demand Is Synthetic a Priori

Take a look now at the illustration of this demand duality in Figure 2, which contrasts and at the same time integrates the transcendental (possibility) with the empirical (actuality) dimensions of an economic decision. Consider first the observable consumption quantity x and income m used to estimate the Marshallian demand $x(p^{o}, m)$ at the right of the figure. On what ground do we assert that m is "explaining" x here? Wouldn't it be the concern of the person making the purchase decision? And in order for m to be relevant to this concern, it would have to be projected onto the problem that x might solve, in contrast to what it might solve if m is spent elsewhere. The worry in the first instance then is over one's income, which by way of $m = e(p, u)$ draws one back to one's 'sense' signified in u. For, prices constant, the added u that another unit of x offers requires more units of m; and m is scarce.[20] The intention of your food choices may be to green the environment as well as feed yourself. If both intentions are successful, the real cost of your food will turn out to have been less than what shows on your receipt because it greened as well as nourished. On the other hand, it may turn out to pollute the environment instead, in which case the receipt was an understatement rather than overstatement. It is impossible to ever eliminate this uncertain and thus interpretive aspect of consumer cost, and in turn therefore of demand.

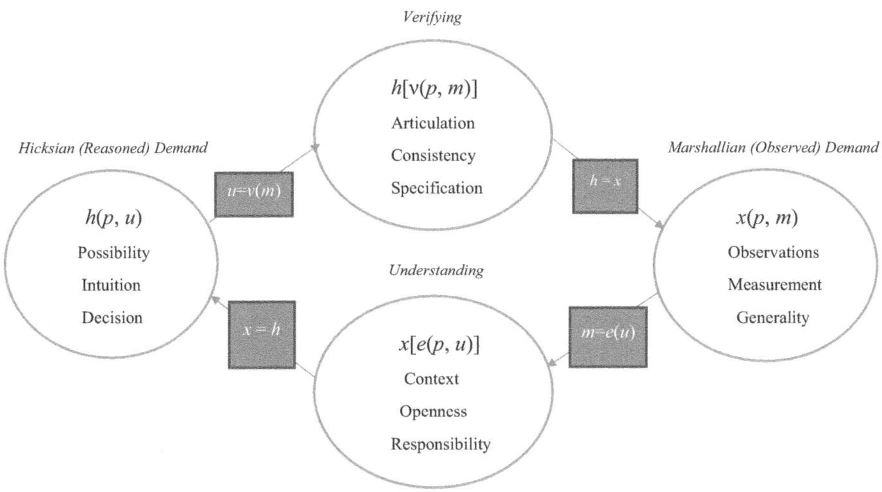

Figure 2 Reason and Observation (Interpretation) in Mainstream Economics.

In fact, we can say the buyer's possibility u – her openness to and sense of the world where she finds herself, in Kant's words, her pure intuition – *constitutes* her income, where 'constitutes' means 'gives income its meaning.' Substituting for m with this now-interpreted income $e(p^o, u)$ generates the prototype of the Marshall-Hume demand $x[p, e(p, u)]$ shown at the bottom of the figure, namely the demand *as the economist interprets it* and, as we've just seen, explains why $x(p, m)$ can be an ordinal concept despite lacking any explicitly ordinal determinant. That is, when the economist encountering $x(p, m)$ interprets it, he 'sees' it as the Hicks-Kant demand $x[p, e(p, u)] = h(p, u)$ at the left of the figure. This means neither minimized expenditure $e(p, u)$ nor demand $x[p^o, e(p, u)]$ can ever be sharply defined because utility, in which every intention is possibly joint with every other one, can't be sharply defined either. So – to paraphrase Frank Knight (1956, 167) – they also can only be estimated or forecasted, never observed.

We have depicted the path from the empiricist or Humean $x(p, m)$ to the transcendental or Kantian $h(p, u)$ as the buyer's pure intuition or anticipation, drawing her back to an interpretation or understanding of herself and which in economics we call u. *Data alone, without u, had been meaningless.* Now take a look at the reverse path, from $h(p, u)$ to $x(p, m)$, which in contrast to the predominantly intuitive route from $x(p, m)$ to $h(p, u)$ is a generalizing route, what Kant calls schematizing and Heidegger would call 'thought.'[21] The food buyer's utility, an intuition of her situation or possibility, can be actualized only in the income she surrenders for it. Income 'provides' the utility and in that sense proxies for it. This proxying is expressed in the indirect utility function $u = v(p, m)$, which, when substituted into $h(p, u)$ to give $h[p, v(p, m)]$, projects the buyer's possible utility onto the income that makes it actual. Kantian pure intuition, what for economics is preference u, is being expressed or unpacked here into its income stand-in.

On the strength of this phenomenological unpacking, the economist is now in a position to specify the structure of the decision base point $h[p, v(p, m)] = x(p, m)$, where $x(p, m)$ is estimated from the empirical data (x, p, m) and in which indirect utility $v(p, m)$ informs the testable hypotheses. On this unpacking by way of equation specification, most of the economist's time is devoted. For the final arrow in Figure 2, the regression of x on p and m, is simply mechanical because Marshallian $x(p, m)$ *alone* is a mere abstraction – blind searches for correlation. Though essential for communication, Marshall's empirical (observable) demand functions are heterogeneous to, transcended by, the pure intuition underlying them, which to the contrary is 'structured anticipation.'

Although we've pointed to it implicitly here, we haven't yet shown explicitly how this correspondence between $h(p, u)$ and $x(p, m)$ is a unity, unique to *this* person and situation.[22] In particular, we haven't shown why the apparently circular structure of Figure 2 isn't tautologous. If $h(p, u)$ and $x(p, m)$ are unifying instead of tautologizing, they must be mediated in some manner. There must be a space in which the unity takes place; and we will have a proof of that unity when we have identified where in Figure 2 this space resides. Now consider that it must be either a sense *or* a generalization that we seek, as these are the only two poles of judgment. I will now show it to be the former of these, the decision maker's pure intuition u.

We start where Heidegger (1927, 135–284) would suggest: thrown down, as we are at every moment, in a world of potential emptiness, the barren empirics of the literal David Hume which, in economics, would be a statistical regression of one object on another without any interpretive model or foundation. The drive for meaning then drives us to minimize this initial alienation in the form of minimizing our expenditure $m = e(p, u)$, the slippage, one could say, into empty curiosity and game playing. That would be to accept full responsibility for the condition we find ourselves in, to be open to all that is to come. This recognition is the phenomenological process of recalling the situation context which comprises u and so underlies Hicksian decision $h(p, u)$. Reflection on this goal moves us along the top of Figure 2 in the way of articulating a formal model, providing the consistency essential to model specification. If preferences are strictly quasi-concave (i.e. if the world is finite), consistency is achieved at the income m^* where indirect utility $u = v(p, m)$ is maximized subject to price and any other constraints. Assembling the relevant data and estimating the associated parameters gives us the Marshallian demand function, promptly emptied of this newfound meaning (sense and context) unless continuously renewed via its duality with the Hicksian demand and the personhood it represents.

Have you noticed that utility enters this judgment process in two ways? It is first in your anticipation and grasp of a matter – your pure intuition of it – underlying your latent demand $h(p, u)$ for particular services. It is next in the associated minimized expenditure $e(p, u)$ and its inverse, your maximized utility $v(p, m)$, guiding you to a decision. In this, pure intuition $e(p, u)$ is joining your Hicksian with your Marshallian, connecting anticipation with observation and in this way anticipation and sense with consistency. In short,

> *The uniting of the intuitive Hicksian* $h(p, u)$ *with the estimable Marshallian* $x(p, m)$ *is itself an intuitive act: the minimization of expenditure* $e(p, u)$. *We "get that we get it."*

Coincidentally, we have now solved the key difficulty of explaining how, as Frank Knight argued for but never demonstrated in detail, concepts like income and demand can be estimated despite that they are unmeasurable. The *unmeasurability* of minimized expenditure $e(p, u) = m(p, u)$ is clear from the fact that the u it reflects cannot be measured.[23] Their *estimability* is clear from the fact that it is u that provides m's meaning, and meaning *is* specification and interpretation. We can take this further. If concepts central to personhood really can be quantified, it can only be an *estimated* quantity because only an estimate can offer a correspondence (Kant's formal, transcendental schemata) between the center of the person, which is uncertainty-bearing, and an empirical category, in Heidegger's phrase a mere looking and watching. Mere *observation* involves, and so produces, no such understanding. It follows for instance that budget constraints in consumer optimization models aren't measurements either, since if they were, there would be no basis for specifying and interpreting them. We would have no way of knowing what to include in a budget and what to exclude. Constraints too, that is, can only be estimates. We have come then to our final distinction between measurement and estimation, which I would name in honor of Frank Knight:

The Knight Principle: Observation vs Estimation

> An observation (measure) is a mere looking-at and recording something. An estimate rather is a quantitative model output, a judgment of a situation or in Kant's words a "representation of a representation" – of the rational (utility maximizing) model structure and the data it employs. Observations therefore are essential to estimates and can be compared to them. But estimates themselves are never observations.

You will note three corollaries to this theorem. *First,* utility can be a maximum only if reality is bounded (finite). Thus, the feasible options in any decision problem are ultimately a strictly convex set. Thus also the decision solution will be unique at that point, i.e. free of the indeterminate play of constructing merely empirical concepts, which assume an infinite, entirely manipulable world.

Second, the Knight Principle applies not only to economic theory but also to econometric testing. An important instance in demand estimation is the sum of squared differences between an observed data point x_i and the corresponding demanded quantity

x_i (p, m, z_i), namely $\Sigma_i [x_i - x_i (p, m, z_i)]^2$, where z_i is the vector of demand-identifying factors. By the duality we have seen above, the Marshall-Hume x_i (p, m, z_i) is set equal here to the Hicks-Kant demand h_i (p, u, z_i) in the neighborhood of the economic decision, i.e. at their intersection point. Introducing this substitution gives

$\Sigma_i [x_i - h_i (p, u, z_i)]^2$, the sum of squares of deviations of the actual (observed, empirical) quantities from the corresponding hypothesized, backcasted ones, which must be utility-based. Just as in our Knight Theorem, we have here the drawing together of the observed with the estimated, the empirical with the interpretive or judged. Backcasting, the substance of econometric testing and meaning, depends entirely on Kant's *synthetic a priori.*

Third and finally, note that the interpreted, backcasted h_i (p, u, z_i) is the model's counterfactual mentioned in Chapter II – the model's specified demand as opposed to the x_i that are observed. Since h_i (p, u, z_i) is the model estimated *as if* it were x_i (p, m, z_i), we can say *h*'s tension with the corresponding data point x_i is the center of modern economics, the point at which, in being contrasted to one another, they give each other meaning.

Supply Is Synthetic a Priori Too

Extending this reasoning to the producer side of the market is straightforward. Wicksteed (1910) has effectively done so in showing supply is ultimately a demand phenomenon, as we can see in models of a household as a production process (e.g. Becker 1993) and from the simple fact that a seller of something must demand it also, namely in the supply reservation price below which he refuses to sell.[24] I will express this here in still another way. To wit, producers seek profit for the sake of utility, as we say in the identity $u(\pi) = u^o$. Let's substitute profit function $\pi(p, r)$, where the p are the producer output prices and r the input prices, into this utility identity to obtain $u[\pi(p, r)] = u^o$. The monotonicity axiom that $u(\pi)$ rises with π now allows us to invert this identity to obtain the extended profit relation $\pi(p, r, u)$. Holding prices constant, this says, profit has the value – the meaning – that the producer's utility projects onto it.

And because utility stands for judgment, profit is, derivatively speaking, interpretive as well – unobservable because it is only a 'sense.' If you ask someone how much he profited from something, let alone how long the profit will last, he won't, with all the data in the world at his side, be able to give you a clear answer. Nor will – despite Piketty's careless income measurements in *Capital in the 21st Century* – anyone else. It will depend on what the 'something' is that generated the profit, or what is the same, the values of the inputs given up for it; and these will always be obscure. Yet despite that u will never be one of its visible regressors, profit function $\pi(p, r; u)$ *can* be estimated and critiqued. How? By way of that same monotonicity intuition thatutility should vary sympathetically with profit. Of course these arguments extend also to a cost-minimizing function $c(q, r; u)$ and to a revenue-maximizing $rev(p, z, u)$ also, being special cases of this same profit function.[25] By Hotelling's lemma they apply to the supply function $q(p, r; u)$ as well – which must also therefore be judgeable only, never observable or subject to any kind of positive proof.

The problem is more, that is, than an inability to define profit or cost – that defining them involves phenomena like utility that are also undefinable, so you will always fail to measure them in themselves. It is also that you cannot see or measure the cost of *this* building or *this* project either. You can draw up the accounts to estimate it, but as Kant would argue, that doesn't tell you what the cost is *itself*. Let's put this more directly. Cost is literally a function of prices and only metaphorically a function of utility. But since the utility is indispensable, cost can only be a formal (transcendental) rather than empirical concept. You don't, in contemporary economics, literally see what a cost is even with every accountant in the world at your side. You only 'get' what it is and, on this basis alone, go beyond the mechanical use of p-statistics or t-statistics to judge the quality of the estimate. Obviously, you wouldn't be forced to bring your intuition to bear on it if you could literally *see* a cost as some thing-in-itself. Consequently, it cannot be the thing it is in a classical economics or in any other rationalist or empiricist thought.

Because profit is simply the change dm in the investor's income, it is worth noting – in fact restating what we've said just above – that profit utility $u(\pi)$ is equivalently $u(dm)$, the additional utility an investment might yield. This marginal utility for example is conformable by way of the Slutzky condition to the welfare improvement obtained from a price cut. So the economics of the producer is an integral part of, and has its meaning in, the economics of the consumer, as Wicksteed (1910) would argue and general equilibrium theory essentially says. Despite the separate handling given to them in textbooks, the principal meaning of economic supply is found in demand. So Figure 2, though directed immediately to the demand side of the market, reaches into every aspect of economics.

Interpretation (Sense, Judgment) as the Core of Mainstream Economics

As we've shown furthermore, modern economics is the only economics that thinks in this receptive, interpretive way. Consequently then, it not only is entirely *synthetic a priori* but the only economics to be so. Rather than rely on me for this claim, we seem to have it on the authority of at least one major positivist thinker. William Barrett (1962, vol 3, 7) notes in his introduction to a collection of positivist philosophical works that "Moritz Schlick himself has said that the whole philosophy of positivism could be summed up in one statement: 'There are no synthetic a priori truths.'" Nor could it be otherwise. The epistemology of the positivist or empiricist is the notion that logic and measurement are all there is to knowing something. Being jointly interpreted *and* empirical, the mainstream economic view could never reduce itself like that. Empiricism therefore has no choice but to reject the mainstream's interpretative spirit wholesale. When it does economics, it must do it the classical, positive way, the successive reduction of 'underlying causes' to strictly empirical – so indefinitely manipulable – concepts.

As the reader probably has noticed, we have now proven from three directions that economics is *synthetic a priori*: in Chapter I by showing (*i*) how Walras' unobservable *rarete* (scarcity) mediates observable price and quantity; (*ii*) how the tangency of the utility indifference curve with the budget line similarly mediates unobservable preferences with observed prices and income; and finally (*iii*) here in Chapter III by demonstrating the duality and complementarity of the unobserved Hicks with the observed Marshallian demand. All these carry the same central insight: that

> Economic concepts such as utility and cost reflect not what is common to particulars, reducing them to what is common, but one-to-one mappings (schemata) from the observed to the unobserved, where each person remains a person, avoiding relegation to an object.

Look to Context, Not Literal Meaning

Here then the entire contradiction and misunderstanding between the classical (rationalist) and modern, mainstream inference is encapsulated. Our intuition of time and uncertainty, and our problematic ability to generalize and articulate it, are the locus of economic understanding. The alternative could only be to avoid these problematics by focusing on what is obvious but simplistic – the human being as object. It is instructive to consider here Milton Friedman's supposed reduction of economics to prediction (Simon 1963, Krupp 1966, Hausman 1992, 2023). This too would be a reduction to an object, where since its wisdom is being ignored, any logic is taken to fail unless 'true' or 'realistic' on some aggregate basis.

Friedman however rejects the entire idea of a generalized, collective access to the 'realism' of economic model logic. Reality is specific to person, time, and place, which are always changing. It therefore is ultimately inaccessible to the objectivity, the third-person plural, of science. Friedman writes, "the construction of hypotheses is a creative act of inspiration, intuition, invention," one suitable to "autobiographies and biographies" and "promoted by maxim and example" (173). These manifestly are aspects of a decision maker's pure intuitions or anticipations, and Friedman is positioning individual choice – a person deliberating *as* a person – quite far from science. Yet even economists who should know better often talk as if human decision were some audible signal, a collective witness, despite that a collective is merely shorthand for claiming to have the 'facts.' The pathos of the realism-of-assumptions literature is that it has so little to do with what is real.

Economics Is the Nexus of Interpretation and the Interpreted

We have come now to the crux of the matter. The incumbent theory of the consumer and producer spans two interconnected domains: pure intuition, which is the locus of the decision maker's sense and anticipation of a situation, and a corresponding generalization where he articulates them. Economics consists that is, of two separate tiers, of a decision maker's inner concern *and* its expression. Total wealth w for instance, as a store of future minimized expenditures on things of value, is this very risk-bearing and concern because it is understood only through u, the person's world considered as projection. And what connects personal intuition to the balance-sheet bottom line u in Figure 1 and 2? Only the Kantian *synthetic a priori* relation itself, the expenditure function $m = e(u)$, which provides that bottom line with its context and meaning. For while data inform the decision, they don't make the decision. Only a person makes it, and only on the basis, finally, of a conjecture or sense.

So also then is dual demand function $x[p, e(p, u)]$ the only possible foundation for interpreting the corresponding data, and consequently *where* the economist's, businessperson's, customer's, and politician's understandings take place. Its inverse schema (indirect utility) $u = v(p, m)$ thus inspires the specification and estimation of that same demand because, as Walras might have said, it expresses utility as the scarcity of the income that must be surrendered to actualize the demand in a purchase. *Of course, the key to this entire schematic is the irreplaceability of the human person that utility implies.*

You might wonder whether equivalent schema are to be found in empiricist or rationalist thought. Indeed they are, in the redacted form of identities. In Chapter I we found that according to David Ricardo, value is identical to labor expense. According to Derek Parfit it is the identity between rationality and being-correct. In Michael Bratman it is the identity of sharing a common knowledge. We've found Brown and Spencer claiming that value inheres naturally in an object, so the problem of knowledge is already solved. In all these, the proposed schema are to be effected – the subject is to be connected to the predicate – by way of an identity, essentially a tautology. Human judgment isn't in the picture.

Note that no one with any utility at stake is ever specified in these accounts, only a distant observer's opinion, which can change quickly. The reduction of reality to abstract thought, to measured objects, lapses in its dearth of any personal responsibility into indeterminacy and why Ricardo slips so repeatedly into self-contradiction, Parfit into the dogmatism of urging us to be correct, Margaret Gilbert into, it seems to me, the self-contradiction of a plural subject. They ultimately are a matter of fancy because the thinkers themselves aren't accountable for the outcomes.

Accountability resurfaces only with the concern that the means we deploy may not have the effects intended, may worsen the situation we'd tried to fix. To this concern contemporary economics stands witness, though in a sympathy for the decision maker and not in any vision of its own, since not bearing the risk itself, the economist is in no position to see what it is to the decision maker. The proof that economists regard their work as *synthetic a priori* – as standing in the decision maker's shoes – is that they wouldn't be going to the pain of estimating demands and supplies if they thought they could simply observe them. To be estimable yet unobservable is what it is to be only judgeable, never dogmatic. Economics' secret, in other words, is that the decision maker's concern lies irreplaceably at its center, not as the disengaged logic of categorizations but as the situation the economist is trying tentatively to illuminate.

We're now in a position to move onto an assessment of utility's close correlative – rationality – and *its* correlatives: uncertainty, completeness, and equilibrium.

Summary Points of Chapter III

1. As we have said earlier, rationalist and empiricist reason are each a classifying, a reasoning down from principles or up from observations, both mechanical processes. Economic reason rather is an intuition of human situations, especially insofar as there are scarcities, united with the quantifiable categories of theory. Mainstream economic modeling is precisely this unification: a projection onto a future.
2. Economics' presumption of a personal decision maker contrasts with the rationalist presumption that value is entirely subjective and the metalogical/empiricist presumption that it is entirely objective. Economics has no theory of value. Utility is discursive, personal, contextual instead, irreducible to feelings or measures.
3. Utility's intuitive, contextual *orientation* points to the inner unity where decisions originate. Its abstract *representations* refer to the consistency and symmetry of economic choice.
4. Revealed preference is an effort to be rid of these personal, unifying aspects, reducing them to publicly observable generalities. Mainstream economic theory instead locates them, as publicly *un*observable, in the duality of price and scarcity, the nexus of what is observed (data) with what interprets it (utility).

5. Cost, profit, income, wealth, demand, and supply then are also transcendental (interpretive, discursive, judged) concepts – estimated, never observed – and because unobserved, only metaphorically expressible.
6. In economic duality, Marshallian demand is essentially correlation, while Hicksian demand is personal concern. Hicks then *interprets* Marshall while Marshall *verbalizes* Hicks. Utility enters twice: as intuition, and as intuition's unity with conception. As in Kant, the unity between intuition and conception is itself intuitive. We 'get' that we 'get' something, or that we don't.
7. Economic duality therefore is Kant's *synthetic a priori*, the link between empirical representation and the structure of conceptual judgment, a mapping between the particularity of a situation (a person) and the categorizations that promote logical consistency (economic theory).
8. All decision structures in economics are *synthetic a priori*, a personally judged correspondence between sense and concept. No essential structure in mainstream theory is not *synthetic a priori.*
9. This unity of sense and category in an economic interpretation is crystalized in the counterfactual: the model-generated estimate of what would have happened had conditions been otherwise. The counterfactual – the rational act of picturing and testing a hypothesis – is the nerve center of mainstream economics.
10. The rationalist reduction of reason to thought and the empiricist reduction to measure sever this nerve. Persons become generalizations, slices of imagination (*noumena*). They resurface in pure intuition and its economic judgments (*phenomena*): one's fallible, uncertain anticipation of a context or situation, jointly conceived *and* observed.

Notes

1 Uskali Maki (2001) for instance introduces his book of readings *The Economic World View: Studies in the Ontology of Economics,* by directing its questions to: "What is the economy made of? What are its constituents and how do they hang together? What kind of general principles govern its functioning? What is utility, or well-being?" (3) With this 'what' question in the forefront, the answers will unsurprisingly concern, as he puts it, "the ultimate nature of the constituents of certain regions of social life," and "the way the world is constituted." (9) These, as we have seen, are rationalist questions – claims to hold the entire reality of the universe in our minds. Typical of much recent language in the philosophy of economics, Maki speaks frequently of a thinker's "ontological commitments," despite that ontology isn't a matter of 'commitment,' whatever that could mean, but with how we understand, interpret, and express the economic phenomena we experience.

2 It is in giving a sense of this fix that Fritz Machlup's writings have been so effective. Inevitably then, as he must use metaphorical language in doing so, he is misunderstood. Bruce Caldwell, for instance, says he comes down in Machlup's favor as "perhaps the most methodologically astute of the analysts," his position falling "somewhere between those of the 'a priorists' and the 'ultra-empiricists.'" (166). Caldwell clearly doesn't mean this to be a literal averaging of an *a priori* and an empirical claim. It would have to

be a unity of the two instead. This would be the Kantian unity, though Caldwell doesn't seem to recognize so and mentions Kant only in a passing phrase.

3 Heidegger and others have called the ultimate principles of a particular discipline 'special metaphysics.' Note that Kant's principles (pure or transcendental categories of the understanding), which include unity, reality, cause, and possibility, are intended for any branch of knowledge. Economics' own ultimate principles, including logic and the moral law, would then in Heidegger's terms constitute their own special metaphysics. Economic textbooks only manage to imply all this, rarely explicating it.

4 For articulating thus, we have Heidegger mostly to thank.

5 We clearly here and elsewhere in this book are not using the word 'utility' in the older way of 'utilitarianism' (e.g. Jeremy Bentham, 1789) and its presumption that welfare and its judgments can be reduced to a measurable pleasure and pain. We are saying indeed quite the opposite. As Hannah Arendt notes, "It is only in Kant that the philosophy of the earlier stages of the modern age frees itself entirely [of the] common sense platitudes.... The reason, of course is that Kant did not mean to formulate or conceptualize the tenets of the utilitarianism of his time, but on the contrary wanted first of all to relegate the means-ends category in its proper place." (155–156)

6 Another positivist claiming Robbins (and Wicksteed!) to be positivists is Don Ross, who writes: "[Robbins] assumes that a genuine science must have the widest logical scope compatible with the possibility of using it as a basis for deriving testable predictions.... He thus follows Wicksteed (1910) in endorsing the doctrine that actions are homogeneous with respect to their describability ...." (87–88) The forcefully and consistently anti-positivist Robbins, who underscored the heterogeneity between abstract thought and sense, between understanding and object (e.g., "the process of ultimate explanation begins just where the description of the technical conditions leaves off") (1932, 37) was somehow, for Ross, a positivist. He in like manner refers approvingly to "early (Kantian) positivism," (89) while Kant himself didn't in the least bit approve, consigning it to the dogmatic period of his life.

7 Jacques Derrida (1997) would, I think, say the professor's view is the irresponsible one since the "place and subject of every responsibility ... is the *person*." [his italics] (26) "The concept of responsibility," he writes, "is one of those strange concepts that give food for thought without giving themselves over to thematization." (29)

8 Kant (1781, 1788 A103–A109) divides the transcendental conditions of understanding into the aesthetic or sensible conditions and the analytic or conceptual ones, respectively intuitive and abstractive. The two must be brought together. We discuss below how this is accomplished by way of Kant's transcendental schemata. Heidegger shows in *Kant and the Problem of Metaphysics* (1929) that Kant's underlying message, in both his A and B editions, is that only sense (receptivity) can integrate sense with concept. In Kant's words, "human reason is by its nature architectonic. This is to say it regards all our knowledge as belonging to a possible system," (161, A474, B502), the possibility being ultimately intuitive or receptive. This issue is strongly debated, especially under the rubric of Neo-Kantianism. More of this in Chapter VI.

9 In the 8th (1920, 821) edition of *Principles*, Marshall offers a brief but compact history of the concept of marginal utility, where he mentions Jevons' and Menger's as well as Walras' contributions to it.

10 From here forward, scalar u will be the consumer's utility, and scalar v be this utility in maximized form. Scalar m will be her income, and scalar e her expenditures from this income when they are set as low as possible to still achieve a given u. $h = x$ will be the vector of the goods quantities she purchases, often shown in boldface to emphasize

they are vectors rather than scalars but here for simplicity left unbolded. Vector p, also left unbolded, is the vector of (assumed constant) prices of those goods. A variable in brackets or parentheses is taken to be a source or cause of the variable level preceding the bracket.

11 See Arrow and Debreu (1954), Debreu (1959), and Hausman (1992, 17–18, 2023, 33–34).

12 In a searching and pregnant discussion, Knight (1956) puts this only slightly differently. He says utility is "quantitative in the sense in which any subjective state is quantitative [but] for which we have no accepted technique of measurement and which consequently must be estimated. The main point seems to be that in the absence of any technique of measurement, there is no clear differentiation between a subjective state and an objective quality…." (166–167) The fact of minimum expenditure $e(p, u)$'s unobservability, I think he is saying, does not mean it can't be estimated, in fact has for instance been estimated by way of flexible functional forms. And the fact that we can estimate it in the absence of any observability is a recognition that in a person, subjectivity and objectivity are nonseparable, the estimate being the subjectivity, and the 'it' in "estimate it" being the objectivity. As we will see below, the same nonseparability is exhibited in the duality between the Hicksian and Marshallian demands.

13 The same insight can be found also for example in the Platonic, Scholastic, Existential, and Phenomenological philosophic traditions.

14 This, the *via negativa,* isn't my idea. In the present context it is Kierkegaard's. I would argue it has, at least in the last several thousand years, been the ultimate way of saying something in depth, and why for instance we find our positive expressions of love to be always inadequate.

15 This ontological or interpretive character of utility is evident in the markedly different ways it is used. Gary Becker (1993) has, at least implicitly, conducted all his work on the rationality of bequests, burglaries, divorce, and education, and of filial love, guilt, and duty, by way of decomposing utility. It is in a (utility decomposed) selfishness-altruism model that he shows parents will *ex-ante* invest more in their children when they expect more back from them in their old age, and less in them when required by law to make cross-generational transfers. Utility enters here not as a measure for Becker but as the negative effects of generational transfer policies on aggregate savings rates. Contrast this with Partha Dasgupta's decomposition of parental well-being into income, life expectancy, literacy, and so forth, which in calling them "measurable and comparable" he clearly intends for redistribution purposes and which Becker argues are self-defeating. Becker's utility is *ex ante* and bounded. Dasgupta's is *ex post* and unbounded, despite their language similarities.

16 Samuelson's revealed preference is of great interest to positivist, metalogical thought too, because as appearing to eliminate utility, it seems to offer a foundation for a totally measurable decision model. The scientist can now not only observe the shopper's decision to buy x but suppose her to have observed x's value before consuming it. In Andrew Caplin's (2008) account for example, the shopper can be said to hold observable 'beliefs and desires' about x's quality. As such they can be regarded as the effects of observable psychological states and the way is fully open to laboratory analysis of decisions, especially in efforts to identify their unconscious sources. "The goal of decision theory is, after all," Caplin writes, "to model 'choice' itself mechanically, … and the issue of what theory accounts for the observed [choice] is open." (360) I mention this to point out how fundamentally different is my treatment of choice and utility here than Samuelson's and Caplin's are. We will have much to say about this scientific

interpretation, for Caplin and others and for expected utility theory as well, in Chapters IV and V.

17 Mas-Colell et al. refer to Marshallian demands as Walrasian. I usually use the more common term 'Marshallian' in this book but either will do.

18 Income data themselves are estimates, as we observe in the continuous updating of Gross Domestic Product figures months after the initial reports. Updates are discontinued not when the 'correct' figure is known but when, in someone's judgment, the costs of going further exceed the benefits. Now here is an interesting question: how do the experts know when that critical point has arrived? The answer is: in their sense of the matter, which, as the nexus of generalization and intuition, is transcendental or interpretational. Economic data then are interpretive also. Just as an empiricist economics would be an extraordinarily generalized one, we can say mainstream economics is profoundly estimative, its pretensions comparatively modest.

19 Lucy Allais also offers an excellent treatment of what we can call the interrelation and yet nonseparability of the empirical and the pure intuition in Kant's philosophy of understanding.

20 This is an immediate implication of Roy's lemma discussed above.

21 Of itself we could call $x(p, m)$ empiri<u>cist</u>. Together *with* $h(p, u)$ we could call $x(p, m)$ empiri<u>cal</u>, now consistent with Kant and mainstream economics.

22 What I am calling the unity between $h(u)$ and $x(m)$ occurs, formally speaking, at the base point of the decision, the intersection of the Marshallian with its corresponding Hicksian demand.

23 For simplification here I assume savings to be zero, so expenditure e is equivalent to income m, the long-run situation.

24 In Wicksteed's words, "what is usually called the supply curve is, in reality, the demand curve of those who [already] possess the commodity….The supply curve is…therefore simply part of the total demand curve." As he notes, most of his *Common Sense of Political Economy* is designed to demonstrate this claim of the final subsumption of supply under demand, though he does so most directly on his pp. 162–169. My own way of explicating it here is slightly different from Wicksteed's.

25 Here r is the vector of input prices and z the corresponding input quantities. We rarely see explicit utility terms in estimated cost, revenue, or profit functions. This is mere convenience because in the absence of the relevant understanding or intention as represented in utility, there would be no reason to care about profit, cost, or revenue.

References

Allais, Lucy. *Manifest Reality*. Oxford: Oxford University Press, 2015.

Allison, Henry E. *Kant's Transcendental Idealism: An Interpretation and Defense*. New Haven: Yale University Press, 1983, 2004.

Arendt, Hannah. *The Human Condition*. Chicago: University of Chicago Press, 1958, 1998.

Arrow, Kenneth, and Gerard Debreu. "Existence of an Equilibrium for a Competitive Economy." *Econometrica* 22, 265–290, 1954.

Barrett, William. "Introduction to Positivism." *Philosophy in the 20th Century, Vol. 3*. New York: Random House, 1962.

Becker, Gary. "The Economic Way of Looking at Behavior." Nobel Lecture, *Journal of Political Economy* 101, No. 31, 1993.

Bentham, Jeremy. *An Introduction to the Principles of Morals and Legislation*. J.H. Burns and H.L.A. Hart (eds.). New York: Oxford University Press, 1970. First published in 1789.

Brown, Andrew and David A. Spencer. "The Nature of Economics and the Failings of the Mainstream: Lessons from Lionel Robbins's *Essay*." *Cambridge Journal of Economics* 36, 2012, 781–798.

Caldwell, Bruce. *Beyond Positivism: Economic Methodology in the Twentieth Century*. London: Allen & Unwin, 1982.

Comte, Auguste. *Cours de Philosophie Positive, Chpts 1 & 2*. Pauls Descours and H. Gordon Jones (Trans.), 1830. Republished in: Indianapolis: Hackett Publishing Co. 1988.

Comte, Auguste. *Cours de Philosophie Positive*. 1842. Partial translation by Frederick Ferre, Hackett Publishing.

Dasgupta, Partha. *An Inquiry into Well-Being and Destitution*. Oxford: Oxford University Press, 1993.

Debreu, Gerard. *Theory of Value*. New York: John Wiley & Sons, 1959.

Descartes, Rene. "Discourse on Method." In: Norman Kemp Smith (Trans.), *Descartes Philosophical Writings*. New York: Random House, 1958. First published in 1637.

Gilbert, Margaret. *Living Together: Rationality, Sociality, and Obligation*. New York: Rowman and Littlefield, 1996.

Hausman, Daniel M. *The Inexact and Separate Science of Economics*. Cambridge: Cambridge University Press, 1992, 2023.

Hedden, Brian. *Reasons Without Persons: Rationality, Identity, and Time*. Oxford: Oxford University Press, 2015.

Heidegger, Martin. *Being and Time*. John Macquarrie and Edward Robinson (Trans.). New York: Harper-Collins, 1962. First published in 1927.

Heidegger, Martin. *Kant and the Problem of Metaphysics*. James S. Churchill (Trans.). Bloomington, IN: Indiana University Press, 1962. First published in 1929.

Hicks, J.R. *Value and Capital*. Oxford: Clarendon Press, 1946.

Houtthaker, Hendrik. "Revealed Preference and the Utility Function." *Economica* 17, 159–174, 1950.

Hume, David. *A Treatise of Human Nature. Book I, Of the Understanding*. L.A. Selby-Bigge (ed.). Oxford: Clarendon Press, 1893. First published in 1739.

Jevons, W.S. *The Theory of Political Economy*, 4th ed. London: Macmillan, 1911. First edition 1871.

Kant, Immanuel. *Critique of Pure Reason*, 1st and 2nd eds. Norman Kemp Smith (Trans.). New York: Random House (Modern Library), 1958. First published 1781; revised 1787.

Kierkegaard, Soren. *Concluding Unscientific Postscript*. D.F. Swenson and W. Lowrie (Trans.). Princeton: Princeton University Press, 1941. First published in 1846.

Knight, Frank H. *On the History and Method of Economics*. Especially "The Ricardian Theory of Production and Distribution" and "What is Truth in Economics?" Chicago: University of Chicago Press, 1956.

Krupp, S. (ed.). *The Structure of Economic Science*. Englewood Cliffs: Prentice-Hall, 1966.

Lewis, David K.. "Survival and Identity." In: A. Rorte (ed.), *The Identities of Persons*. Berkeley, CA: University of California Press, 1976.

Machlup, Fritz. "The Problem of Verification in Economics." *Southern Economic Journal* 22, July 1955.

Maki, Uskali (ed.). *The Economic World View: Studies in the Ontology of Economics*. Cambridge: Cambridge University Press, 2001.

Marshall, Alfred. *Principles of Economics*. New York: Macmillan and Co., 1890, 1920, 1930.
Mas-Colell, A., M.D. Whinston, and J.R. Green. *Microeconomic Theory*. New York: Oxford University Press, 1995.
Menger, Carl. *Investigations into the Method of the Social Sciences with Special Reference to Economics*. Louis Schneider (ed.). New York: New York University Press, 1985. First published in 1883.
Mill, John Stuart. "On the Definition and Method of Political Economy." In: D. M. Hausman (ed.), *The Philosophy of Economics*, 3rd ed. Cambridge: Cambridge University Press, 2008. First published in 1836.
Ricardo, David. *The Principles of Political Economy and Taxation*. Mineola: Dover Publications, 2004. First published in 1817.
Robbins, Lionel. An Essay on the Nature and Significance of Economic Science. London: Macmillan, 1st ed. 1932.
Robbins, Lionel. "Economics and Political Economy." Richard T. Ely Lecture (ed.), *American Economic Review* 71 (2), May 1981.
Ross, Don. *Economic Theory and Cognitive Science: Microexplanation*. Cambridge: MIT Press, 2005.
Samuelson, Paul A. *Foundations of Economic Analysis*. Cambridge: MIT Press, 1947.
Schlick, Moritz. "Meaning and Verification." *The Philosophical Review* 45, 1936. Reprinted in W.P. Alston and G. Nakhnikian, *Readings in Twentieth Century Philosophy*. London: Collier-Macmillan, 1964.
Sen, Amartya. *Collective Choice and Social Welfare*. Oxford: North-Holland, 1979.
Simon, Herbert. "Problems of Rationality: Discussion." *American Economic Review Papers and Proceedings* 53: 229–231, 1963.
Smith, Adam. *The Wealth of Nations*. 1776. New York: Modern Library, 1937.
Walras, Leon. *Elements of Pure Economics*, 4th ed. William Jaffe (trans.). Homewood, IL: Richard D. Irwin, Inc., 1954. 1st edition 1874, 4th edition 1900, definitive edition 1926.
Weber, Max. *The Theory of Social and Economic Organization*. A.M. Henderson and T. Parsons (Trans.). New York: Oxford University Press, 1947. First published in 1922.
Wicksteed, Philip H. *The Common Sense of Political Economy*. Introduction by Lionel Robbins. London: Routledge and Sons, 1933. First published in 1910.

IV Uncertainty, Completeness, Equilibrium: Rationality

We've seen that because contemporary economics takes the view of someone concerned for what is not yet and may never be, it is fundamentally about risk. Choices *h*(*p*, *u*) and *x*(*p*, *e*) are for the sake of a future, even five minutes from now, and it is much truer to say we live in the future than in the present. The frequent to the point of monotonous insistence that economic theory 'assumes' perfect information isn't therefore credible. To the contrary, the pedestrian, the broker, the restaurant owner are already ahead of themselves. It isn't that weather and prices are ever certain, but that the professor treats them so because unknown futures can only be modeled indirectly. Hausman seems to be making this point when saying a perfect-certainty assumption would be the limiting case of the completeness axiom (that any two options can be compared) – meaning, I assume, that the decision maker dwells on only small parts of her world at a time rather than all of it (1992, 15, 26; 2023, 44–46). Since possibility is essentially futural, it is essentially uncertain. Every economic model therefore points to uncertainty even when not modeling it, just as every person does even when not directly aware of it.

The Nonseparability of Decisional Reasoning

The economics discipline has been framed in so many ways, pejorative or otherwise, it is hard to know what to make of them. An economist once said to me in my youth that it is the study of how people make a living. But it is also, as Econ 101 students hear the first week of class, about expectations. Equivalently, it is the worry that the expectations won't be realized. Risk is expectation's alter ego, just as expectations are risk's alter ego. Both then must be foundational to economics – a mutuality of sense, or as Frank Knight (1921) put it, "neither entire ignorance nor complete and perfect information." The first clear explicator of this possibility structure was Knight himself, who in a virtual quotation from Kant and Heidegger – taken up, as we have just seen, in Friedman (1953) – called it an 'image' of the decision maker's future state of affairs (201). This image, Knight says, takes one of two forms: what we call risk, where the parameters of the relevant probability distributions are known, and uncertainty, where they aren't.

DOI: 10.4324/9781003514602-6

The distinction has remained canonical for nearly a century. It ignores, unfortunately, Knight's own critique of it. For as Irving Fisher (1906) had already noted, probability is itself "always an estimate" (222). Or as Knight says more colorfully, "statistics give but a probability of what the true probability is" (227), one that in turn, presumably, would be probabilistic. Probabilities are categories only, mere aggregations, and business settings are far too unique for aggregates to be any more than temporarily interesting to them (231). Yet this caution involves its own difficulties. It suggests the future is ultimately Brownian motion, where uncertainty therefore would be complete ignorance. Knight leaves us with this paradox: empirical data and prescriptions have their truth. But they also need to be shot down. And that quandary, the heart of decision making, isn't a bad one to be left with.

It had already been presaged by Immanuel Kant's formal, transcendental dimension of understanding; and indeed Knight's paradoxical argument is an instance of reasoning in this transcendental, interpretive space. Risk and uncertainty turn out for Knight to be a sort of duality – risk being conducive to empirical *modeling* and uncertainty to *judging* it. Risk modeling involves probability estimates drawn from aggregate data sets that are only distantly related to a given decision – for the reason that the model isn't revealing the risk itself but only proxying for it. Uncertainty is part of an intuitive grasp of a situation, which economic theory, in its consistent but generalized theory, can alone never fathom. In this, Knight takes the quintessentially modern view of decision making, where the economist is "agnostic on all questions beyond the fairly immediate facts of experience" and doesn't claim to be "expressing any view as to the ultimate nature of reality" (200fn). Unfortunately, empiricist critiques of economics do take it to be asserting an ultimate nature of reality.

Uncertainty Is Concern over the Fading-Away of Structure

Von Neumann and Morgenstern (1944) appeared to break from this critical stance in the form of a utility that would be observable, in particular as a probability distribution of weighted future rewards. Their innovation is important to consider here, partly because it's the platform-of-choice in empiricist efforts to find 'the true utility' and which we address more here and in Chapter V. Its main idea is to think of the future as a distribution $f(x)$ of rewards x, so that the preferred option is the one bringing the highest expected utility $\int U(x)f(x)dx$, or sum of the future reward possibilities as weighted by their probabilities (e.g. Boadway and Bruce (52, 226); Mas-Colell et al.) (173). The key to our ability to determine such a point on $U(x)$ is that, because U must be concave, any random move below position x^o would reduce U by more than any random move above would raise it. So, all that matters as you move along U is its slope change $d(dU)$. U's meaning, in other words, is confined to a suitably normalized $d(dU)$.

We are then with VN&M utility poised between the empiricist and mainstream view. The mainstream rejects any observable, measurable preference at all. The empiricist – Partha Dasgupta's social orderings for instance – claims to measure utility in the full or ratio-scale sense of the word, so that even zero utility is asserted to have meaning.[1] In a fully empiricist world, you literally run out of utility like you run out of toothpaste. This of course implies that proportionate utility variations du/u are literal as well: we can say, on a ratio scale, that Harriet is 15% better off than Karl and mean it absolutely. Von Neuman and Morgenstern offer between that and what was then called the neoclassical approach (where utility is ordinal only) a compromise: preferences will be measured but only in their curvatures rather than levels.

How far does this compromise carry us in the metalogical, empiricist direction? The Taylor expansion offers a playful clue. If U is cardinally measurable (origins, intercepts, are arbitrary), utility can be approximated as an expansion around U consisting of its present level $U = U^o$ plus a weighted first-order (1st derivative) term dU/dx, plus a weighted second-order term $d(dU)/dx^2$, and so forth through nth-order d^nU/dx^n (Chiang 1967, 256–257). As this routine itself takes all such terms, $n \Rightarrow \infty$, literally, while under Von Neumann and Morgenstern's cardinal metric the first or level-term U^o isn't observable, we can say, assuming some rough but not unreasonable utility parameters, that expected utility invites us approximately one-quarter of the way to the empiricist or literalist.[2] VN&M utility therefore seems in this way to remain largely in the mainstream orbit, where language is pre-eminently metaphorical only.

If it is, we should be able to show more specifically how. We've argued in Chapter III that demand and supply in economics are transcendental rather than direct or metaphysical, since if they aren't, we could never understand any attempt to estimate them. The moderate compromise that expected utility now proposes with standard utility theory, by partly parameterizing the utility maximization process, has the virtue of illustrating this transcendental character.

In particular, expected utility can be expressed parametrically as $E\left[U(x)\right] = \int U(x,\alpha)\cdot prob(x,\beta)dx$, where the x's are the relevant economic actions, $\int prob(x,\beta) = 1$, and α and β are respectively the utility and probability parameters (e.g. Boadway and Bruce 52, 226). Providing as it does a sense or estimate of curvature, E must explicitly incorporate the utility $U(x, \alpha)$ of every possible outcome. If we think we know $U(x, a)$ and $prob(x, b)$ in the sense of knowing how each possible event is incorporated in the parameters α and β, then we think we have succeeded in computing the actual – not a possible, interpretive, illustrative – expected utility of this decision. That is to say, we think we know the actual structure of our random future, as Maki, Guala, Dietrich and List, and others would have it. This is the setting Frank Knight (1921) called risk, and which most economists today, especially when punctilious in their wording, do too. If however – and which is the case for many or most decisions – these parameters are *un*known because $U(x)$ and $prob(x)$ are never quite knowable to begin with, then we have, I believe, what Knight (1921, 19, 232) called uncertainty.

We can take this a step further. It is to first imagine, as detached analysts are tempted to do, that they 'know' α and β, and with them, the actual stochastics. If so, they know with mechanical precision what the rational choice is. Now imagine they become gradually undeceived of this assertion of clairvoyance. As they do, α and β fade gradually into obscurity, so the entire expected utility problem becomes blurry, losing *its* own structure. This sense or suggestion of surrendering one's control of a decision's outcome parameters, of accepting whatever the future has in store, is, I would argue, what Knight was essentially driving at in his notion of uncertainty (235). Uncertainty is a Kantian unravelling of the claim to know the parameters themselves. In this gathering obscurity and its focused calm, we are in the situation of the hiker beginning his perilous mountain ascent, of the restaurateur opening her new restaurant. They are prepared for what is to come, for the unknown along with the known.[3]

Separability Is Useful Metaphor, Nonseparability Is Reality

Importantly, we couldn't have gained this particular acceptance had we not estimated the parameters, because it is in our act of doubting them that the genuine uncertainty emerges. We always knew it wasn't literally true that α and β are 'known' despite writing them that way, but only, in Mas-Colell, Whinston, and Green's words, that they "provide a valuable guide to action" (178). "It is very easy to work with expected utility and very difficult to do without it," they say. Conversely, and as we've also shown, it is personal experience that provides the meaning of the estimates.[4] For it is the risky experience of opening a restaurant that allows us to recognize the significance or validity of the empirical model built to represent it, despite that its parameters will never be literally known. This mutuality between intuition and generalization is what we mean when we say economics stands in an *as-if* – a symbolical or metaphorical – position to the decision maker.

> *But note what this implies. It implies economic models use metaphorical rather than literal language.*

We can see this in three ways:

Distinguishing between Cause and Effect. A first way to recognize this symbolical character is that in its absence, expected utility flatly contradicts itself. For the location of the probabilities on the right side of the above $E(U)$ expansion implies that the risk is the cause and utility the effect. That is, a choice can't be conceived without first grasping in some way its risk. With dramatically opposite meaning however we can think of the expansion as a *decomposition* of the utility, in which case the risk resides *in* and unfolds *from* the utility. Risk is now the effect and utility the cause. Unless then this model is to be taken as obviously confused, it must be understood as asserting no causality assertions whatsoever. It only provides us with alternative views of a picture. Decision and risk always go together, a question of judgment only.

Distinguishing between Expectation and Risk. A second way to see expected utility's metaphorical sense is that in its Taylor expansion, only the variance and higher probability moments of x are supposed to reflect unpredictability. They are additively separable from the first or expectation term, which as shown in footnote 47 is assumed, as $\ln(x)$, perfectly known. If the mechanics of the model are to be taken literally then, the future's risky and non-risky aspects are, being additive, independent of one another. That might be fine for manufacturing operations, where risk is, say, random electrical failure with known probability support and density. It wouldn't be fine for a person's total experience of facing what is to come, which as we've seen resists any reduction to a density. It is only interpretively or for the sake of consistent judgment therefore that expected utility theory can ever be useful.

Distinguishing between Risk and Risk Bearing. A third way to recognize expected utility's symbolical nature is the apparent claim in $E[U(x)] = \int U(x;\, \alpha) \cdot prob(x;\beta)dx$ that risk can be distinguished from the willingness to bear it. Risk is supposed to reside in the probabilities (or what is the same, the probability moments) and risk-*bearing* in the $U(x)$. Risk and the courage to face it have their separate domains. If so, however, why do economists never talk of the intellect and the will as the medievals and even Nietzsche did, the one being the decision maker's *grasp* of what confronts her and the other being her *strength* to face it, or of her related psychological conditions of fear and celebration?

If the separation of courage from risk is to be successful, what unifying principle will bring them back together? The multiplication (as opposed to addition) of each utility prospect by its probability does imply a tentative jointness between utility and risk. But this is immediately undermined when the products are added together in the form of $\int U(x,\alpha) \cdot prob(x,\beta)dx$. Additivity after all is flagrant nonjointness.[5] We have an apparent denial of the integrality of human experience, of the possible jointness of every aspect of experience with every other that accounts for the unity of our understanding. And unlike the Slutzky decomposition of demand into substitution and income effects, a distinction in which no one claims to know the effects themselves, $E(U)$ terms are commonly advertised in the metalogical and behaviorist literature as explicitly revealing utility.[6] This advertisement is especially egregious because expected utility models are supposed to depict uncertainty, and uncertainty is precisely what can't be measured.[7] We cannot then take expected utility theory literally. It can only be an interpretive aid.

All three of these apparent inconsistencies, that is to say – between cause and effect, expectation and risk, and risk and risk bearing – can, in the mainstream economic spirit, be put aside. That spirit is to stop advertising expected utility, or any other model, as an expression of actual preferences or chances, but like the Slutzky equation mere projections of integral meaning onto a screen of supposed separability, *as if* they were separable. They offer ways in which sense and conception can be brought together in a single cognitive frame. They help, that is, to inform intuition, provided we remind ourselves they do nothing else, are never anything actual or literal, are metaphor only.

Preference and Risk Measures Have an Identification Problem

Expected utility is useful in other ways too. Like the revealed preference theory developed around the same time, it was part of the mid-century impetus toward measurement, toward escaping the onus of a utility that sounded too ethereal. It would henceforth be positive, confirmed in psychometric labs and observed price variations. Its only problem, mocking its instinct to bring a fresh new clarity to economics, was how to obtain the parameters. As $E(U)$ isn't observable in market data, it must be extracted, if it can be, in labs and surveys. Either way, the subjects are assigned a certain context on the basis of which they are to think of the dollar amounts (certainty equivalents) they would accept or pay for given risks. The result was a collision or collusion between the lab operator's and subject's attitudes: a group phenomenon therefore, *about* an average, never about a person.

It isn't surprising then to see positivists like John Harsanyi use Von Neumann Morgenstern utility to rationalize interpersonal utility comparisons, because in the laboratories needed for eliciting the parameters it is an aggregate already. *u* had offered no toe-hold for doing so, no positive content in someone's utility allowing it to be aggregated with someone else's. Expected utility had now begun – I emphasize only begun – to offer that toe-hold.

An important development in the social sciences has been an effort called mentalism to shift the locus of human choice from a judgment to a brain event. Utility is to be an aspect of brain phenomena, which as empirical are in the domain of bioscience. Preferences, now to be distinguished from utility, are positioned in a subsequent behavioral (including economic) arena, to be assessed by the experimental psychologist on the basis of stated emotions and wants (Samir Okasha 2016, Dietrich and List 2016). Psycho-economic data, anchored in and *guided by* the cranial, are then scientific ('true'), in Okasha's view for instance entirely expressible in empirical categories. The expected utility model is attractive for this purpose but only if both utility and probability are determined by neuroscience and its psycho-economic counterpart.

Now here is an important inference of this claim. Okasha argues that if we're interested only in economic forecasts ('positives'), the originating or biological stage here can be dispensed with. Psychological methods are enough for prediction purposes because brain functions are manifested in psychological form anyway, in turn impelling action. Only therefore if we're concerned with *causation* do we reach back to the brain, which as the more basic and important aspect of reality has the right to be called normative. The advantage of the positive-vs-normative distinction for Okasha is this implication that psycho-economics is mere convenience (brings good predictions), while biology gets to the real underlying matter and cause (tells us what truly is).

If it does, however, the obverse would hold too: a failure to distinguish between positive and normative would imply a failure to distinguish between convenience and underlying cause. And it should be clear from our discussion of *u* in Chapters I and III that there indeed is no ultimate distinction in contemporary economic theory between positive and normative, so that, by Okasha's reasoning, there would be no basis for dividing choice between psychology and biology. What I plan to do and what I should do in modern economics are finally the same (see Chapter VI). Positive and normative differ no more from one another than a risk model does from a deterministic one. They are interpretations, there already in *u*, whether you call them preferences or utility, and so are a matter of emphasis only. In any event, as we've just shown, expected utility isn't a measure of anything at all. It is only a way of glimpsing or interpreting a problem – of guiding oneself into a future. It can't therefore be any basis for distinguishing the roles of a neural from a psychological science.

In particular, Okasha is trying to draw a distinction in $E(U)$ between use and cause. Construed psychologically, he says, which he conflates with economics, expected utility is just a "convenient mathematical device," a way of *indicating* that x is preferred to y (415–416). Construed mentalistically on the other hand, it is a "potentially valid causal explanation" of a choice, so would *determine* the choice of x over y. Since however we've shown above that expected utility has little to do with either prediction *or* causation, because it is only estimable rather than measurable, Okasha's conflation of psychology with economics here is baseless. The language of *as-if*, of the unity of the formal with the empirical dimension of understanding, is as foreign to most empirical psychology as it is to neuroscience – so if anything, it is these two sciences that can be merged. Neither are they interpretive because, being purely empirical, both are blind to the distinction between actuality and possibility, between 'truth' and human judgment.[8]

It is important here to recall from Chapter III, that because the u in the optimized Hicksian demand function $x[p, e(p, u)]$ is an ultimately ordinal phenomenon, it leaves preferences structurally unspecified. And it finally must leave them so because even in aggregate data it is to individual persons that u finally points. We are attending to those, represented by u, who *have* preferences. So also are we in expected utility $E(U)$ but only in the sense of a decomposition *of* u, and in that way an additional fosterer of intuition. This is not so in $E(U)$'s psychological and neuroscientific renditions, where it is about objects, not persons. To whom in that case will $E(U)$'s linearity in utilities and parameters refer? Just *who*, to a scientist, is this modeled entity? Until this is answered, literal expected utility will be inadequately identified. It will remain useful, but offer no basis for reducing a person to the mechanical computations that empiricism is looking for.

The Problem of Equilibrium and Disequilibrium

Utility, we've been saying, is the unity of a person's concern for a situation, including the future, and which is Kant's pure (as opposed to empirical) intuition. Like, in contrast, the doctrine of revealed preference, *expected* utility is an effort to expose this view to public inspection. In doing so, it has both revealed and covered it up, and in this respect is no different than one's own future possibilities as they start to actualize. New uncertainties immediately surface.[9]

Economizing as a Substitute for Utility

In sympathy or mimicry of the increasingly mechanized and specialized nature of science in the late 19th century, economics turned in the 20th to a better understanding of the 'how' of decision making. It would be a 'how' in the sense of further elaborating the means-vs-ends framework canonical in optimization problems and ordinary economic vocabulary, and which Robbins had again brought to the fore. But though the problematic nature of any measurable objective had always been obvious to economic introspection, there now seemed an irresistible draw to particular economic measures that might encapsulate, vivify, or justify the others. Utility was a likely target for this purpose because from the classical standpoint, still clinging to thinghood, utility was unacceptably narrow, while from the mainstream standpoint it had already been taken off the table as any *thing* at all.

If any economic objective could be held up as an obvious substitute for utility, either by logical deduction or direct observation, it would seem to be 'economy' itself. In the mid-20th century the thought began circulating that economic theory and real economic decisions did harbor a single unifying principle: it would be to economize, to avoid waste. The principle, A.L. Macfie (1936) wrote, "that scarce means should not be wasted, or should be used to the best advantage," appears to be a universally reasonable goal, regardless of activity. Uncomfortably, however, the universality of 'goals' begins to sound circular. Macfie, remarked on by Kirzner (1960, 141), says for instance, "the realization of an objective which is reasonable is in some sense good in itself." Economy would, that is, be a self-evident value, free of any particular context and so logically deducible or easy to see.[10]

The advantage of 'economy' over utility, in Macfie's mind, is that its antithesis is waste, a universally deprecated practice. The notion of waste is one of the more interesting and paradoxical problems in economic thought. Waste could be nothing other than the difference between the actual and minimal expenditure on a given purpose. What Macfie doesn't broach is how such a minimum could ever be recognized in absence of an understanding of what those purposes are, especially say if they include taking-it-easy and maintaining your health. As no one would rationally surrender more than needed to reach a goal, expenses greater than necessary were likely for goals that an analyst, looking on from a distance, hadn't perceived – or perhaps random events diverting inputs to unintended directions. Ex-ante, that is, waste is irrational. So, in appearing to have discovered waste, Macfie must have been thinking ex-post – that you never be caught appearing to *have tried* to waste. Only ex- post, for goals merely speculated to have been envisaged at the time of the expenditure, could waste be identified. The idea of economizing and avoiding waste, then, is a useful intuition-building exercise. But ex ante, it speaks to meaning and motive only and isn't anything different from utility: it cannot be observed.

In *Human Action*, von Mises proposes another utility substitute: *action*. Mises' starting point, like revealed-preference approaches, is to note an asymmetry between a decision maker's means and ends. Means are clear because evident in a transaction. A trader accepts p amount of a good – money – in exchange for q amount of the thing given up. We see nothing of why the transaction took place, nor the ends it satisfied, other than that the good was wanted more than the price it was exchanged for. From this principle, Mises argues that any important finding in economics can be derived syllogistically. He is constructing then a rationalist, Leibnizian science in which economic truth is implicitly contained in its axioms – in Mises' case, the axiom of 'action' – so that only logic is needed to draw out the truths. Daniel Hausman mistakenly calls this view of reason *synthetic a priori* (1992, 303). As Mises is proposing that economics be derived entirely from principles, he is appealing entirely to an *a priori* instead, rejecting any need for a synthesis between the *a priori* and the empirical (*a posteriori*) dimensions of understanding that would constitute a *synthetic a priori.*[11]

This point deserves some elaboration because, in an important confusion, Hausman extends Mises' rationalism to Kant as well. Hausman writes in his 1992 edition, apparently referring to philosophers rather than economists, that

> Empiricism remains dominant. But it is not unchallenged. Kant argued in his *Critique of Pure Reason* that there are 'synthetic' truths about the world that can be known '*a priori*' – that is without empirical confirmation.
>
> (303)

This remark is misleading on two important grounds. First, to know something *a priori* for Kant doesn't rule out our epistemic need for connected empirical experience. Second, it doesn't eliminate the accessibility of these experiences either. And 'experience' can be taken in two quite different senses, pure mathematics engaging us in a manner different from how GNP and unemployment numbers engage us. That math is indeed *a priori* is clear, as Kant notes, from the necessary character of its conclusions – that they are necessarily true. To use his example, once we know that 5 + 7 equals 12 we know it cannot equal anything else. By way therefore of its obvious necessity, $5 + 7 = 12$ is an *a priori* reality, no data required. Surprising to some, however, it is synthetic as well, confirmed by the universal practice of confirming the various arithmetical equations in tangible *ways*, even if imagined ones. As Kant writes, "We have to go outside these concepts and call in the aid of the intuition which corresponds to one of them, our five fingers for instance... adding to the concept of 7, unit by unit, the five given in intuition." "Arithmetical propositions therefore are always synthetic" (B15–B16).

If arithmetic doesn't in this way avoid for Kant the synthetic side of a *synthetic a priori*, it would seem that the GNP data can't either, requiring as these numbers do the careful, fallible matching of empirical economic signals with their relevant economic categories. And surely it wouldn't in the kinds of understandings met with in microeconomics, where the prices and quantities of purchased and sold goods, say, are obviously observable and measurable and thus immediately subject to empirical confirmation. To be in contact with the empirical dimension of understanding is part of being grounded – economic or otherwise – and it is our empirical intuitions, including engagements with our hands, that place us in this contact.[12] Mainstream economics is in no way to be identified with the rationalist thought of von Mises.

Measurable Concepts Can't Fathom Equilibrium

An important decision concept that served as a challenge to, rather than duality with, utility appeared in the form of Leibenstein's *x*-efficiency (1966), which in its implied unnameability did suggest a transcendence over the empirical. In an *x*-inefficient situation, more inputs than necessary are being devoted to a given output, evidenced for instance when another producer is using less of it. Resources are being wasted, so this is another version of the waste idea. As David Lewis later declared, to every empirical effect there is to be an empirical cause, and Leibenstein proposed – what really was a hypothesis auxiliary to *x*-inefficiency – that the reason for the waste is an inadequate motivation to work hard. 'Motivation,' in its elevation from mere verb to noun, became then this auxiliary empirical concept.

George Stigler's 1976 *American Economic Review* article criticizes the Leibenstein motivation hypothesis and along with it the assumption that inefficiency is observable as some bad thing on its own. In Leibenstein's case, it was to be eliminated by worker incentive plans and in that way virtually net costless to the firm. Failure to motivate would imply a wasted resource: too much labor, because ill-encouraged, is being used to produce what other firms can produce with less. The failure was to reveal itself as operating at a point below the firm's or industry's production function or to the northeast of its production isoquant, appearing in that way to be a technical inefficiency although nothing of the kind because it isn't technical. The problem was motivation instead, and the solution was to deploy a better motivation policy.

In his critique, Stigler asks in the first place why these workers shouldn't have additional goals like security and flexibility. If they did, the presumption that motivation policies are costless would go by the board – at least in the opportunity sense that a motivation policy will attract workers less inclined to security and flexibility goals and so be more expensive to hire, while repelling the current workers more inclined to them. As it recognizes this input supply shift and the expense of paying for it, the firm soon recognizes what it really had been doing. It had been engaged in producing not only goods but information useful for guiding its inputs toward the manager's objectives, which may involve security and flexibility too. Motivation, in the sense Leibenstein uses the word, therefore has no underlying reality. As a measurable and therefore separable element, it simply *isn't*. And because a similar argument can be made for any other non-technological cost factor, neither can there be any '*x*-inefficiency.' It has deserved its self-effacing name. We must however give it its due. It stimulates rational curiosity about where the workers have gone that the new policy has chased away, where the new workers have come from, and why. In other words, what it really raises is the question of equilibrium.

Leibenstein simply hadn't taken his thinking far enough. If the point on the boundary of the feasible technology set really were an optimum, so the firm was doing its best there, why had it, or a competitor, not done its best when found to be at the supposed interior ('less efficient') point as well, in which case *it* is on the real frontier? Why wouldn't it be devoting, to some *other* best use, the input that had disqualified it from the official frontier? In asking this why-wouldn't question, I am posing a reduction to the absurd: it is absurd (inconsistent) that the producer would behave optimally at a point the analyst considers efficient and *not* continue to behave optimally at points the analyst considers inefficient. Because he is irrational? Then how did he begin rationally? This is a burden-of-proof issue. And the distant, external viewer, the poser of an empirical category like 'motivation' or 'waste,' carries the burden of proof.

Equilibrium Is Formal Only

Haven't we come to a puzzling juncture? Economics is supposed to be the one discipline where incentives matter. Yet here has been posited an incentive mechanism specially tailored to a certain management question, like a key to a lock, and been found wanting. For if motivation is something you can literally watch, isolated from everything you *cannot* literally watch – from what is possible that is – you have been boxed into that corner we could really call irrational: an insistence on isolating any one question from any other. If so, a rational decision's peculiarly rational aspect would have to be a sense or openness to its possible ramifications for your other prospects. This openness we could call the form or possibility of equilibrium. I therefore advance the following two conjectures:

> *Empirical Equilibrium: There is no empirical concept (e.g. a measured 'motivation', 'effort', or 'inefficiency') held up to explain a defined economic reality – that is, there is no ex-post categorical interpretation of a given economic choice or outcome – that isn't an implied substitute for equilibrium.*

Obversely,

> *Formal Equilibrium: There is no formal, transcendental (nonmeasurable though estimable) concept (e.g. utility, cost, or income) held up to explain a judged economic reality – that is, there is no ex-ante interpretation of economic choices and outcomes – that doesn't imply the possibility of equilibrium.*

The attitude that reality is immediately empirical, so you can know it by just watching and reporting it, is one that can never recognize an equilibrium, which is never meant to be empirical or actual. Equilibrium is nothing but continual anticipation of a future and a consistent application of reason to it, including others' responses to yours.[13] Equilibrium says, and only says, that no anticipation can be clearly isolated from any other anticipation – ever.

How then does economic theory express this isolation-resisting character? One way is the tangency of the budget line to the utility indifference curve between two goods (Figure 1). If to equilibrate is to abhor isolation, it must be a giving-back for what was taken and a taking-back for what was given. Near the tangency base-point of the figure, this is what is happening. A small movement to the southeast means surrendering utility by giving up some y while gaining an equal utility from a bit more of x, so spending on the new x what had been saved on y.[14] Robbins reminds us of what this implies: "…our knowledge of the statical foundations is fundamental. We examine change by comparing small differences of equilibrium" (103). In particular, because any marginal change must originate at the tangency, which is a tentative equilibrium, you will want it to be one that minimizes cost, and that is to move along the gradient vector orthogonal to the tangent. Sentimental adjectives like 'appealing' in Amartya Sen (1979), dogmatic ones like 'real' in Samir Okasha (2016), and scientistic ones like 'causal' in

Francesco Guala (2019) are only a *righting* of an inorthogonality in the gradient, so a *substitute* for equilibrium.

This same giving-back occurs in a market transaction. When all the higgling and calculating are done, you are supplying me what I demand and accepting from me what you demand. In absence of this equality, exchange would be an arbitrary jerk of the arm or brain. So would be any transaction that fails to rely for its anticipations on what we can call the Houtthaker Sequence (Chapter III) of those stemming from ours.

As anticipation then – and *only* as anticipation – does quantity supplied equal quantity demanded. And we already know from Chapter III that both these quantities are functions of utility – the demands directly so and the supplies because, by way of Roy's lemma, they are functions of the supplier's *indirect* utility. Equilibrium $E = q^d(p, u) - q^s(p, u) = 0$ therefore is a utility (so a *synthetic a priori*) concept. This is why even Alex Rosenberg (1992) and Marc Blaug (1980), together with much of the mainstream tradition, are right in saying that general equilibrium is fundamental to economic thought, that absent a clarified path to one, models are only 'toys,' or more charitably, mere particles of complete reasoning (67).

Interestingly, we have in the inverse of a quantity equilibrium a liquidity one. Inverting demand and supply to price-dependent form and setting its difference to zero gives the expression for perfect liquidity $L = p^d(q, u) - p^s(q, u) = 0$, where the highest price someone will pay (the demand price) equals the least price someone will accept (supply price). Trade is now instantaneous on terms everyone anticipates. A denial of the possibility of perfect equilibrium $E = 0$ is therefore a denial of the possibility of perfect liquidity $L = 0$, in which $E = 0$ if and only if $L = 0$. Liquidity is a *synthetic a priori* concept too, just as demand, supply, equilibrium, cost, profit, and income are. And utility is their essential rationale. In particular here, equilibrium and liquidity aren't entities that can be found to 'hold' or 'exist' as empiricist critiques maintain. They cannot be detected and measured despite that they *can* be estimated and interpreted. They are a necessary form of any thought, even in the denial of it.

As Is Disequilibrium

We can see this even more easily by considering their counterfoils, disequilibrium $|E| \neq 0$ and illiquidity $|L| \neq 0$.[15] The syntax of disequilibrium is revealing: it amounts to asserting equilibrium, then retracting it. Disequilibrium has no independent cognitive or phenomenal status, depending instead on the very possibility it denies, for in absence of an ability to deny there is no ability to assert. In this respect, however, it does have an advantage, since in its shadowy identity as a mere *not*, it at least can't pretend to be anything visible, while equilibrium can ever so briefly suggest such a pretense. Disequilibrium *can* be estimated, by way of $q^d(p, m)$ and $q^s(p, m)$, but *their* reality is in the realm of interpretation too. And interpretation, we have shown, is a Kantian unity of intuition and generalization, which is equilibrial. It is the restaurant owner on opening night *and in the deepest uncertainty* who is in equilibrium, the true concretion. There we have the stasis point without which there would be no fluctuation or dynamics. Thought, even of a disequilibrium, must itself be equilibrial, so those who laugh at the idea that markets equilibrate ironically do so by way of equilibrium.

Methodologists put considerable store on knowing whether general equilibrium is essential to economic thought. Mark Blaug asks, "can we ... infer that the manifest failure of an economy to exhibit an equilibrium in all markets also falsifies ... the utility maximizing theory of consumer behavior and the profit maximizing theory of the firm?" No, he rightly answers, because "some of the initial conditions of GE theory aren't satisfied; GE theory is, therefore, inapplicable rather than false" (187). By inapplicable he means it has no empirical content to start with (189). In a remark that might have come directly from Kant's *Pure Reason* or Heidegger's *Being and Time*, Blaug writes, "we could hardly verify the existence of GE in all markets simply by looking." The theory rather "attempts to establish the logical possibility of GE ... without claiming it will actually come about" (188). Yet, he says, the logic of this possibility has become economics' strength by providing the context for the non-general equilibrium models that do the yeoman's work of explanation and forecasting.

Frustratingly, Blaug often backpedals, for instance complimenting "orthodox, timeless equilibrium theory" for being, "of all the contending economic doctrines of the past," the only one "willing to be judged in terms of its predictions" (262), when he has already told us that GE theory is inapplicable to much empirical forecasting. Blaug often confuses his understanding of foundational economic thinkers, as when he dissects J.S. Mill word for literal word what Mill had never intended to say because he was never a literalist thinker.

Daniel Hausman (1992, 2023) allows himself to be misled too on this question of equilibrium. To a partial and a general equilibrium, Hausman assigns a sharply differing epistemic. On the one hand, he says, are economics' bedrock assumptions – consumer rationality axioms like preference completeness and decision axioms like profit maximization, jointly implying a demand and a supply function which, to be intelligible, must interact with each other. This bedrock interaction, says Hausman, is non-general or partial equilibrium (1992, 81, 98–99; 2023, 87–96). Additional, non-bedrock presumptions are now introduced allowing the equilibration to be a total or general one, to wit that agents know everything, compete rather than collude, have unassailable property rights, and take futures as well as cash positions. The latter, in contrast to the bedrock assumptions, can be established only empirically Hausman says. In the event, he finds them empirically so unlawlike in a "real" or "actual" economy (1992, 273; 2023, 94) – as distinguished from a "make-believe" one (2023, 460) – to be unworthy of even statistical testing and calls, along with Brown and Spencer and others, for keeping our distance from general equilibrium until we can establish it in more realistic fashion.

I challenge Hausman's claim that economics' bedrock axioms are any more fundamental than its empirical hypotheses are. The cost-minimizing tangency in our Figure 2 for instance, the most fundamental diagram in economic theory, assumes, in the bidirectionality of its gradient from A, that traders can go short as well as long. And since the neighborhood of this tangency is where – as a central tendency – purchases and sales are made, they require property rights. Yet Hausman says property rights are an optional hypothesis. We have the sense in Hausman that if we can't isolate a small subset of claims for axiomatic status – like force in physics – and leave the rest to be tested empirically, we won't have a science. And since he insists on science, he insists on such a protocol.

Here most of today's English-speaking philosophers appear to agree. Economics differs from other sciences only in being inexact, they argue, and this is because it requires a gaggle of hypotheses from other disciplines in order to proceed. Why economics requires them, condemning it to an inexactitude, they don't tell us. It simply hasn't yet found the right auxiliary hypotheses. I do however, along with economics' founders, have an explanation: economics is about persons rather than things, so its bedrock categories must be formal, discursive, and suggestive rather than empirical despite paying attention to statistical fit as well. It speaks only, and even then just on occasion, *as if* it were exact. It is enlightening analogy or metaphor. It will never *be* an exact science for the simple reason that it isn't a science, and this is because its locus is a decision maker facing a future and only that. Economics makes no claim that we 'reach' equilibrium.

Necessary and Sufficient Conditions for Economic Rationality

If we could draw a sketch of the positivist, metalogical vision of uncertainty, it would be of dust on the lens of a moon's-eye view of earth, to be brushed away with the advance of technology. Auguste Comte (1830, 1842), the first after Bacon to formally declare a positivism, called this cleaning-of-a-lens "social physics" (13). The uncertainty of the person is quite different. It indeed is dust on a lens but the sharpest of clarities too – the immediate concentration of the whole self in an act of choice. This immediacy is what we've been calling form or judgment, what cannot be constrained to any particular future but extends potentially to every one of them, imagined and unimagined.

Uncertainty, Completeness, and Equilibrium Are Rationality

Here, Houtthaker's completeness theorem has a central place. If x is revealed preferred to y, y to z, z to $(n-1)$, and $(n-1)$ to a limiting case n, then x must be revealed preferred to n. Most importantly, Houtthaker shows x brings the greatest utility. I take x over n, and there the matter rests. It wouldn't however rest if I promptly preferred n instead, but an inner turmoil that one could really call irrational. Now note that this state of rest I achieve, even briefly, when I've made a decision is what we're calling equilibrium. To have regard then for all future possibility – to satisfy the completeness axiom *in the sense of remaining open to the entire future* – is equilibrium. In Houtthaker I argue, equilibrium and completeness are mutually dependent states, a Kantian matter of context. Speaking of which, the transitivity axiom is inessential *for* either of these principles, following *from* them instead. For if I did promptly turn about and choose n, acting intransitively, I never made a choice to start with.

To come to rest, to make a decision, to be decisive, is the question: whether to cross the street or open the restaurant, where amidst uncertainty, you are at rest because you are open to all that the future holds. Peace amid tumult. This is the 'all' of the completeness axiom's "all options can be ordered" and why I argue the transitivity axiom is only an additional elaboration. Transitivity is little different from assuming that someone has chosen something.

Let's express this more systematically. Uncertainty, equilibrium, and completeness are joint rather than separate concepts. They have the character of jointness rather than severalness because each implies the other two as the integrality of utility demands. To wit, in the act of deciding ('maximizing utility'):

(i) *Uncertainty* is what fixes your mind, a staying-open to all consequences (completeness), a possible future (equilibrium).
(ii) *Equilibrium* is that sense of possibility (uncertainty) to which you are open, involving total responsibility (completeness) for its implications.
(iii) *Completeness* is the totality of responsibility you have assumed, not as a plurality of likelihoods but as the unity (response to uncertainty) achieved in standing open to the whole of possibility (equilibrium).

Jacques Derrida (1994, 1997), though never an economist, captures this unity of the meaning of economic theory and its applications perhaps better than anyone:

> One must love the future. And there is no more just category for the future than that of the 'perhaps'. Such a thought conjoins friendship, the future, and the *perhaps* to open on to the coming of what comes – that is to say, necessarily in the regime of the possible whose possibilization must prevail over the impossible. For a possible that would only be possible (non-impossible), a possible surely and certainly possible ... would be a poor possible, a futureless possible.
>
> (29)

Just as completeness, uncertainty, and equilibrium imply one another, guaranteeing logical consistency, so do incompleteness, certainty, and disequilibrium guarantee *in*consistency. It is easy to show for example that in a permanent disequilibrium, and with suitably shaped supply and demand curves, that the money pump rears its head again, and again we've all gotten rich from someone else by just changing your mind. Rest assured then. You yourself don't reason disequilibrially even when you teach it. Completeness, uncertainty, and equilibrium are unified in the structure of reason itself, which 'realism' alone – where you're dogmatically sure that your measurements encompass, or will encompass, everything that exists – leaves inexplicable.

All this, like all joint phenomena, is unobservable if only because too close to us, too obvious, to see if all we do is 'look around' (Heidegger, 1927, 177). We encounter them in our awarenesses of situations (utility), so can be aspects of reflection only – cannot be tested, are not hypotheses, do not comprise any theory.

They are what *give* tests, hypotheses, and theories their meaning rather than constitute the tests and theories themselves. This won't prevent literal-minded thinkers from taking them to be theories – of perfect competition, perfect foresight, and so on. And they may be theories for those thinkers. But for contemporary economics, where equilibrium, say, is interpretive rather than tape-measured, they are a matter of attitude only.

A question equivalent to rationality, it seems to me, is whether economics can grasp its counterfoil – irrationality – in any way at all, let alone test for it. Let's first put aside a probably cheap way of posing this problem. The cheap way is to ask, if we really are irrational, how we could ever persuade ourselves we are, a persuasion that would require rationality. The deeper way is to reflect on economics' rationales for its own formal concepts. The rationale for utility is that it points to a source of personal understanding that will always be publicly unknowable, but to a person, each person, alone. The rationale for equilibrium is that social relations are impossible in its absence, that because economics is about persons and the economist is a person, she cannot stand outside her own project. She cannot, in this setting, be a scientist. Rationality is so fundamental that it resists any effort to deny it given that the insight employed in denying it involves rationality. As David Walsh (2016) puts it, "It is because all things are open to reason that they are capable of being known. It is through reason that everything becomes intelligible, while nothing else renders reason any more intelligible" (111). Reason is just the unity of your judgment, your understanding. If it weren't, it wouldn't be there for you to understand anything else, including reason.

Economics Is in Lieu of the Person

Much of what I'm saying here is consistent, at least in spirit, with Mark Kaplan (2002), J.-C. Spender (2011), Paul Erickson et al. (2013), and Christopher Clarke (2016) for instance, of whom we will have more to say in Chapter V. The basis of economics is free choice in the face of uncertainty, projected onto a screen of mathematical logic that seems, in the armchair of its apparent objectivity, to say that you and I recline in it too. We on the contrary are a complex of possibility comprising our relations with our world. This complex is so far from being observable to the scientist, to the economics professor, even to ourselves, that we must say economics can never be a science in the sense of starting and ending with what can simply be 'looked' at – observed in the sense of measured. It rather is a way of understanding a domain of human experience and behavior, in particular the making of a living but never reducible to that, as we each are bound up with the entirety of our possible connections and experiences, ever bringing something new and unpredictable to the table. The utility of economics rises above economics, permitting even economic motives to be absent from what appear to the bystander to be economic acts. Gross Domestic Product in this sense is less than the real economy, just as – as many have argued on environmental grounds – it is more than the real economy. Consequently, we will never get anywhere by saying the GDP is 'right' or 'wrong,' but an interpretation only, some better, some worse.

What economic theory brings to the table is our capacity to talk about it. Absent generalization we can't *say* anything about what we sense. Necessarily then, it remains a pointing-to. Economic theory knows it is a mere projection of the unseen but that it must proceed as though seeable, a mathematical clarity about what is unclear, an articulation of the inarticulate. 'As if' – analogy or metaphor – is the language of this realization. It is a concession that the words aren't descriptive but suggestive. It is *as if* the phantasms passing before David Hume's eyes were causing and affecting one another; *as if* the matrix of individual income-seeking behaviors converges to Adam Smith's market equilibrium; *as if* demand-price effects were divisible into substitution and income terms; *as if* a risky situation – that is, everyone's situation – were the products of given outcomes and their probabilities; *as if* demand were literally cardinal rather than the ordinal, deliberative state it must be. It is *as if*, in other words, the joint possibility comprising human concern were some kind of mechanism. As-if's are projections from the phenomenal (interpretable) horizon to counted, measured ones, pointing to the unity and meaning beneath. It is the mutuality of the measured and unmeasured, as if the unmeasured could be measured. It is *synthetic a priori*, the connection between the literally seen and the conceptualized. The sort of understanding economics finally claims for itself, then, is nothing literal or observable, only estimable.

The alternative is to suppose everything is in our pocket from the start. That would be ex-post reason, of ratio-scale utility and its claims to know directly someone's pain, happiness, and 'well-being.' Metalogical, empiricist economics, a ceaseless shuffling of categories and assertions, of ever-new empirical pigeonholes, is inadequate for rationality because it lacks a facing of the future *as* the future, and with it, a capacity for a decision as a person makes one.

If we are right that economic theory stands in only a symbolic relation to a deeper reality – the formal, interpretative, transcendental and, by way of morality and freedom, the metaphysical – we would find its ultimate mode of demonstration to be a reduction to the absurd. Being unobservable, freedom is in little position to support either direct argument or derivations of conclusions from principles. It is interesting that in Aristotelian and Thomistic metaphysics, as in today's empiricist, indirect proof was regarded inferior to direct proof because it doesn't explain *why* the claim one is trying to prove is true. It only eliminates the alternative. Yet reduction to the absurd, we can see *via* the Kantian Enlightenment, might finally be the deeper way to demonstrate something.

Has the Slutzky decomposition not already done so in its unpacking of the demand effect of a price rise into a substitution effect and income effect? As a price goes up, you effectively become poorer and so normally,substitution effects constant,demand less of the good than you did before. On the other hand, you wouldn't demand less had your marginal utility of money been insensitive to how much money you had, and indeed would be insensitive had you an infinite amount of it. The world would be infinite, and it is easy to show then that everyone would be identical to everyone else. Individuality, personhood, would be meaningless, precisely the empiricist's metaphysical view. Only constraints give persons their significance, their reality, and this the Slutzky decomposition shows.

Let's move on then to the implications of this harder world – what a John Updike character once called "this hard planet" – for economics' relations with its neighboring academic fields. We will focus especially on the economics of knowledge, information, and machine learning, bellwethers of much of our era.

Summary Points of Chapter IV

1. Even under a 'perfect certainty' assumption, economic demand and supply are references to, and reflections on, a future. The mainstream economic attitude therefore is one that suggests a certitude and then doubts it: an exercise in judgment.
2. This method is embodied for instance in the distinction between risk and uncertainty, risk implying that the future's parameters are known, uncertainty implying they are not. If a risk is what is to be estimated, uncertainty is the foundation of the judgment made in view of the risk estimates.
3. Such relation is encountered in expected utility, where the joint ground of uncertainty and the bearing of it are modeled as a measurable probability and a separately measured satisfaction. In a symbolic switch, utility's metric is upgraded here from the neoclassical ordinal to the cardinal.
4. We find this switch doesn't contravene the mainstream. To see the switch has been symbolic, we only note that if it were literal, causalities between risk and utility, expectations and risks, and risk and risk-bearing would collapse.
5. In the rationalist or empiricist, utility can be taken as brain phenomena, transferring the locus of choice from personal judgment to a scientific measure. Interpretation, the Kantian unity of sense and generalization, is ruled out. Distinctions between normative and positive, only tentative in economics, become absolute.
6. Utility's tentative, interpretative, Kantian character invites still more imaginative, object-like terms such as 'economizing' and 'mental states,' with their observed-entity (scientific) air. Persons become disconnected from situations, so essentially infinite.
7. There appears to be no empirical (measurable) economic concept – 'inefficiency' for instance – that isn't an implied substitute *for* an equilibrium. Obversely, there appears to be no transcendental (formal, estimable) economic concept, cost for instance, that doesn't imply the possibility *of* an equilibrium.
8. Every act of decision is an *equilibration* in the sense of a mutual consistency of possibilities, a *completeness* in the sense that the equilibration rules out arbitrary limits on what should be considered, and an *uncertainty* in the sense of a responsibility for the consequences, known and unknown.
9. As these factors are nonseparable, they are nonempirical.
10. And because they comprise the act of personal judgment, which is understanding, they comprise economic rationality.

Notes

1 A physical substance has a ratio scale; you can scale its dimensions up or right down to zero where, despite still holding its shape, it vanishes. It is easy to show (e.g., Mas-Colell, Whinston, and Green, 836) that any comparison of two individuals' utility levels requires a ratio scale, so that, say, a zero utility means you get nothing. See Boadway and Bruce (1984, 144–169) for a more extensive discussion of the associated metric spaces.

2 I only half-jest here. The half-jest part is as follows. Note expected utility's Taylor expansion $U(x) = U(x_o) + [dU/dx)(dx)]/1! + (d^2U/dx^2)(dx)^2]/2! + ... + (d^nU/dx^n)(dx)^n]/n!$. Let's focus on the first three terms, assume a log utility function $U(x) = \ln(x)$, and let $x_0 = 2$ and $dx = 1$. U(x) then resolves into $U(x) = \ln(x_o) + (1/x)\, dX - (1/2x^2)\, dX^2 = \ln(x_o) - 0.125 + 0.042$, namely the utility level plus the utility curvature terms d^2U/dX^2 and d^3U/dX^3. As even in a cardinal utility metric the utility *level* cannot be known (Boadway and Bruce 17–18, 50–60), expected utility theory here is asserting that only (0.125 + 0.042) / (0.5 + 0.125 + 0.042) or 25% of the utility shape that a literalist economics thinks can be asserted can really be asserted.

3 Far then from eliminating the feasibility of economic modeling and prediction, uncertainty is what facilitates it by sharpening one's focus and incentive. The literature seems confused on this subject. See for instance Blaug's (1980, 259–260) view that the Austrian school regards the future as too uncertain to allow forecasts, when all of us are making forecasts every minute, before we step into the street for instance.

4 We can call this writing-out of the parameters, the projection of subjective intuition onto a screen of objectivity, 'thought,' while the fading-away of that objectivity – experience's influence on our intuition – 'phenomena,' to be examined transcendentally or phenomenologically. Heidegger (1927) depicts the fading-away of objectivity or thinghood as the "withdrawal of being" which lights up that from which it withdraws, because the anticipation of loss is how we recognize what is valuable.

5 The independence of irrelevant alternatives property, a condition of the expected utility theorem, is only one implication of this additive nonjointness (Mas-Colell et al., 171).

6 On this see Chapter V below.

7 Some models have incorporated, along with an outcome's variance, the sampling variance of each of its statistics (the variance respectively of the mean, variance, skew for example). The practice has largely been abandoned, likely because total variances of such kind are embarrassingly large.

8 For additional doubts about the credibility of isolating a true utility, see Roberto Fumagali (2013).

9 Von Mises (1949) speculates – in what could be an anthropology instead of an economics – that there would have been no need for money in human history in the absence of this kind of rolling uncertainty, since gradual asset liquidation alone would have been adequate for continuous consumption demand. The arrival of money in history and its instant convertibility thus marks the point at which people became explicitly aware they were at risk, or as we could say, human. If so, our official money supply measures are understated because they ignore the supply of credible promises, which compensate for the fixity of the remaining, non-money assets. A credible promise is itself liquidity, just as a noncredible one is illiquidity. Most promises don't include formal tokens, and some economies, cultures, and eras are undoubtedly blessed with greater promise-credibility than others are. No wonder central banks have such difficulty getting the money supply right, when it changes every time a promise is made with even a small possibility of fulfillment.

10 Kirzner (108-145) spends considerable time parsing Robbins' sense of scarcity as a choice "between ends and means that have alternative uses." Some parsing here is necessary because, he says, Robbins hops back and forth between the idea of economizing and the idea of maximizing, the latter requiring we know the decision maker's ends, which are "abstract" and slippery. (124) Taking Robbins' words mechanically, Kirzner is perfectly right. And he does often take Robbins mechanically. If, however, Kirzner had made explicit as well as implicit to himself the distinction between the formal or phenomenological and the empirical – which Robbins always did keep in mind – he'd have saved himself and his readers much trouble.

11 Mises' follower Murray Rothbard confirms this depiction of Mises by arguing that the minor premises to be conjoined to his major or 'action' premise are themselves "so generally true … as to be seen by all as obviously true once they are stated," and hence "not empirically falsifiable." (316) In contrast, he says, "positivists of all shades boggle at self-evident propositions." As I have pointed out frequently in this work, the metalogical or empiricist also has its self-evident propositions.

12 Kant applies syntheticity also to the claim that the shortest distance between two points is a straight line, noting that this is a qualitative rather than quantitative – and so an empirically intuitive and thus synthetic – argument (B16). Hausman refers to such claims more generally as Euclidean geometry and argues they are false. In reference to the current presumption that parallel lines can converge if stretched out far enough, Hausman says "modern physics has refuted Kant's view that the axioms of Euclidean geometry are *a priori* truths." Does such convergence however refute Kant or only serve as a current working scientific hypothesis? As what can prevent it from later becoming scientifically false again?

13 Jacques Derrida (1994) evokes something similar to this idea in his paradoxical concept of isolated friends: We are "friends who are alone because … incomparable and without common measure, reciprocity, or equality." (35)

14 The Edgeworth box depicts this kind of equilibrium in a slightly fuller though correspondingly more complicated way.

15 Disequilibrium is sometimes interpreted as a reflection of trader error, a plausible suggestion after the fact. Ex ante though, disequilibrium must always be unforecastable in the sense that every expectation is an equilibrium of some kind. It is hard then to see how there ever could be an ex-ante theory of error, though many ex-post theories of it.

References

Blaug, Mark. *The Methodology of Economics*. Cambridge: Cambridge University Press, 1980, 1992.

Boadway, Robin W. and Neil Bruce. *Welfare Economics*. Cambridge, MA: Blackwell Publishers, 1984.

Brown, Andrew and David A. Spencer. "The Nature of Economics and the Failings of the Mainstream: Lessons from Lionel Robbins's *Essay*." *Cambridge Journal of Economics* 36, 2012, 781–798.

Chiang, Alpha C. *Fundamental Methods of Mathematical Economics*. New York: McGraw-Hill, 1967.

Clarke, Christopher. "Functionalism and the Role of Psychology in Economics." *Journal of Economic Methodology* 27, No. 4, 2020, 292–310.

Comte, Auguste. *Cours de Philosophie Positive, Chpts 1 & 2*, 1830. Pauls Descours and H. Gordon Jones (Trans.). Republished in 1988, Indianapolis, Hackett Publishing Co..

Dasgupta, Partha. *An Inquiry into Well-Being and Destitution*. Oxford: Oxford University Press, 1993.

Derrida, Jacques. *The Politics of Friendship*. Paris: Editions Galilee, 1994. Trans. George Collins, Verso Press, 1997.

Dietrich, Franz and Christian List. "Mentalism vs Behaviorism in Economics: A Philosophy of Science Perspective." *Economics and Philosophy* 32, 249–281, 2016.

Erickson, Paul, Judy Klein, Lorraine Daston, Rebecca Lemov, Thomas Sturn, and Michael Gordon. *How Reason Almost Lost its Mind*. Chicago: University of Chicago Press, 2013.

Fisher, Irving. *The Nature of Capital and Income*. New York: Macmillan, 1906.

Friedman, Milton. "The Methodology of Positive Economics." *Essays in Positive Economics*. Chicago: University of Chicago Press, 1953.

Fumagalli, Roberto. "The Futile Search for True Utility." *Economics and Philosophy* 29 (2013): 325–347.

Guala, Francesco. "Preferences: Neither Behavioral nor Mental." *Economics and Philosophy* 35: 383–401. 2019.

Harsanyi, John C. "Cardinal Welfare, Individualistic Ethics, and Interpersonal Comparisons of Well-Being." *Journal of Political Economy* 63, 309–321, 1955.

Hausman, Daniel M. *The Inexact and Separate Science of Economics*. Cambridge: Cambridge University Press, 1992, 2023.

Heidegger, Martin. *Being and Time*. John Macquarrie and Edward Robinson (Trans.). New York: Harper-Collins, 1962. First published in 1927.

Heidegger, Martin. *Kant and the Problem of Metaphysics*. Bloomington, IN: Indiana University Press, 1962. James S. Churchill (Trans.). First published in 1929.

Houtthaker, Hendrik. "Revealed Preference and the Utility Function." *Economica* 17, 159–174, 1950.

Hume, David. *A Treatise of Human Nature. Book I, Of the Understanding*. L.A. Selby-Bigge (ed.). Oxford: Clarendon Press, 1893. First published in 1739.

Kant, Immanuel. *Critique of Pure Reason, 1st and 2nd eds*. New York: Random House (Modern Library), 1958. Norman Kemp Smith (Trans.). First published 1781; revised 1787.

Kaplan, Mark. "Decision Theory and Epistemology." In: Paul K. Moser (ed.), *Oxford Handbook of Epistemology*. Oxford: Oxford University Press, 2002, 434–462.

Kirzner, Israel M. *The Economic Point of View*. 1960, 1976. Menlo Park: Institute for Humane Studies.

Knight, Frank H. *Risk, Uncertainty, and Profit*. Boston: Houghton Mifflin, 1921.

Leibenstein, H. "Allocative Efficiency vs. 'X-Efficiency.'" *American Economic Review* 56, June 1966, 392–415.

Leibniz, Gottfried von. *Theory of Knowledge and Metaphysics*. In: Philip Wiener (ed.), *Selections*. New York: Scribner & Sons, 1951. First published in 1676.

Macfie, A.L. *An Essay on Economy and Value*. London: Macmillan, 1936.

Maki, Uskali (ed.). *The Economic World View: Studies in the Ontology of Economics*. Cambridge: Cambridge University Press, 2001.

Mas-Colell, A., M.D. Whinston, and J.R. Green. *Microeconomic Theory*. New York: Oxford University Press, 1995.

Mill, John Stuart. "On the Definition and Method of Political Economy." In: D. Hausman (ed.), *The Philosophy of Economics*, 3rd ed. Cambridge: Cambridge Univ. Press, 2008. First published in 1836.

Mises, Ludwig von. *Human Action: A Treatise on Economics*. 3rd ed. Chicago: Henry Regnery Co., 1966. First published in 1949 by Yale University Press.

Okasha, Samir. "On the Interpretation of Decision Theory." *Economics and Philosophy* 32 (2016): 409–433.
Robbins, Lionel. An Essay on the Nature and Significance of Economic Science. London: Macmillan, 1st ed. 1932.
Rosenberg, Alex. *Economics – Mathematical Politics or the Science of Diminishing Returns?* Chicago: University of Chicago Press, 1992.
Rothbard, Murray N. "In Defense of Extreme Apriorism." *Southern Economic Journal* 23, No. 3, January 1957, 314–320.
Sen, Amartya. *Collective Choice and Social Welfare*. Oxford: North-Holland, 1979.
Smith, Adam. *The Wealth of Nations*. 1776. New York: Modern Library, 1937.
Spender, J.-C. "Human Capital and Agency Theory." In: Alan Burton-Jones and J.-C. Spender (eds.), *The Oxford Handbook of Human Capital*. Oxford: Oxford University Press, 2011.
Stigler, George. "The Xistence of X-Efficiency." *American Economic Review* 66 (1), 1976.
Updike, John. "The Sea's Green Sameness." *Museums and Women, and Other Stories*. New York: Vintage Books, Random House, 1960.
Von Neumann, John and Oskar Morgenstern. *Theory of Games and Economic Behavior*. Princeton: Princeton University Press, 1944.
Walsh, David. *Politics of the Person as the Politics of Being*. South Bend: University of Notre Dame Press, 2016.

V The Economics of Knowledge and Information

Knowledge and information have been the economic hot topic since the mid-20th century. In the age of what some call classical liberalism (say the 75 years before 1940), few economists claimed to be privy to what decision makers know about a market beyond the institutional rules and data directly relevant. This changed with the introduction of information and knowledge as topics in themselves.

Philip Mirowski (2009) is one of the more picturesque and polemical critics of the information age. He and Edward Nik-Khah (2017) divide it into three phases, though admitting it hard to in any neat way. In the first or neoliberal period, information was handled obliquely, simply as news relevant to decisions. This sort of information is associated with the University of Chicago school of Gary Becker, Milton Friedman, and George Stigler. In the second period, information is treated more explicitly – as inductive or analytical statements, decision trees, state-space models, and transition probability matrices of likely states of the world. This Mirowski and Nik-Khah center at the Cowles Commission (first at Chicago, then Yale) including Koopmans, Arrow, and Hurwicz and to a lesser extent at MIT and Harvard, prominently in Samuelson, Ackerloff, and Stiglitz. The third and most recent has been information in the still freer form of computational and numerical processes, emphasizing the dynamics of number management.

With information in the picture, both a prospective analyticist and a current mainstream economics can, each in its way, raise the notion of a 'mind' framed as how and how much someone knows. In the mainstream view this is the entrée to, for instance, mechanism design and the theory of contracts, of separating equilibria and asymmetric information, of transaction cost and agency theory. In instruction and academic modeling, utility remains the center. It was the rise we saw earlier of the duality between Hicksian and Marshallian demand, and on the supply side between producer intentions and technology, where the symbolic, as-if character of the mainstream was indeed further asserted and from which information modeling detracted nothing, accentuating and enlivening the symbolism instead. If information brought anything to the economic table during these periods, it was a symbology inviting us to think provisionally of mind and knowledge as distinct factors, despite continuing to reject the medieval and positivist metaphysics of a mind and body as separate entities. It could be interpreted to have added another

DOI: 10.4324/9781003514602-7

and powerful set of analogies and metaphors to economics' repertoire, additional latent, nonliteral concepts serving economic intuition and judgment.

The postwar idea of information did however also quicken the empiricist and pragmatist impulse toward what had already been its interest in epistemics. Far from the mainstream metaphorical representation of knowledge, positive epistemology continued to ask 'what' a decision maker would know at a given deliberation point. It answered 'how' questions only as reduced to sequences of steps, each a 'what.' Over in this corner the philosophy of knowledge was being reduced to processions of entities, each influencing its neighbor. In the wake of David Hume's literal side, thence of Whitehead and Russell, Ayer, Schlick, and others, the 'who' – the person – was being pushed more and more out of the picture, though most economic textbooks and instruction remained as before.

Persons and Things in the Economics of Information

The positivist spirit did influence economics, and as Hunter Heyck (2012), Paul Erickson et al. (2013), and several others have said, did shift a portion of the applied modeling rhetoric from chooser to the abstract 'choice'. The notion of a choice as a thing-in-itself explains how Mirowski and Nik-Khah could say Stigler (1961) and Becker (1993) regarded information as an object, even if unmeasurable. This 'thing' phase, however, like decision trees, state spaces, and probability matrices, remained consistent with an economics of a person in the sense that in none was there any claim to be privy to an actual decision process. Markov chains remained probability estimates rather than observations, never a claim to be the true probabilities and hence the true paths to any absolutely right or wrong decision. They remained, that is, unmistakably anti-empiricist frameworks. Mirowski never gets around to distinguishing mainstream from metalogical in this manner because, like most recent writers, he doesn't address the dimension of economic understanding as such.

Organized vs Disorganized Complexity

Friedrich von Hayek (1974), whose interests spanned economics, psychology, and biology, did address the question of understanding, especially in the incommensurability he saw between scientific and other kinds of knowledge. Hayek draws on the language of the philosophy of science, the notion for example of an unorganized versus an organized complexity – but with a new twist. It is the natural world for Hayek that is unorganized, despite our casual impression that nature is the more predictable. Here he shows the influence of the Kantian epistemic critique, for it is the human interpretation of nature, Hayek says, that is organized, not nature itself. Natural objects cannot be trying to organize themselves because there are no 'themselves' there to organize, consistent with Kant's metaphysics of morality discussed back in Chapter I and below in Chapter VI.

Organized phenomena remain however the more difficult problem for Hayek because they are subject, as he puts it, to the intangible "manner in which individual elements are connected with each other" (4). This phenomenology of connection that occurs in an act of knowing is the Kantian question, and Hayek gestures here to Kant's answer: that it originates in immediate experience. In particular, he says in his Nobel Address, "in the explanation of the working of such structures we [cannot] replace information about the individual elements by statistical information." Each of us dwells in a context unmeasurably different from others,' so markets will finally resist any mechanical construct, being actuated and observed only in tomorrow's prices. "Nor can we," therefore, "statistically test our theory that it is the deviations from that 'equilibrium' system of prices and wages...." (4).

Hayek here flirts with or falls into the rationalist fallacy. For the inaccessibility of the relevant empirical data, he says, is that it is complicated: "the social sciences, like much of biology but unlike most fields of the physical sciences, have to deal with structures of *essential* complexity" (4). The Kantian critique, as we have seen, faces and solves this difficulty. For Hayek and others here are referring to the essential freedom and indeterminacy of the metaphysical dimension. This indeterminacy doesn't forestall any intelligibility in the formal, transcendental dimension, namely by way of the synthesis of one's empirical signals with one's *a priori* capacity to conceptualize and judge.

Organized Complexity in Mechanism Design

Not that the difficulty of facing complexity hasn't grown with technology, inviting a turn from the chooser to the choice. A turn toward choices is a turn toward 'knowledge' in either the rationalist or empiricist mode, in either case considered as generalizations as opposed to specific personal choices. On the other hand, an interest in knowledge does raise the question of its form or possibility, and with it the person in whom it is embedded in the act of understanding. An important example of form is Leonid Hurwicz' concept of mechanism design. Hurwicz and Stanley Reiter (2006) consider the following story, and a story it is. A certain manager's job is to coordinate the activities of certain agents – employees, customers, suppliers, creditors – toward a goal Z in which the information needed to do so is in their hands and not his. In other words, it is the usual management problem. The situations of the agents holding this information are represented by the distributions among themselves of the relevant goods, resources, technical capabilities, and preferences, which we call environment $\theta \varepsilon \Theta$. An example of $Z = F(\theta)$ is a company's stock valuation, a function F of the company agents' dispersed resources and preferences. Because they are dispersed, so must the firm's decision-making be, the combined effects of which will, through the manager-unobserved θ, determine outcome Z. The manager sets the mechanism and lets the agents make the specific decisions, conditioned by the relevant resources and preferences, of which the manager knows little and that collectively will either hit or miss the target.

The problem is to find the least-costly 'message' mechanism inducing agents to make the choices producing management goal Z^{o}. The virtue of keeping the cost low is that the cheaper the system, the more will be left for Z. A way to solve the cost-minimizing problem is to imagine agents sending information to the manager in the form of $M = \mu(\theta)$, where M is the matrix of messages sent and μ converts the individual agents' resources, preferences, and actions into message form. Or what is the same, agents respond to the manager's message setup according to their own situations. Now here is a critical point. Agents send two kinds of message: the literal ones of filling out reports and the nonliteral ones of their actions, of how well for example they improve their skills and services and that the manager only partly sees. Just how such actions constitute a message to the manager – or equivalently how, under conditions θ, actions can be interpreted as responses to the organizational setup, is what $M = \mu(\theta)$ provides. It is the decentralized agents who for the most part 'know' $\mu(\theta)$. Only M reaches the manager.

With M then, or at least its nonliteral aspects like actions, the manager faces a difficulty. M has been returned to him in code and he must interpret it. This interpretation Hurwicz-Reiter call $Z = h(M)$, where M again is the entire message set, literal and nonliteral, and Z the interpretation the manager ascribes to it, h being the interpretation process. The manager interprets the agent's 'message' as if it were a fact, though he understands it isn't one and takes this into account in his interpretation. Substituting now the agent's outgoing interpre*tive* message $M = \mu(\theta)$ into the manager's incoming interpre*ted* one $Z = h(M)$ gives net message $Z = h[\mu(\theta)]$: *the manager's interpretation of the agent's interpretation.* h maps the agent's resources and consequent actions, as well as any formal messages, into the economic outcomes Z relevant to the manager's goal Z^o. Management then is in a position to design the least costly decentralization structure for achieving Z^o.

As Hurwicz and Reiter note, preferences enter this mechanism design in two places – in management's goal function $F(\theta)$ and in each agent's message transmission function $\mu(\theta)$. If we have N agents, we have then $N + 1$ preference sets. In $F(\theta)$, utility enters as the manager's own, and in $\mu(\theta)$ as the N agents' own. In any but a formal or transcendental sense, all are generally unobserved not only to one another but – being largely implicit – to themselves. Note too that because factors $\theta \varepsilon \Theta$ enter $\mu(\theta)$ and $h(M)$ in generally nonlinear fashion, the literal and nonliteral, namely the empirical and the *a priori, affect one another* in both the N message sets M and in management goal Z. Yes, this is a Kantian model though Hurwicz and Reiter may be unaware it is. *We interpret what someone does in light of what he says and -what he says in light of what he does. Action and interpretation are joint,* as the *synthetic a priori* calls for. Gross domestic product, company earnings and public health outcomes can be read from empirical reports. But their meanings are another matter: every purchase and sale, employee sales effort, and public-health promotion is both a physical event (actuality) and a message (possibility). This I think is the point of Hurwicz-Reiter mechanism design.

$Z = h(M) = h[\mu(\theta)]$ is an information mechanism, converting – via messages – latent, purely intuited situations (what we have been calling utility) to aggregate outcomes. We can call h itself a 'thing,' and Hurwicz-Reiter insist it is by asserting it is a mechanism. If so, it is one in which persons are intimately involved, given that only persons can interpret. N personal interpretation models generate message outputs and send them to a center, there to be interpreted in yet another light, the manager's. Messages must be observed in order to be sent; so they must be mechanical as Hurwicz-Reiter insist, if only because h (M) is an estimated model *outcome*, which must be readable literally as a machine does. Yet being an *estimated* outcome, it is also an interpretation; and as we have seen in Chapter III, interpretations are expressions of utility and can never have the quality of a 'thing.' Message-reading h (M) therefore is not a thing but the Kantian bringing-together of thing and interpretation, the observed and unobserved, in what we have been calling judgment and that in the present discussion we are calling information. Information is what *in-forms*. So although it involves data, it must be of an order distinct from data. Observables are never knowable in themselves, but only in their duality with – interpretation through – preferences.

We can say still more about mechanism and market design:

(i) Although it is a model of information, it is also a model of hiddenness because the persons remain hidden even as the public is revealed.
(ii) It is an optimization and thus an equilibrium because every optimum (see Chapter IV) is equilibrial. Not that there is any actual equilibrium here but that it can be rationally and usefully *modeled* that way. And it is Walrasian in particular. As Hurwicz-Reiter note, unobservable goal function $F(\theta)$ can as a special case be modeled as $P(\theta)$, the equilibrium price vector, in which Walrasian *rarete* and the corresponding price ratio are equated to one another.
(iii) It is a minimization of the cost of information at a given output, public or private, at a given opportunity cost to the agents. Utility here is the manager's pure intuition of the situations that the agents, and thus the organization, find themselves in and to which the manager and agents can now best respond. And finally, it isn't married to any organizational or political program.

So, it is thoroughly mainstream economics.

Economics as a Critique of Knowledge

We are now ready to re-examine the mainstream/empiricist conflict – from the beginning as it were but interpreted now in knowledge and information terms. Let me consider three recent writers I take to be mainstream economists and two I take to be metalogical or empiricist: Christopher Clarke (2016) and Faruk Gul and Wolfgang Pesendorfer (2008) on the one side and Andrew Caplin (2008) and Francesco Guala (2019) on the other. You will note something important. The mainstream takes its job to be critique. The empiricist takes its to be liberation – to break free from shackles and go further into causes than economists do.

Critiquing the Dogma of Observed Choices

Clarke's critique of empiricism, unusual and effective, is to interrogate its apparently innocuous claims about the legitimacy of economic reasoning. Here is my abbreviated version of Clarke's critique, at an angle different from his but I think consistent with it. The apparently innocuous claims he considers are the following: Because (a) science's aim is to explain less-familiar empirical conditions by way of more-familiar ones, and (b) economics has this very aim when showing how observed choices are affected by prices and resources, it follows that (c) economics is a matter of observing price and resource effects on observed choices. Since furthermore (d) economics needs no help in this task from psychology or neurobiology, it is a confirmed, if penurious, science (193). Clarke notices something suspicious about (c) and (d): that they compliment the economic for being scientific despite its own denial it is. The dunce has been dressed the professor to look the fool.[1]

How had the dunce been tricked? Clarke takes for his critical model a certain Eve who chooses one evening between a restaurant item *x* and another *y*. Suppose, following the revealed preference language looked at in Chapters III and IV, she weakly prefers *x* to *y* in the sense that, in at least one instance, she was seen to choose *x* over *y* when *y* was available too. A commonsense, nonscientific way of expressing this decision is that Eve 'might possibly' prefer *x* to *y*, because she did choose it over *y* in the present circumstances. Note the advantage of this sort of diction. It is part observation and part interpretation. It leaves open the possibility that Eve might have selected *y* over *x* had her circumstances differed enough to justify *y*, the possibility that economics calls (as we've seen earlier) the counterfactual. Clarke names this counterfactual approach the "short-hand" story of Eve's choice – the economist's story, the one expressible in commonsense language. Despite its plebeian ring, common sense for Clarke requires an insight deeper than just watching Eve order dinner. It is the recognition that, despite that she ordered *x*, she would have ordered *y* had she judged the situation right for it. Her act of ordering *x stood under the possibility* she might have ordered *y*, which because she *didn't* order *y*, means *y* is potentially counterfactual, potentially a model prediction.

Now contrast this story, of which the counterfactual is the essential part, to the literal-minded one Clarke calls "face-value." A literal mind only observes. And because counterfactuals are only model-projected, not observed, it takes no account of them. They simply *aren't*. The literal mentality asserts only what it can see, and what it sees is that Eve chose *x* over *y*. It concludes therefore that she prefers *x* over *y*.

Let's now return to the language of models Clarke uses in epistemological claims (a) – (d) above and take them the following way. Both the short-hand and face-value rendition of Eve's choices can be expressed as a model construction. The empiricist way of construction is to regress Eve's choices against a group of measured factors and choose the subset with the best statistical fit. The economic way is to develop a theory of rational decision so that an interpretative model can be specified in its light. The interpretations will fall under a discipline, namely that the model counterfactuals *as well as* the actual choices must be consistent with the rational theory (in order to obtain low *p*-values). Counterfactuals, that is, are unobservable and a matter of estimation (interpretation) only. Clarke (and I with him) then have a problem with empiricist, metalogical comments (b) – (d). All three are false because all three assume economics to be a scientific effort, a matching of observables to observables rather than of counterfactuals to rationality restrictions, which can be interpretative only. The claim that economics tries to be a science but in the absurd way of ignoring scientific evidence had been an empiricist claim. *As* empiricist, it must fail to understand economics.

Clarke considers the distinction between the face-value and short-hand attitude, which he also calls the real-content attitude, *a distinction between belief and acceptance*.[2] Eve had to judge which menu item best matched her situation at the time. That involved forming her own mental model of it, the graver the situation the more careful her model. "This highlights the crucial and intuitive distinction," Clarke writes, "between belief and acceptance: to accept a model is to be willing to use it for various purposes, but it need not involve believing the model's face-value language," which for instance may misleadingly exclude any mention of Eve's uncertainties (198). I would add that acceptance – what elsewhere I have been calling openness – applies not only to the economist's model but to Eve's too, which no analyst is in a position to replicate. Neither Eve's nor the economist's model is relevant to the face-value attitude, where the goal is to know what Eve's preferences are in themselves. That goal is conveniently fail-proof because it assumes that to *see* x chosen is to *know* it is preferred. Circularly, x's preferredness to y has significance only if it is observed, since to be significant is to be known for sure, and to be known for sure is to be literally seen. In its mere estimability, economics is tautologically trumped by the measurability of the empirical.

This last inference, that any claim to know the world-in-itself is a tautology, is my own rather than Clarke's. But the economics he defends is the same that I do.[3] It would have been unlikely before mid-20th century to find the economic viewpoint elaborated in Clarke's way – over some isolated choice (see Erickson et al., 2013). We live in an information era and Eve's fixation over an isolated x and y is itself a piece of information: "According to the shorthand story," says Clarke, "the content is that there is some circumstance in which Eve would choose lobster over steak when steak is on the menu." 197 My emphasis has rather been on structure, on Eve's personhood. The failure of the face-value story, I argue, is its presumption that it takes place in the metaphysical plane, with all the 'truth' that literally intended language implies. But this, I believe, is Clarke's underlying point too. The shorthand, commonsense theory is what I and others have been calling the *as-if*, the metaphorical stand-in for and preservation of the formal, possible, latent, analogical, interpretive dimension of understanding, the inviolability and irreplaceability of the person, where angels fear to tread.

The Data Become the Axioms

In his "Economic Theory and Psychological Data" (2008, Andrew Caplin offers an instance of the virtually unbounded reason that 'beliefs' bring to the table, in his case efforts to render economics psychological. His train of thought works this way. To: (i) read Samuelson's revealed preference theory as a matter of recording what someone buys and doesn't buy; (ii) include the not-buying as well as the buying in the choice data; (iii) wonder at economics' restricting itself to the buying only, and (iv) invite in the not-buying, overthrowing utility.

Undeterred by the fact that nonpurchases aren't data, Caplin imagines a world in which they are, and at coincidences the thinker selects. Possibilities therefore are infinite.[4] "I propose … essentially limitless expansion in the psychological data that economists model." It must – here is the catch – be *data*: "Psychological and neurological constructs modeled in this manner will end up being characterized precisely in terms of observable counterparts, as has been the case [sic] for utility and choice. In this sense [Caplin's proposal] represents no more than a broadening of Samuelson's original proposal to broader settings" (337).

I leave aside for a moment that revealed preference doesn't succeed in eliminating utility and that, other than in the much earlier 'utilitarian' movement, it was never intended to be addable to someone else's revealed preference. I also leave aside my Chapter III demonstration that, in light for instance of Houtthaker's proof that reason draws us toward an equilibrium, it also doesn't reduce economics to observed choices. I want only now to emphasize the extraordinarily loose frame Caplin's specifications bring to the table, a tolerance for any measurable abstraction the thinker wishes as long as appealing to his "underlying intuitions," or as Kant would retort his *noumena*, his fancies. One almost misses, but soon recognizes, an additional assertion: that because it is the modeler's rather than the decision maker's preferences that drive everything here, it is the modeler's data that really are being axiomatized. *The data become the axioms*.

Caplin seems to recognize this. There will be, he says, a "single axiomatization of all measured data" around the modeler's data picks. As with other empiricists trying to leverage revealed preference theory, it is the modeler who dictates the model transitivities and with them reason's bounds, which because he is the one who dictates them, are generally infinite (363).[5] Consequently, there are no bounds or axioms whatever. Caplin in other words is proposing a machine. To what purpose? Likely not Eve's, who can make her decisions for herself. More likely it is *for* Eve under the assumption that she can't. Still more likely it is an even grander purpose of a device that would make humanoid decisions, that stands for – or against – a human person.

Caplin's offer of 'richer settings' to an otherwise, for him, barely tolerable mainstream economic view falls easily under Clarke's critique. Let's see how it fares. First, Caplin's reasoning steps (i) and (ii) do match Clarke's steps (a) and (b), depicting how the empiricist reads the economist. In both, economists are said to concede that everything important to choice is measurable. Caplin writes, "the goal of [economic] decision theory … is to model 'choice' itself mechanically" (360). Second, Caplin's steps (iii) and (iv) are a critique of Clarke's steps (c) and (d). Economists are wrong to reserve their attention to choices only and prices and resources only. And as, in Caplin's way of thinking, this restriction is one economics imposes on itself, there's no reason to continue imposing it. Caplin writes, "…the issue of what theory accounts for the observed realization is open" (360). Thus, Caplin belongs to Clarke's subset of positivists who tolerate economics simply because they don't understand it.

And Data Need a Brain

If, however, this subset is really non-empty, so must its mirror image be – the set of those who dismiss economics because they do understand it. Francesco Guala's "Preferences: Neither Behavioral nor Mental" (2019) is a test case of such a category. Guala says the old controversy over what preferences are, and that seemed to converge toward agreement by mid-20th century, has flared up again. The main dispute he says is whether preferences "should be given a *behavioral* or *mental* interpretation."

> Do these [preferences] refer to overt behavior, patterns of choice that are readily observable and inter-subjectively measurable? Or should we take them to describe psychological states, hidden in the minds of the decision makers? (383)

The ready observability Guala speaks of here, presumably the revealed-preference theory we've just discussed, fails to rid itself of utility – a pure (pre-empirical) intuition. Contrary to Guala then, it isn't inter-subjectively measurable at all because it ignores the uniqueness of the person and situation that utility or preference represents. Preference is unobservable not because held as a secret in someone's mind but because it is a capacity to visualize only, a pre-empirical grasp, as how otherwise might one subsequently claim to empirically observe it? A claim to empirically observe that someone else is empirically observing something is pure tautology. It is precisely on the grounds of such a critique that the mainstream economic consensus rejects the behavioral-*vs*-mental dichotomy Guala speaks of.

But this very confusion will speak to our point, and it is worth first seeing how Guala proposes to integrate the behavioral with the mental aspect of human choice. It is, following the usual metalogical categories (Chapter II), to think of an agent's dispositional states (measurable 'beliefs and desires') as generating – providing the causal mechanism for – behavior. Crucially, they are both economic and behavioral for him because in both, he thinks, preferences combine with 'beliefs' to form decisions. Economists are merely those who insist on strict rationality rules like transitivity, he says, while behaviorists allow simplified (generally intransitive) ones as well.

Now Guala stresses that these dispositional states may include more than just beliefs and preferences. They also include more robotic phenomena like habits and instincts, where computations aren't involved. Here psychology drops out of the picture because the sources of these rote functions are biological, to accommodate which Guala posits a brain factor coming prior to the dispositional. Following Okasha, Dietrich and List and others (Chapter IV), brain is acted upon by events, which as determined by circumstances induce various psychological instincts and habits. This animal-like linkage between brain and disposition is what he and others call mental. A science or mechanics of decision is conceived, and economics is an honored one of the children.

It is significant that Guala calls the mental phase of this choice process ontological (389). Given his usage of this word he evidently means it in the sense of Cartesian metaphysics, the reduction of meaning to homogenized objects differing only in level of processing, so that human reality can finally be stamped, say, in brain patterns. For Guala's purpose in locating the brain at the originating, causal side of the mental dispositions chain is to assign final reality to cellular activity, whether later determined to be specifically rational or merely habitual. As with the metalogical and empiricist generally, it is science that claims to show us what things really are. In his case, it is physical science: the brain is what choice really is, so even psychologists and economists are just mediating lab techs. Nothing rids itself of this data aspect as it moves along the knowledge assembly line. Pointedly, no formal – intuitive, transcendental, interpretive – dimension is acknowledged.

Has however, in telling this story, Guala not drawn on the formal dimension of his *own* thought? Most certainly he has. The question is only whether he has accounted for it in his system. And the answer is that far from doing so he has hardened personal decision making – except his own – into a mechanical apparatus.

At least in this respect Guala qualifies as one who welcomes economics into the fold because he doesn't understand it. But there is an additional prospect. In a meditative aside, Guala writes:

> The [economic or psychological] interpretation casts a shadow of mystery….The mystery disappears once we realize that the controversy concerns different scientific programs and explanatory frameworks within the sciences of behavior. Anti-mentalists in economics avoid the identification of choice theory with psychology in order to … make its application possible in a wider domain.
>
> (398)

Guala must tell us however what this wider scientific sphere would comprise or he can't credibly be waving economics into it. In his reticence here, the empiricist Guala may indeed be getting economics right in realizing the futility of his pigeon-holing it, though as a scientist he feels driven to. The attributes we've seen earlier of a classically Humean attitude remain: an implied preference for the general over the specific and the separable over the nonseparable, where the analyst's hand rests heavy.

Economics as a Critique of Machine Learning

From the spirit of a quasi-mechanistic economics in Andrew Caplin (a psychology), to the associational, Humean spirit of Francesco Guala (biology) comes a third spirit – of an *entire* economic mechanism that, it seems to me, sets the stage for the machine learning and artificial intelligence our society is beginning to deal with. This third way is worthy of some discussion.

Nature and Machines vs Causal Autonomy

An introduction to this new mechanistic spirit is well provided in Nancy Cartwright's clarification of the difference between the 'Humean' – strictly associational – take on science versus the earlier 'natural' take on it that has become prominent again. The natures of things, Aristotle had said, are primary and their regularities or behaviors only derivative (290). And in contrast to Hume, Aristotle had argued that objects are knowable in themselves, that the knowability of something is inside it rather than outside it, so that, one way or another, we are able to grasp this thing directly. And a direct grasp of something is in turn, she says, to know its capacities. She writes, "all that is law-like on the Humean picture are associations between measurable quantities – and that's it," whereas "we aim in science, I urge, to discover the natures of things … what powers or capacities they have…." In particular, "I want to recall the Aristotelian idea that science wants to understand what things are, … a large part [of which] is to understand what they *can do*" (276–277).

Cartwright raises the question, as we did earlier, whether economics' evident differences from science in this regard are metaphysical – implied by the structure of reality itself – or only economics' asserted weak performance in understanding the world. The latter seems to be the position of Daniel Hausman (2009, 2023) for instance and the majority of analyticist philosophers. But Cartwright argues for the former: that science and economics differ metaphysically, that the capacities of physical objects may be easier to understand than the capacities of economic objects are. A possible holism in economic entities, that is, may be standing in the way of perceiving their capacities, and she notes that even Aristotle would often take account of such 'organics' in his explanations (290). Their holism could explain why the natures of economic entities don't stay "fixed long enough to manifest themselves in the [required] regularity" they do in science.

Yet for Cartwright they do remain directly understandable, if only with effort. Economics thus is, like science though less successfully, a systems view – of a great mechanism with mechanical subparts. "Where we say 'mechanisms,'" she writes, "I think we mean 'mechanism in this literal sense – the structure or adaptation of parts of a machine'" (282). "Models in economics…are more appropriately represented as a design for a socio-economic machine which, if implemented, should give rise to the behavior to be explained" (278). Now here is something crucial in Cartwright's account: this economic machine is not to be taken as running on its own. It is to be operated by a singular analyst. "No behavior results from either the supply or the demand mechanism operating on its own…" (280).

Would it not seem here that Cartwright is an economic rationalist in the sense we've used: a follower of Descartes and Leibniz? Consistent with this, she's chosen for her example of an economic machine the U.S. Federal Reserve, a monopolist supplier of a nation's currency in which the Board chair, the Leibnizian seer, initiates and everyone else reacts. But this example too falls quickly apart, for the contents of physics, being particles, are far easier to compare and generalize in covering laws than those in economics are. So, Cartwright says, the reliance of economics on individual models becomes especially important, a scientific setback indeed because to be noncomparable or generalizable, thus nonpredictable, is precisely to be nonscientific. The solution too of ranking models according to their statistical fit is invalid because in relying on regularities it denies, in its Humean anti-Aristotelian denial of nature, true causality. Economics then in Cartwright's framework must collapse entirely, something she does little to deny in reducing it to "a repeated triggering of determinate systems."

It is a useful exercise then to compare Cartwright's critique of economics with John Dupre's, which as we shall see are on a paradoxical collision course. Economics, Dupre says, "has developed in the context of a broad set of metaphysical assumptions that have existed in parallel with the last four hundred years of science" (308). And with it, he says, is a determinism, reductionism, and essentialism – respectively a claim that human action is entirely predictable, reducible into parts, and reassembled in some new and better way. Econ in other words is a claim to know what human behavior is in itself, what it 'really' is as Aristotle would say (309). And how do we know it is so, that reducing-into-parts is fundamentally how economists think? Because, he says, they build it literally into their theory.

That for Dupre such economic rationalism is a classical metaphysics fits with what we have argued throughout, that classical *economics* originates, like Cartwright's, in Aristotle and then Descartes, Leibniz, and Ricardo. And Dupre rejects this classical approach, arguing that causality and thought are of an order different in science than they are in economics. For in the latter, goods and services fall into particular types, any subdivision inviting further division and so inevitably arriving at some particular situation. Here at least then, fact and value would merge, and "it is impossible to escape the conclusion that value judgments are increasingly embedded in that constructive [subdivisional] process" he claims modern economics to be (321). Consequently, "there is no sensible prospect of a value-free economics. The fact/value distinction, in short, should go the way of the Berlin wall" (324).[6]

All this argues, Dupre says, "for the causal autonomy of economic agents" – by which, as taken from Kant's *Metaphysics of Morals*, he means the absolute moral freedom of every economic decision maker. Put differently, Dupre writes, "reality does not determine a uniquely correct set of economic concepts" (324). Indeed if the economic world can be modeled as a set of machines, then "my world…has room for all kinds of machines" (326). "There is no reason to expect any causal completeness at the economic level" (329).

Now here is the crux of the issue. Dupre says, as if in an allusion to something backstage, that his own frequent reference to economic machines "doesn't mean they are really there" (326). They wouldn't, in the mainstream economist's thinking, be actual entities. Dupre would be marking it perfectly here, seeing through the klieg lights below the stage to what lies above. Those constructions were fully analogy. They aren't 'real.' There is no machine there whatsoever unless an administrative or political one. Dupre regards human and economic reality to be deep-set, so deep they cannot be directly expressed. If so, they can only be *in*directly expressed, and indirect expression is analogy, symbol, metaphor. Dupre may not see that economics sees this as well and thus is in full agreement with him. Certainly Hurwicz' mechanism design is of this analogical character, as in no other way could it represent persons' preferences without implying they are in a literal machine shop. Even for Cartwright to speak of a 'machine' that an economist operates is to use metaphor, as certainly no one can literally be tapping it with his hands.

Ergo, the Struggle for Machine Learning

Francesco Guala's knowledge system is unquestionably a mechanism as well, though not at all in the sense of Hurwicz. In Guala's – in line with Leibniz rather than Kant – incoming event-signals trip nerve impulses to subsidiary economic and psychological stimuli, translating them into behavior. Brain conditioning ensues, generating the choice regularities that explain statistical significance. Signal novelties interrupt earlier ones, restarting the process in new directions. This machine 'does' learn.

Economics will soon have its own interpretation of such a machine. Suppose for starters that inputs are divisible between capital and labor and a machine is set the task of learning something. Then labor must, because machine learning is a substitution of capital for labor, begin planning for retirement. Let's think this through. A bureau or firm, say, wishes to hire a study of an economic snafu in some sort of retailing operation. Let x_a be the quantity of analysis it contracts-in. Equivalently it hires a combination of analytical capital K_a and analytical labor L_a to produce analysis quantity x_a. That is, $x_a = x_a\,(K_a, L_a)$. x_a can be either observed (written down and transcribable into action) or unobserved (tacit in an employee).

Now suppose the firm shifts away from human, interpretative learning and toward machines. This can be visualized in the form of a learning isoquant by holding analysis quantity x_a constant at x_a^{o} and solving $x_a^{o} = x_a\,(K_a, L_a)$ for K_a to obtain $K_a = K_a\,(L_a, x_a^{o})$, the rate at which capital skills trade off with labor skills. As machine learning intensifies, knowledge-capital is substituted for knowledge-labor along the $K_a = K_a\,(L_a, x_a^{o})$ frontier. In the limit where machine learning is entirely untended, $K_a = K_a\,(L_a = 0, x_a^{o})$ and the analysis isoquant touches the K-axis, where labor's interpretation services are entirely dismissed at $L_a = 0$. I ask two questions. First, is it possible to operate at a corner of the isoquant like this? Second, if it is possible, what does it mean to be operating there?

It might help in answering these questions to first spell out how a machine might learn. Your bureau wants to know what it takes to hold onto a customer for at least a month. You organize customers into two categories or labels – those who continue coming back for a month or more, and those who don't. You propose N categories of service features (product characteristics, service speed, package design, and so on) that may have influenced customer retention. For each customer contact, you list the N x 1 vector of service features (the feature vector) present at time of contact. If machine learning is, as they call it, supervised, the supervisor will know during the machine training session whether or not the customer was retained for at least the desired month, so can associate the current feature vector with that customer retention success. In doing so for the success or failure of each customer contact, you now compute the N-dimensioned vector of parameters, and with it the product and marketing characteristics, providing the clearest demarcation between retention successes and failures. As everything in this model is measurable, a prediction mean square error can then be computed showing a given service strategy's retention performance.

Given it is future rather than past customers you care about, you now deploy these estimates to forecast the following month's customer retentions, the out-of-sample (future) prediction errors which you won't know until the month passes. Thereafter nothing in theory prevents the process from continuing on its own: waiting for retention results, computing the prediction errors, generating – in the direction of the greatest retention rate – a new customer service ('feature') vector and its correspondingly revised parameter estimates and forecasts, and with them a new customer contact policy. We now have capital alone.

An Economic Interpretation of Machine Learning

At risk of the objection that no machine is ever left completely untended, let's think along the path that could lead us there. Most obvious is that the machine itself, both what we literally see as well as, say, Francesco Guala's synaptic reproduction of one, is something quintessentially empirical. Lacking a formal, transcendental (judgeable, discursive, interpretive) dimension, which could subsist only in the designer of the circuits and the reader of the predictions, *the machine* cannot interpret. Rather it is what will *be* interpreted, and for this a supervisor is needed. In the context of our Chapter III discussion, the machine itself is the empirical demand phenomenon $x(p, m)$ which, in offering us by way of duality $m = e(p, u)$ a measure of the customer's empirical demand $x(p, e)$, looks to the corresponding Hicksian $h(p, u)$ for the intuition providing the insight for the impending policy decision. Hicksian demand then would be the supervisor if there were to be one.

If there weren't, what will be left for us in machine learning? I will argue: metalogical, empiricist economics, the Marshallian demand left alone and isolated. Its theme will be that it grasps, or will eventually grasp, the customer retention factors *in themselves*, to be provided by observation and correlation alone. Machine and AI enthusiasts are anything but shy about this. The quick search routines of the future, the promise of their advance to sharper, more self-confirming correlations and thus certitudes, are a source of excitement. The excitement is precisely the prospect of freeing ourselves from the incertitude of new, unexpected situations and to which only intuition can be privy. What the prospective machine or AI proudly *lack,* indeed *stand against*, is intuition, an openness and receptivity of what is to come, as it itself would *be* what is to come.

Prospects for decision centralization presumably would grow as the population of individuals with access to the relevant decision context shrinks, reducing and sterilizing the sense necessary to comprehend them. Modelers would increasingly rely on outcomes of other models, copycatting and conforming themselves accordingly. Sense and context would decline even further.

Labor versus Capital: Which One Will Survive Artificial Intelligence?

On the other hand, can there ever finally be an unsupervised machine learning or artificial intelligence? Could, that is, learning ever avoid being some*one's,* who then would be the supervisor? This would be the person, the seat and symbol of the heterogeneity between – yet radical mutual need of – intuition and category. For the machine alone is just conceptualization. Only the supervisor needs intuition. And intuition, a sense of a matter, is useless unless matched, in the *synthetic a priori* act of judgment, with the appropriate categories.

Let's look first at labor, then, because it allows starting with Karl Marx (1849, 1867), whose concept of labor is especially well-defined and indeed rules over capital. This will in turn raise the question of capital in the form of its integrality with labor.

Labor in the Shadow

Hannah Arendt brings context to the subject of Marx and labor in her account of the gulf separating the life of the household from the life of the artisan in ancient Greece. The household (*homo laborans*) was the locus of privacy, the means of sustaining life alone, of little interest to anyone else. It was the endless round of the life-giving functions of eating, sleeping, cleaning, and procreating, of a certain futility because the moment a task was finished, it had to be repeated. The work of the artisan (*homo faber*) in contrast was productive of what could endure – buildings, laws, art – that everyone could know and value in common. As a shaper of materials, *homo faber* became "lord and master of the whole earth" (139). Objectivity came into being because lasting works are public reference points, so that people "can retrieve … their identity by being related to the same chair and the same table" (137).

This distinction between private and public didn't however survive modernity and its notion of society, which Arendt describes as "…the collective of families economically organized into one super-human family" (28–29). "In our [current] understanding, the dividing line is entirely blurred, because we see the body of peoples and political communities in the image of a family whose everyday affairs have to be taken care of by a gigantic, nation-wide administration of housekeeping" (28). The public has conquered the private space but only to be absorbed by it.

By the mid-19th century writers like Marx were drawing the implications of this convolution for the making of a livelihood. The laborer labors, writes Marx, because he must, expending energy as he does and requiring additional work to provide that additional energy. Following Ricardo, productive activity "is the expenditure of simple labor power, that is of the labor power which, on average … exists in the organism of every ordinary individual." Crucially, Marx understands this conjunction of public life with survival, and of survival with energy, to be a *universalization* of labor: "All labor … in its character of identical abstract human labor," he writes, constitutes the value of commodities.

If labor is homogeneous, it is also pure quantity. Marx reminds us of this repeatedly: "Skilled labor counts only as simple labor intensified … a given quantity of skilled being considered equal to a greater quantity of simple labor." The redaction of labor to an energy that moves in synchrony with a machine, in the coordinated motion Marx stresses, is the redaction of capital to machinery too. The capitalist employing labor, and the laborer whose energy is diverted to the capitalist's uses, are equally a matter of quantity. But note then there finally can be only one input besides the capitalist, and it is capital itself. The Chief Interpreter (to draw on our above figure of machine learning or artificial intelligence) will be the only labor. Just as untended machine learning must ultimately be tended – by the person who finally must interpret it – so must the Chief Interpreter be the one to give final meaning to the output. Economics is now, absent the interpreter, fully scientized because if the input must be abstract so must the output be.

Arendt describes Marx's depiction of a worker then as virtually a machine, bound up in the rhythms and synchronies of the tools he labors with and the consumption it affords. The laborer is reduced *to* the machinery. Arguments are often heard that something like this is going on in the economics discipline. For utility's quasi-concave tradeoff between labor and leisure implies that as wage rates fall, work is sacrificed to leisure. And leisure is a form of capital, since it is the spare time and energy to think and create that capital development requires. Leisure in current thought then is the freedom to form capital, and in that way is one with it. In Marx on the contrary, labor and capital compete with each other for dominance. Compete they must because, while in mainstream theory labor and capital are at least partly complements, for Marx they are always perfect substitutes – identical to each other. It is true as we saw in Chapter I that in an economic model there can be no final distinction between labor and capital. This isn't however because of any homogeneity or perfect substitutability between them but because in modern economic thought the worker *chooses* to be at leisure – and so to form capital – and thus not to work. The freedom to choose, to say no rather than yes, is what resists reduction to capital, as Sartre no doubt would agree.

Human Capital in the Sunlight

The economic theory of human capital it seems to me is founded on this heterogeneity, this complementarity, of labor with capital, indeed is what 'tacit knowledge' is. It nevertheless, as the distinction between tradable and untradable human capital shows, has a substitutive aspect also. Usage forms such as patents and copyrights separate oneself from the capital one has produced, liquidating the capital and in that sense substituting it out of oneself. Human capital as commonly understood then is what hasn't yet been fully liquidated so retains aspects of complementarity with oneself. In a useful collection of papers on economic human capital edited by Alan Burton-Jones and J-C Spender (2011), the types of tacit knowledge satisfying this requirement include abilities, skills, traits, knowledge, health, energy, capabilities, multicultural insight, education, communication tools, cultural intelligence, rent-generating assets, competitive advantage, experience, and interpersonal competency.

Are these empirical concepts or formal only? It is their contexts that will give the clues. In the Burton-Jones and Spender volume, Margaret Blair argues that statistical estimates of education, training, and experience capital are valid for aggregates but not for individuals (54–57). And because only individuals have contexts, she says, an epistemological problem arises for we scholars who are far from the scene. Brian Loasby reflects on the heterogeneity and indefinite variety of human capital and our efforts to restrict its bounds (244, 258). Russell Coff emphasizes the unobservability of competition in particular: "Competitive advantages are like icebergs. The bulk of the rent lies below the water line" (374). Robert Grant and James Hayton are suspicious of catch-all notions of social capital, generalized only for rhetorical effect. They draw their own notions from interconnected stories, suited more to developing a manager's judgment than to any synthesized definition (424). I wonder then, following their lead, whether novelists and poets shouldn't be included in the next book on human capital.

Spender's (2011) own sense of human capital might, in its way of walking us through every kind of human knowing, come closest to the poetic:

> It expands from 'know what' to cover 'know how' and 'know why' – for how we know something depends on our intentions and utilities. We admit 'risk propensity' as a dimension of 'know how'. The embeddedness of social and network capital indicates 'know who', [and] something of 'know when' – awareness of … the moment of appropriate action – and 'know where' – a spatial appreciation of the situation.
>
> (186)

It is integrated in the agent:

> It points to the agent's…ability to note, negotiate, and manipulate a specific situation. …[It] presupposes social, organizational, or structural capital, that it is simply one of several 'capitals' that are mutually constituting and defining.

And it is bounded there: "Under Knightian uncertainty we discover our identity and bounded rationality….This is incommensurability."

Much of the present book is on that same theme. Incommensurability is another word for the unique, integer (thus discursive) character of the link between an expressible concept on the one hand and an intuition on the other – an opening to a *given*, to a *this*, where science is ultimately excluded. Science too then has its bounds. In a borrow from Heidegger, Spender says (209), correctly I think, that the kind of capital which grasps and uses particular situations isn't anything "ready to hand" like a chisel, but "the appearance in the world of our agentic capability to make something happen as we respond to the possibilities of our uncertain space-time situation" (209). In this originary, creative, entrepreneurial act, causality has no place. Entrepreneurs bring "their own human capital to bear in a particular situation that is neither fully known nor," again following Heidegger, "fully determined by 'causes'" (186). Surprisingly, Brian Loasby seems not to recognize that an agentic capability to make something happen in our space-time situation is what – though usually only in an implied way – mainstream economics is. He unaccountably says economics' "rational choice theory … would have no place for entrepreneurship or firms" (258). Granted, I answer, it needed a century to begin saying so and isn't very articulate in saying it. But neither, in the entrepreneurial act, is the entrepreneur.

We need therefore ask more directly: if there is a human capital, where is the capital part? And what has happened to labor? What is the relation of labor to capital – and so of the human to the capital – in human capital? If it is the same as that between a person and a thing, and it must be, it is a figure for the stability and identifiability of the relations between the two of them. Hannah Arendt had, as we noted earlier, written: "The reality and reliability of the human world rests primarily on the fact that we are surrounded by things more permanent than the activity by which they were produced….Human life, in so far as it is world-building, is engaged in a constant process of reification, and the degree of worldliness of produced things, which altogether form the human artifice, depends upon their greater or lesser permanence in the world itself" (95–96). The modern economic rendering of the supply of capital as the decision to delay consumption serves this reifying role because as a rate-of-return it constitutes a 'making,' which in contrast to an understanding, is what Heidegger and Arendt call thinghood – ontic or measurable reality. Krogh and Wallin in the Burton-Jones and Spender volume also point to a making in their notion of creating knowledge. Capital assumes the role of a 'thing,' a technology, though integrated with us through intentions.[7]

Where capital is a thing, then labor, the burden of a laborer, can't be one. The laborer as no-thing therefore would be a person, never to be used like an object despite herself using objects. Labor, as the person side of this person-thing relation, needs capital; and capital, on the thing side, needs labor in order to remain the thing that it is. *Consequently, neither can absorb the other*. Nor can they be distinguished from the other by observation. Both have their source in utility, our pure intuition or anticipation of, our free openness to, the future.

Beware then taking too seriously the syllogistic linkages among various human capital theories. Syllogism carries us only so far because it devolves quickly into objectification, upending the unity (in economics, 'duality') between sense and data and distorting the writer's intentions, which are always partly inarticulate. Human capital, skilled labor, are merely useful narrative devices. We have capital when the emphasis is on capacity or capability, labor when on sacrifice, risk-taking, and meaning – the crystallization of personhood. The multitudes of qualities imputed to human capital are useful starting points but have no final status. Distinctions between capital and labor, for this reason, have no final status either. They are matters of context and interpretation, never dogmatic in the sense of derived from something more general. They are phenomenological rather than empirical, which is why we estimate them, never observe them.

Sparked by the Bayesian probability debate but germane to where we've come here is Mark Kaplan's (2002) critique of the idea of a categorical belief – that statement *x* can be flatly true and *y* flatly false. In invoking categorical beliefs says Kaplan, "some have sought reflections on the metaphysical structure of the world... scientific study...analysis of the way actual human inquirers behave, the findings of cognitive psychology, the application of evolutionary biology to human cognition." But they are misguided. "I will not call the thing I am defining 'belief,' he writes, "I will use a much more flexible term of art, 'acceptance'" (13). Acceptance will be an attitude, an "assertion in the context of [an] inquiry"(14). Can acceptance too be dissolved into 'beliefs'? Only at the price of ignoring contexts: "Distinct though they are, acceptance and confidence do not occupy entirely disjoint spheres" (15). They are different but nonseparable, a clarity of thought balanced by an acceptance of uncertainty.

Summary Points of Chapter V

1. The idea of information and the mind that uses it is a mark of postwar economics. The metalogical drive to codify learning, taken as mechanical object, has intensified. So too has the economist's interest in knowledge, incentive, and strategy, but as sense or anticipation, only *as if* mathematical.
2. A signal feature of information is its complexity. In the economic view, complexity is resolved into unity in an act of choice. In the metalogical, empiricist view, it remains just complexity.
3. Mechanism design exemplifies the mainstream economist's stance toward understanding. Information is dispersed but serves centered goals. Agents express preferences in actions (messages), which as interpreted by a coordinator determine joint outcomes. Economic coordination is, following Kant, an interpretation of an interpretation, a representation of a representation.
4. Opposed to the interpretative is the empiricist concept of messaging, which as restricted to measures, assumes agent and coordinator are too. What was chosen (a factual) is admitted to reason while what was not chosen (a counterfactual) is not. Empiricist economics thus excludes itself from persons, where interpretation – judgment – is always a counterfactual.
5. The presumption of an infinite view – an objective cognition of data – is deaf to the limitation of a decision maker's sense. It thus: (i) cannot distinguish irrationality from error; and (ii) is urged to suppress both by accumulating data. As a finite modeler, only economics can empathize with a decision maker, who is a finite modeler.
6. The empiricist drive to observe and measure terminates at the brain. Psychological phenomena assume biological, synaptic import. Neural patterns induce habitual as well as psychological and economic response. Brain becomes the underlying reality, economics a handmaid.
7. In this machine theory of reality, economic behavior becomes ever more difficult to control, requiring an ever-firmer central coordination. The Leibnizian

seer, rationalism at its peak, takes charge of this literally minded economic machine.

8. Enter then artificial intelligence, the reduction of human understanding to measured capital. As a search for regularities, machine theory and AI are claims to a direct knowledge of reality – the computer's knowledge as read by a final reader
9. Capital now the center, an obverse view interposes: human capital. Here the discursive, contextual character of the labor-capital relation is emphasized, a duality of person (subject) and thing (object), a tension of opposites. Human capital is form rather than matter: an unmeasurable 'getting' of a situation.
10. The positivist view of the capital-labor relation allows the two to be substitutes (separables) only. Economics allows them to be complements as well. Complementarity – nonseparability – is the locus of the fallible, uncertain (Kantian) character of human capital: measurable no, interpretable and estimable yes.

Notes

1 The sense of Clarke's version is that empiricism compliments economics because it misunderstands it. My version here is that empiricism compliments economics facetiously because it does understand it. Both versions I think are logically consistent with Clarke's intention. Mine is a rhetorical as-if device only, as is Clarke's, and I'm not implying either of us is really being facetious. Separately, following usage in some of the philosophy literature, Clarke calls behavioral economics what I've been calling the mainstream, and mentalist what I'm calling the behavioral or psychological. I am staying consistent here with mainstream usage.

2 See also Mark Kaplan (2002) and Keith Frankish (2004) on the attitude of acceptance. Kaplan is discussed further below. In his concept of a supermind, Frankish accords acceptance a central place, which he describes, following Cohen (1989), as "having a policy of premising…committing oneself to doing this, on appropriate occasions, in appropriate contexts." (91) This acceptance, like Clarke's, sounds identical to Kant's and Heidegger's phenomenological dimension of understanding, which as founded on intuition is a receptivity of some kind – and in that way an acceptance – of what is around us. The questionable element of Frankish's term 'acceptance' and Nicholas Georgalis' (2006) similar notion of 'subjectivity' is that they're presented as aspects of a mind and its beliefs and desires, namely as objects, undermining an intuition of a *this* and so of any personhood. They begin on the wrong (namely objective) foot and so, I think, end up there, with the positivist standpoint even when called acceptance or subjectivity.

3 At the same time and as shown in our earlier treatment of revealed preference, I think Clarke is incorrect in saying that the commonsense view avoids appealing to preferences or utility. I am arguing the commonsense view is constantly in touch with utility.

4 One could say that every time someone doesn't do something we can count it as a zero. But then we have an infinite number of zeroes and so an infinite amount of data, so Samuelson's revealed-preference theory (Chapter III) again collapses on its own terms: its claim to empirical reality. A 'not-buying' something is a matter of free imagination (Kant's *noumena*) and nothing more.

5 The modeler decides for example whether to enforce the Weak Axiom of Revealed Preference or not. One can't help seeing the similarities with sociology's C.W. Mills (1959), who pled with great eloquence for sociologists to invent their own axioms, an influential message in academic circles today.

6 With this distinction also goes – as we've argued in this book (e.g. Chapter I) – any univocal economic *definitions*, as the correct ones will depend on the person and setting involved, and with each, any determination of an isolable empirical value. (322)

7 See for instance our discussion earlier in this chapter and in Chapter III of the integrality of technology with producer intentions.

References

Arendt, Hannah. *The Human Condition*. Chicago: University of Chicago Press, 1958, 1998.

Ayer, Alfred J. *Language, Truth, and Logic*. London: Victor Gollancz, 1936. Esp. in "The Function of Philosophy." 2nd ed, NY: Dover, 1952.

Becker, Gary. "The Economic Way of Looking at Behavior." Nobel Lecture, *Journal of Political Economy* 101, No. 31, 1993.

Blair, Margaret. "An Economic Perspective on the Notion of 'Human Capital." In: Alan Burton-Jones and J.-C. Spender (eds.), *The Oxford Handbook of Human Capital*. Oxford: Oxford University Press, 2011.

Burton-Jones, Alan and J.-C. Spender. *The Oxford Handbook of Human Capital*. Oxford: Oxford University Press, 2011.

Caplin, Andrew. "Economic Theory and Psychological Data: Bridging the Divide." In: A. Caplin and S. Schotter (eds.), *The Foundations of Positive and Normative Economics*. New York: Oxford University Press, pp. 336–371, 2008.

Cartwright, Nancy. "Ceteris Paribus Laws and Socio-Economic Machines." In: Uskali Maki (ed.), *The Economic World View*. Cambridge: Cambridge University Press, 2001.

Clarke, Christopher. "Preferences and Positivist Methodology in Economics." *Philosophy of Science* 83 (April 2016), 192–212.

Clarke, Christopher. "Functionalism and the Role of Psychology in Economics." *Journal of Economic Methodology* 27, No. 4, 2020, 292–310.

Coff, Russell. "Maximizing Value from Human Capital." In: Alan Burton-Jones and J.-C. Spender (eds.), *The Oxford Handbook of Human Capital*. Oxford: Oxford University Press, 2011.

Cohen, L.J. "Belief and Acceptance." *Mind* 98 (1989), 367–389.

Descartes, Rene. "Discourse on Method." In: Norman Kemp Smith (Trans.), *Descartes Philosophical Writings*. New York: Random House, 1958. First published in 1637.

Dietrich, Franz and Christian List. "Mentalism vs Behaviorism in Economics: A Philosophy of Science Perspective." *Economics and Philosophy* 32, 249–281, 2016.

Dupre, John. "Economics Without Mechanism." In: Uskali Maki (ed.), *The Economic World View: Studies in the Ontology of Economics*. Cambridge: Cambridge University Press, 2001.

Erickson, Paul, Judy Klein, Lorraine Daston, Rebecca Lemov, Thomas Sturn, and Michael Gordon. *How Reason Almost Lost its Mind*. Chicago: University of Chicago Press, 2013.

Frankish, Keith. *Mind and Supermind*. Cambridge: Cambridge University Press, 2004.

Friedman, Milton. "The Methodology of Positive Economics." *Essays in Positive Economics*. Chicago: University of Chicago Press, 1953. II, IV, V.

Georgalis, Nicholas. *The Primacy of the Subjective*. Cambridge, MA: MIT Press, 2006.

Grant, Robert M. and James C. Hayton. "Interdependencies between People and Organizations." In: Alan Burton-Jones and J.-C. Spender (eds.), *The Oxford Handbook of Human Capital*. Oxford: Oxford University Press, 2011.
Guala, Francesco. "Preferences: Neither Behavioral nor Mental." *Economics and Philosophy* 35: 383–401, 2019.
Gul, Faruk and Wolfgang Pesendorfer. "The Case for Mindless Economics." In: A. Caplin and S. Schotter (eds.), *The Foundations of Positive and Normative Economics*. NY: Oxford University Press, pp. 336–371, 2008.
Hausman, Daniel M. "Laws, Causation, and Economic Methodology." In: Harold Kincaid and Don Ross (eds.), *The Oxford Handbook of Philosophy of Economics*. Oxford: Oxford University Press, 2009, 2023.
Hayek, Friedrich A. von. "The Pretence of Knowledge." Nobel Memorial Lecture, December 11, 1974. Reprinted in *American Economic Review* 79, No. 6, December 1989.
Heidegger, Martin. *Being and Time*. John Macquarrie and Edward Robinson (Trans.). New York: Harper-Collins, 1962. First published in 1927.
Heyck, Hunter. "Producing Reason." In: Mark Solovey (ed.), *Cold War Social Science*. New York: Palgrave Macmillan, pp. 99–116, 2012.
Hicks, J.R. *Value and Capital*. Oxford: Clarendon Press, 1946.
Houtthaker, Hendrik. "Revealed Preference and the Utility Function." *Economica* 17, 159–174, 1950.
Hume, David. *A Treatise of Human Nature. Book I, Of the Understanding*. L.A. Selby-Bigge (ed.). Oxford: Clarendon Press, 1893. First published in 1739.
Hurwicz, Leonid and Stanley Reiter. *Designing Economic Mechanisms*. Cambridge: Cambridge University Press, 2006.
Kant, Immanuel. *Fundamental Principles of the Metaphysic of Morals*. T.K. Abbott (Trans.). New York: Bobbs-Merrill, 1949. First published in 1785.
Kant, Immanuel. *Critique of Practical Reason*. Lewis White Beck (Trans.). Chicago: University of Chicago Press, 1949. First published in 1788.
Kant, Immanuel. *Critique of Pure Reason, 1st and 2nd eds*. New York: Random House (Modern Library), 1958. Norman Kemp Smith (Trans.). First published 1781; revised 1787.
Kaplan, Mark. "Decision Theory and Epistemology." In: Paul K. Moser (ed.), *Oxford Handbook of Epistemology*. Oxford: Oxford University Press, 434–462, 2002.
Koopmans, Tjalling. *Three Essays on the State of Economic Science*. New York: McGraw-Hill, 1957, 2013.
Krogh, Georg von and Martin W. Wallin. "The Firm, Human Capital, and Knowledge Creation." In: Alan Burton-Jones and J.-C. Spender (eds.), *The Oxford Handbook of Human Capital*. Oxford: Oxford University Press, 2011.
Leibniz, Gottfried von. "Theory of Knowledge and Metaphysics." In: Philip Wiener (ed.), *Selection*s. New York: Scribner & Sons, 1951. First published in 1676.
Loasby, Brian. "Human Capital, Entrepreneurship, and the Theory of the Firm." In: Alan Burton-Jones and J.-C. Spender (eds.), *The Oxford Handbook of Human Capital*. Oxford: Oxford University Press, 2011.
Marshall, Alfred. *Principles of Economics*. New York: Macmillan and Co., 1890, 1920.
Marx, Karl. "Wage Labor and Capital." In: Robert C. Tucker (ed.), *The Marx-Engels Reader*, 2nd ed. London: WW. Norton & Co., 1978. First published in 1867.
Mills, C. Wright. *The Sociological Imagination*. Oxford: Oxford University Press, 1959, 2000.

Mirowski, Philip. "Why There is (As Yet) No Such Thing as an Economics of Knowledge." In: H. Kincaid and D. Ross (eds.), Oxford Handbook of Philosophy of Economics. Oxford: Oxford University Press, 2009.

Mirowski, Philip and Edward Nik-Khah. *The Knowledge We Have Lost in Information.* New York: Oxford University Press, 2017.

Okasha, Samir. "On the Interpretation of Decision Theory." *Economics and Philosophy* 32 (2016): 409–433.

Schlick, Moritz. "Meaning and Verification." *The Philosophical Review* 45, 1936. Reprinted in W.P. Alston and G. Nakhnikian, *Readings in Twentieth Century Philosophy*. London: Collier-Macmillan, 1964.

Spender, J.-C. "Human Capital and Agency Theory." In: Alan Burton-Jones and J.-C. Spender (eds.), *The Oxford Handbook of Human Capital.* Oxford: Oxford University Press, 2011.

Stigler, George. "The Economics of Information." *Journal of Political Economy* 69 (3), 1961.

Stiglitz, Joseph. *Selected Works.* Oxford: Oxford University Press, 2009.

Whitehead, Alfred N. and Bertrand Russell. *Principia Mathematica.* Cambridge: Cambridge University Press, 1920.

VI Will the Philosophies of Economics Converge?

In asking this question about a 'belief' versus a tentative assertion, I will emphasize again the phenomenon of counterfactuality we have discussed above. That is, counterfactuality will be the focus of a mutual critique between a would-be metalogical, empiricist economics and the current practicing mainstream. An important source of the empiricist is, as we saw in Chapter II, David Lewis, who, though never much involved with economics himself, I will show to have implied one. Lewis is broadly representative of a reductive modern philosophy, a term he proposes himself. My source for the mainstream economic side will, as above, be the economics of the textbooks, teaching, and most research.

Counterfactuality, and with it causal reason, differs fundamentally between these two opponents, so much that they can hardly be said to speak to one another. How could this be otherwise, as metascience is an economics only at its proposal stage while its mainstream competitor is one developed by economists – though implicitly and sub-professionally – from a philosophy. It is a matter of, from the mid-20th century at least, a philosophy proposing or dreaming of an economics versus an incumbent economics expressing, mostly in an implicit way, a philosophy. Between the philosophical and the economic profession there is a prevailing epistemological asynchrony. I summarize this asynchrony in Table 1, general though it be.

We will first here take up the empiricist side. I will argue, consistent with the above chapters, it is the one with a metaphysics focusing on occurrences or events. Reality for it is reducible to these events. In that case, its epistemics would be a matter of cause and effect, or in the language of phenomenology (e.g. Heidegger, Merleau-Ponty), the ontic. As Lewis emphasizes, it is a matter of actualities. In fact, possibility for Lewis is a reduction to a set of specific possibilities in the sense of having value or interest only if or when they merge into an actuality. As this depends on the presence or absence of the necessary and sufficient conditions for becoming actual, Lewis's principal interest is in such a process or mechanics. I will note that this will imply a language that is mechanistic in the sense of being entirely literal, in fact is what defines literality. Its corresponding economics then will be an entirely literal expression, of mechanical causes and effects as determined by one's observations and measures of them (Caplin, Guala, Okasha).

DOI: 10.4324/9781003514602-8

Table 1 **Reductionist *vs* Mainstream Economics**

School	*Sense*	*Structure*	*Status*	*Epistemics*	*Metaphysics*
Reductionist, Analytic	Literal, Mechanical	Separable, Facing	Measures, Observations	Cause, Actuality	Thing, Necessity
Mainstream, Contemporary	Symbolic, Metaphorical	Nonseparable, Uniting	Estimates, Judgments	Model, Possibility	Persons, Choice

As we have seen, the contemporary discipline operates on the opposite side of this metaphysical divide. Reality here is a matter of a person making a decision, a free choice. Because personhood, and expressly so in decision making, can never be reduced to an event or object (although it will have an objective dimension), it also can't be reduced to causes and their conditions. Cause and actuality instead are replaced by models and their possibilities, causality being identified or referred to only symbolically. Literal meaning falls largely away, so that observations and their measures are replaced, with some exceptions, by model estimates and their associated judgments, although with a causal ring to them. One can easily see then, that though counterfactuality remains essential to reason in economics, it will have a nearly entirely different meaning than it has in a reductively empirical discipline.

An Actuality Theory of Counterfactuals

Is a 'counterfact' not an arresting word, effacing itself in this very way? Wouldn't to counter a fact be, in this very countering, an undoing of itself? Little wonder that what we call commonsense language usually avoids the word. For how else than by being avoided might a concept that says No to itself continue to survive? A counterfact would seem then to be a concept with no underlying status of its own. On the other hand, a refusal of any independent status may be its very purpose. The history of the word has in any event differed greatly in empiricist philosophy from the mainstream, formal economic.

In his *Counterfactuals*, Lewis's first thought is to ask into 'truth values' or what a 'truth condition' could be (1). And it becomes clear that a 'fact' or a truth for Lewis is something that *did* happen as opposed to something that didn't. To be, in other words, is to happen and to happen is to be. I thus take 'true' in Lewis to be merely the adjectival form of 'fact,' in turn an event or a happening. "Nots" do not, in Lewis's world, qualify as true or therefore caused. An instance of this is a fact's opposite, a counterfact, which for Lewis is a nonhappening, with his well-known illustration:

> If we had finished packing Monday night, then we would have departed Tuesday morning.
>
> (3)

It should be evident at the outset that the instance Lewis offers here is a thoroughly economic one. For although I will offer the reader no definition of economics – as there is no definition – it would, if it existed, involve weighing the alternative means, including the packing-up to leave, against the importance of the end, the departing Tuesday morning. And so, especially because Lewis frequently touches on this packing example, I presume he has economics at the back of his mind in much of what he does in *Counterfactuals* despite his more overt allusions to science.

You will note that one implication of the packing-up reference here is that they *didn't* manage to leave Tuesday. Since an event or occurrence is what truth is for him, it makes sense for us to think of the presumed failure to pack Monday evening to be a non-truth, one that contains no truth conditions (3). For if the truth were that they did pack, how would they explain why they didn't get on the road Tuesday morning? Lewis writes in this regard, "it is difficult to find out the truth conditions of counterfactuals with true antecedents [those in which they did pack Monday night], since they would [given that they didn't leave Tuesday morning] be asserted only by mistake..." (3). As Lewis says, the old Humean science of empirical regularities or facts is inadequate here because "what would have happened if one had *not*" done such-and-such is also a legitimate – in fact essential – question. It isn't just, for Lewis, that we must deal with didn't-happens but also with how they introduce to our imaginations the prospect of something failing to occur as against its not-failing to, and as weighed against the significance of the purpose of leaving Tuesday. In other words, some of the burden of truth is to be laid on the one who denies that any successful packing Monday night would have put them on the road on Tuesday.

A counterfact is something that didn't happen, and in not-happening, raising questions about what did. A counterfactual, an initially ambiguous claim to the source of any Tuesday morning departure, is therefore a challenge – and yet a potential aid – to a causality structure. Can we for instance *demonstrate* they wouldn't have made the trip even if they packed Monday night? If so, we're on our way to finding the truer causes, in Lewis's mind, of any successful departure. Untruth – an unactual antecedent – would then have been essential or at least helpful for reliably discovering the truth. Nevertheless, it is the "actual" world Lewis cares about. He says, "we are ultimately interested only in the actual truth values of sentences..." (61). In conceding also that "counterfactuals are, for the most part, contingent," he is assigning them to the lower level of reality, the shadow world of the merely helpful. Only the actual is true in itself. And to be actual is to be a thing in an entirely literal, observable way. The purpose of the counterfactual is, despite its lowly metaphysical status, to reveal the loftier status of the factual.

The state of possibility itself is a state of vagary, explaining why Hume had largely, though not entirely, left it behind. It is in this sense the enemy of the strict, the disciplined, and the determinate. Possibility therefore is of value to Lewis only to the extent it leads to actuality. The literality of Lewis's thought on this emerges in his meditations on what actuality is. "I emphatically do not identify possible worlds in any way with [merely] respectable linguistic entities." "I take [possible worlds] to be respectable entities in their own right," that is to say, as *actually* possible. By this I conclude he means a possible world *as* literally imagined and expressed, *as* actual. We bring tentatively to our minds, as an actuality, what we know to be not or not-yet actual. Referring for instance to someone puzzled at what 'similarity' might mean, Lewis says, "I only ask him to admit that he knows what sort of thing our actual world is, and then explain that other worlds are more things of that sort, differing not in kind but in what goes on at them" (85).

The purpose of a counterfact, in sum, is to introduce 'if not' to the scientific consciousness. While 'if' is a conjunction among possibilities, pointing us in the direction of what might have happened, the 'if not' points us the opposite way. It is not so much, at this juncture, with the *empirical* force of not knowing whether it happened, but with the *logical structure* of how a 'what *if*' is to be connected to a 'what *if not.*' The immediate goal is to focus on and define possibility itself. Lewis says, "we have been trying to give [a claim's] truth conditions in general: to say how the truth value of a counterfactual at *any* world depends on the truth values of various worlds, of its antecedent and consequent" (61). The nature of dependency is the nature of the possible. To inform ourselves of how important it was to have packed Monday if they'd wished to leave Tuesday is to imagine what it would have been like on Tuesday had they not packed on Monday. Connected with this latter counterfact is its obverse: whether, had they not packed Monday, they would themselves have compensated for this lapse by doing something else to ensure getting out Tuesday (3). The goal of Lewis's science is to minimize the unclarity otherwise represented in these possibilities by facing them directly.

Because the strictness of the actual is the inverse of the variety and looseness of the possible, the variety of testing needed to infer actuality should be minimized. "I subscribe to the general view," says Lewis, "that qualitative parsimony is good in a philosophical or empirical hypothesis..." (86–87). And metaphysics, he says, is an effort to systematize – in our present example to minimize – the variety of opinion. "Realism about possible worlds is an attempt, the only attempt that I know of, to systematize these pre-existing modal opinions," where modal refers to the merely habitual, lazy ways of surmising how a thing could have happened (88).

Here Lewis makes clear the starkly literal, yet simultaneously metaphysical, quality of his thought – literal being another word for empirical, namely real for him, the real being the metaphysical. Lewis's main question, which ever looks in the direction of the real and actual and so the causal, then is to ask: what is the range of actuality phenomena over which a causality assertion is valid? He answers: "when I profess realism about *possible* worlds, I mean to be taken literally. Possible worlds are what they are, and not some other thing" (85). They are in other words indefinite although prepared to be definite and thus of ultimate interest. Reality for Lewis is preeminently a seeking-to-be-definite. We want something to *be*, he says, and to really-be for him is to be definite.

The Logic of Reductive versus Contemporary Economics

Lewis fails to note that the earlier decision to leave Tuesday morning, and the intervening one to not-pack Monday night, were essentially economic. Planning a trip – planning anything, even technological – involves economic judgment. In each one we balance opposing goals and interests with the paths to reach them. We will call these plans 'phenomena' or, as economics does, counterfactuals: 'phenomena' in the sense of projecting of ourselves onto a risky plan as a part of other aspects of our lives, 'counterfactual' because they are distinguished from any actual taking-of-a-trip and which we will call facts or data. Taking account of the fact that professional economists are studying our own personal reasonings, we have mainstream economics going on at two widely different levels: the level of the prof and the level of the decision maker. Note that we aren't calling any of this science.

It is important to see how different from the reductionist, scientistic literature this mainstream form of counterfactuality is. I would put it this way: if we take economic theory and its modeling to be the locus of economic *reason*, we must take its counterfacts to be the locus of economic *understanding*. Consider a simple model of the decisions whether to pack Monday night and leave Tuesday morning. The economic model will generate an estimate of: (*i*) in what we will call $z_{i,t}$, the gross benefit of your leaving Tuesday morning relative to the net opportunities you missed by not leaving at another time; and (*ii*), in what we will call $y_{i,t-1}$, the *cost* of your preparing for it by packing Monday night relative to the cost of other packing-date alternatives. Then $z_{i,t}$ and $y_{i,(t-1)}$ are the counterfactuals, the output of our planning model. They are, that is, what *ex ante* seem best to the modeled decision maker relative to other packing and departure dates and so are necessarily interrelated with each other. To wit, packing Monday puts cognitive heat on leaving Tuesday, and leaving Tuesday puts cognitive heat on packing Monday. Input and output, means and ends are, according to the decision maker's utility, in optimal tension. Utility or preferences here are the decision maker's inner intuitive (not psychological outer) capacity to visualize alternative outcomes.

An Economic Model Is *the Mainstream's Counterfactuality*

Step out of the model now and let everything happen. Then compare the *measured* gross benefit $\mathrm{z}_{i,t}$ with the cost $\mathrm{y}_{i,(t-1)}$ of packing Monday and departing Tuesday. Note these symbols are now un-italicized, as they comprise the facts, the observable prices and income, of the matter. They are empirical observations, not formal, phenomenological estimates or judgments (which are always italicized) as examined above. Indeed, differences between counterfact and fact, e.g. $z_{it} - \mathrm{z}_{\mathrm{it}}$, will constitute this model's error terms and hence the indicators of the model's goodness-of-fit to the data. Fact and counterfact, empirical and *a priori* reason, will have shared the stage in this causal inference drama.

The dramatics have thus generated an empirical relation between packing and leaving. But does this relation tell us much without knowing more about the decision maker? The phenomenal reality is that she has made her own choices in the matter. Lewis wants to know whether the hour of packing 'caused' the hour of departure. And it can be useful to think of it this way, especially the further one gets from the situation at hand. The purpose of the modeling, which the decision maker herself conducts in her own head or sense at the time – and which professional economists do more formally and elaborately in classrooms and research papers – is simply to develop more wisdom about whether and when to pack. And counterfactuality, the backcasted values (over earlier time periods or over a cross-section) of the model's two endogenous variables (the packing and the leaving time), has been a necessary part of this liberation from being-caused.

For notice that in any Humean or Lewisian (metalogical *cum* empiricist) reasoning, an *event* was to be the starting point. Yet it was logic that quickly took center stage when thinking about, or making sense of, this event. And so it was logic itself and its capacities to form counterfacts that we were finally left with. Where, however, had the events themselves then gone? More importantly, what was their significance for what we are about? For in some respects at least, we will ever be involved with balancing or allocating scarce resources (time, space, capability, insight) with some purpose or good in mind. The question of clarity and definition that always arises when these balances are involved in turn raises the question of what exactly *is* being balanced. The answer would have to be: human purpose itself. If so, one certainly cannot begin, as Lewis does, with events, as *they* will bear on still other events. And because human purpose and its fulfillment can always usefully be cast as a balance between means and ends, and this balance is perhaps the central theme of contemporary economics, we must ask what sorts of situations one might have in mind that would require allocating means to ends. And to this question only empirical *and* pure (non-empirical) intuitions, collectively a getting-hold of a problem and visualizing its possible implications, could initially speak.

Note already the departures we've made here from a simply empirical metaphysic. Lewis's *exclusively* empirical, data-filled space had involved us in a conundrum: it had provided no formal structure that could guide us to a plausible outcome. It would have to be a human structure, namely in which one decision is connected to other decisions and thence still others in a concatenation with no clear stopping point (recall Houtthaker's theorem in Chapters III and IV). In economics, such a structure is indeed present: in a person's situations and the models symbolically representing them, where nothing can be reduced to a mere event like a leaving Tuesday morning. Economic *counter*factuals instead represent what actions would rationally have been taken in the situation the model has posed and the solution to which the model hypotheses are directed. For the model requires a foundation, including a respect for the uniqueness and individuality of the person making the decision and for her situation and context that the model represents.

The uniqueness of the person cannot *itself* be known. But if there is one 'itself' that for Kant *can* be, it would be a model of her, a representation consisting of a minimized expenditure $e(\boldsymbol{p}, u)$ and its modeled solution for u and in which we do 'know' her counterfactual situation.[1] The counterfactual also requires, for a complete template, the prices p of the services offered for sale and the money income m with which to purchase them, together comprising the observable data the decision maker takes into account when judging her demands. As $e(\boldsymbol{p}, u)$ is equivalently $\boldsymbol{p} \cdot \boldsymbol{x}(p, m)$, the sum of the quantities of the demanded goods each weighted by its respective price, it is easy to see that the *model-predicted* demands x_i (p, m) *are* the counterfactuals of the problem. The pure (*a priori*) elements are being brought together with the empirical ones m and p in the act of judgment.[2] A model's estimate of a decision maker's judgments then, which is vector $\boldsymbol{x}$ in the case of a demand model, is precisely a counterfactual. While it does depend on empirical signals $\boldsymbol{p}$ and m, it cannot, given that pure preferences u remain central, be reduced *to* these empirics as Hume's and Lewis's 'events' are.

Hume's and Lewis's counterfacts were *didn'ts*. But they could never have conceived of a *didn't* had they not the prior capacity to perceive the difference between a 'didn't' and a 'did.' For in the absence of this capacity, how would they ever have recognized a 'not-packing' Monday night? Could there not for instance have been a *partial* packing that evening instead? *How* partial, then, would this 'partial' be? Nor furthermore could we have synthesized such partials as a Monday evening semi-packing into a 'whole' packing unless we *already 'knew,' as intuitive possibility, what the 'whole' would constitute.* Neither would empirical experience be able to show us what this whole means or constitutes unless we can 'see' a complex state in the form of a 'whole' in the first place.

If this pre-conceptual *a priori* capacity to grasp possibility in its various emptinesses, partials, and wholes is only dimly needed in some fields, it certainly is needed in economics, where every decision, on both the buying and selling side, involves looking ahead in at least some manner, an uncertainty which will ever cast doubt on someone's claim to what a 'full' packing might comprise. We must for these reasons distinguish the *empirical* intuition of Hume from the *pre-empirical*, pure intuition of Kant, in the latter of which the empirical and conceptual are synthesized into a determinate, though fallible, articulable judgment, always singular to a given situation.[3] The decision maker's *a priori* pure intuition then – the capacity to synthesize intuitive sense with abstract thought, empirical intuition with concepts, creating an order or pattern – is what I argue utility u represents in mainstream economics. I correspondingly argue that this logic, our *a priori* capacity to synthesize, the *synthetic a priori* of Immanuel Kant, constitutes the center of economic logic and reason.

Note that this synthetic structure isn't itself entirely intellectual or entirely empirical; it makes no claim to any inner understanding of the 'truth' nor to any obvious or persistent regularity. *Contra* David Lewis, not-packing Monday isn't a counterfact merely because Monday-night packing didn't happen. A Martian landing didn't happen either. A decision qualifies as a counterfact in contemporary economics only when one senses, in one's view of the whole situation, that it bears on the entire picture of which their not-leaving Tuesday morning was only a part. If therefore there is to be an accord between Lewis and Kant – between the reductionist and the mainstream – it will have at least to begin reckoning with these problems.

The Nonseparable (Thus Analogical) Character of Mainstream Economics

Economic counterfactuals cannot therefore be the same as those in the reductionist literature. They are estimates or judgments of, in the present instance, demands $x(p,$

m), not any antecedent – or any failure to be an antecedent – in a causality chain. Viewed humanly, we can say the claim of causality – of how a situation came into being – is intended formally or transcendentally, a judgment, not a metaphysical claim to be 'true.' Only in a scientized economics is there a claim to tell us how an event 'actually' comes about, how a person is 'actually' motivated. Mainstream theory therefore cannot be science, as its concern is with a person *as* person, one who makes free choices, who when viewed at a distance as an observer must view it, can only be addressed in a metaphorical, analogical manner, cause-and-effect being part of this metaphor.[4]

Counterfactuality in both economic and econometric theory then is an estimate of how choices would or might, in analogical terms, come about under given conditions, keeping in mind that they will be choices. In this subjunctive sense Lewis does take a step, though in direction only, toward contemporary economics. But because empirical science makes predictions about events instead – that is to say about facts – it preempts itself from viewing a counterfactual in the way economics does. As entities are by nature separable from other entities, measures from other measures, the character of scientific causality, and so of any scientific economics, is *always one of separability*. By separable, what we have meant in this book is to be *movable about* in search of more predictive postulates.

In contrast as we have seen, every demand $h = x$ in economics is nonseparable from every other, as all are connected by way of u, and with it the inseparability of intuition from the concepts or categories through which they are articulated, expressed as trade-offs among possibilities. *The nonseparability of every demand from every other, each a relativity to the others, is the character of any economic judgment.*

The way out, then, from reduction is a nonseparation or unification. In the neighborhood of an economic decision in particular, the following counterfactuality relations in mainstream economics have now emerged, each understood to be judged, so only metaphorically expressible:

$$h = x$$

the estimated demand h is the counterfactual of observed demand x;

$$e = m$$

the estimated minimum expenditure e is the counterfactual of observed income m; and

$$u = v$$

the estimated pure, pre-empirical intuition u is the counterfactual of observed acceptability v,
where in each and in Kant's terms, an intuition is being conjoined with a concept, the same unity (understanding itself) involved when someone judges between two alternatives in an economic decision. Together these comprise a Kantian *synthetic*

a priori: a unity of sense and conception in the act of judgment and decision (A79/B105)

If we think of these nonseparabilities as starting intuitively, then reaching toward or appealing to a capacity within itself to articulate – specific and particular in terms and thus subject to error – then we have what Kant and Kant scholars are calling discursive. An intuition for Kant is a 'singular representation,' i.e. "immediately related to an object" and so nonseparable from it (JL 9:91;589). Quoting Henry Allison, "as discursive, such cognition requires not merely that the data be given in intuition but also that they be taken under some general description," or quoting Kant, "recognized in a concept" (80–81). What forms this unity is "some third thing" or "mediating representation," which "must be pure, that is, void of all empirical content, and yet at the same time, while it must in one respect be intellectual, it must in another be sensible" (A138/B177). No 'empirical turn' in econometrics can alter, or is altering, this Kantian integrality in economic reasoning and which constitutes the meaning of any econometric estimate.

And discursive reason can never be expressed reductively either because this very reduction would assume a reason beneath *itself*, and in requiring it, bind us in a circle. Freedom, choice, cannot be modeled *as* freedom or choice because models must always be expressed in causal-sounding language. The conditions and constraints to which a situation is subject, the unfree aspects, we can model directly. But the final freedom, Jean-Paul Sartre's final 'No' with which one can finally reject what isn't acceptable, is inarticulate beyond that one-syllable epithet and which itself is only symbolic. This is why economic models must always have an 'as-if' character – expressed *as-if* choices were mechanical though they are not, something that the vast, confused literature on *homo economicus* will never grasp. Efforts to express choice in literal terms, a mechanical process and in that way no choice at all, takes us instead back to biology and thence to brain physics. Choice and freedom, *as* choice and freedom, can only be hinted at: in particular in the form of an optimization, a seeming mechanism but only an analogy to judgment and choice – the center, theme, and hallmark of mainstream economics. This is despite that engineering, empirical psychology, and other sciences are frequently deployed with some success as economics' auxiliary hypotheses.

Do we not find ourselves continuously *choosing* to remain economists and philosophers? Do we not see in doing so that we are constantly modeling for ourselves the possible effects of these earlier decisions, yet in no way forcing us in any particular direction? What we can call our 'internal models' then, which are fully economic (not only because about finance but about what we *want,* for ourselves and others), aren't a matter of something being caused but only an assistance in reconfirming, or disconfirming, our choices. And in this way it can only be in *as-if*, symbolic language. And (I promise to stop now), do we not see that all this is to reason in terms of counterfactuals as we understand them in economics?

Counterfactuality then is the principal output or expression of economic reason, and in particular of its formal, *synthetic a priori* character. We never say something is 'worth it' or 'not worth it' without thinking economically, and the inevitable metaphor in such language, in the 'worth' of a situation and which need have nothing to do with money, marketplaces, or 'selfishness,' is precisely what identifies it as economic.

Possibilities for Conciliation

Our question now turns to the possibility of any accord between the empirical reason of Hume and Lewis and the synthetic *a priori* of Kant, so of any economics that they might mutually condone. To help in this regard, Table 1 offers a way of summarizing the present chapter's conclusions. The contrasting character of the two schools – the mainstream and the metalogical/empiricist – suggests that nothing like a compromise between them could be possible. Nor could their epistemologies, and correspondingly their metaphysics, ever appear to be further apart. Then again, as each school constitutes its own way of reason in general, and economics has a rational as well as an empirical foundation, perhaps some accommodations can be found. Might a reductivist causality theory, say, not be brought closer to contemporary economics by way of a suitably broader definition of (to use Lewis's terms) 'world' and 'accessibility' that overlay mainstream language and sense?

I turn for this purpose to several philosophers speaking to, if not deriving from, the empiricist tradition although with some openness to the Kantian contemporary economics. We then can examine any possible flexibilities between these two main schools.

Did Friedman Urge a Positivist Economics?

Ambiguities and misinterpretations will surface as we do. An instance is the widespread misreading of Milton Friedman and especially of his praised and reviled "Methodology of Positive Economics" (1953). We've already cleared up in Chapter III some major misunderstandings of Friedman's work. But some additional emphasis will be useful. It begins with this methodology essay, in which he honored John Neville Keynes' (1891) demarcation between positive science and what Keynes had called 'mere normative' conjecture, a demarcation that was essential, in Keynes' words, to "recognizing a distinct positive science of political economy." Throughout Friedman's long authorship, he too continued to call 'positive' what he thought economics does and ought to be doing. Ergo, says much of the methodology literature, Friedman was a positivist. In his introduction to *Philosophy of Economics* (2008), for instance, Daniel Hausman says Friedman "attempts to show that economics satisfies broadly positivist standards." Consider however, despite his frequent use of the word 'positive,' that Friedman was a thoroughgoing mainstream economist.

In the first place, he was continuously aware of the mutuality of, the simultaneous dependence between, economic theory and observation. Because, he says, "a theory is the way we perceive 'facts', ...we cannot perceive 'facts' without a theory" (166). It is why we put 'facts' in quotation marks: "A theory cannot be tested by comparing its assumptions directly with 'reality'" because perceptions of reality come to us *via* theory. More generally, "... the very concept of assumptions of a theory is surrounded with ambiguity" (159). Does this co-dependence between concept and observation sound even remotely like a metalogical economics? Mainstream modeling requires optimization, which is a normative act. And optimization is what one does to estimate backcasts (counterfactuals) of earlier events – so help estimate goodness of fit – together constituting its positivity. Contemporary economic modeling therefore is both fully normative and fully positive. The two are inseparable, so in this sense Friedman is right in calling it positive.

And his recognition of this nonseparability between theory and perception is clear. He was fond of mocking the positivist presumption that we can know which of a decision maker's possible intentions are 'realistic' and which aren't. Meaning is contextual: "everything depends on the problem; there is no inconsistency in regarding the same firm as if it were a perfect competitor for one problem and a monopolist for another" (168). Nonseparability implies we have no direct access to how people make decisions but only to how to think of them consistently. And for consistency, all we can resort to are generalities.

Because then economic hypotheses are useful only, subject to the judgment of the modeler and user, their efficiency is what is central. Friedman says a theory "is important if it 'explains' much by little" (153). By the climax of this important paper, Friedman has made clear he stands at the epicenter of modern economics. Its theory is interpretive only, no claim to reduce economics to either an objectivity or subjectivity: "Firms behave *as if* they were seeking rationally to maximize expected returns … and had full knowledge of the data needed to succeed in this attempt, *as if*, that is, they knew the relevant cost and demand functions…," (158). Imagining they or we know the actual ones is absurd.

Articulating Mainstream Thought: An Embarrassment of Riches

The modern economic revolt was a rejection of the claim that human persons can be understood only in massed form, the boundaries between which can be determined by distant administrators and scholars, alienating them from individuals and so from any sympathy for their motive and intent. This I think is what J.S. Mill (1836, 230) meant in his remark that economic laws derive from introspection; what Max Weber (1903, 1917, 1922, 89–96) meant by ideal types,the inner- and other-directed man for instance of David Riesman's *The Lonely Crowd* (1950); what the characters' existential situations implied for Thomas Hardy's *Tess of the D'Urbervilles* (1891); for Rainer Rilke's *Duino Elegies* (1923); for T. S. Eliot's *Four Quartets* (1943) and the protagonists of every great novel. It is Joseph Schumpeter's (1949, 212) market innovator, a "vision or intuition," a "pre-scientific act of fancy or common sense" stimulated and disciplined by the unease of an unknown future; Kenneth Boulding's (1950) comment that "aggregates and averages are at best merely mathematical constructions and not 'real' in the sense in which their individual components are" (8).

It is James Buchanan's (1969, 23) argument that there is no objective 'truth' in utility theory but only ways to channel "self-interest toward mutually compatible goals" (Ayres 1976, 127); is Fritz Machlup's (1978, 296, 283–301) reference to the "literal minds" thinking *homo economicus* to be an assertion about how people 'really' are instead of the simplification it is intended to be; is Israel Kirzner's (1979, 109, 225) "entrepreneurial input," an employee's insight into an opportunity that becomes visible only in the successes or failures to utilize it. It is Robert Sugden's (2000) demonstration that the rationality of the group resides in each participating individual; is Daniel Klein's (2012, 108–111) notion of the 'deepself,' the vacationing 'director' of the mind's sub-areas which, in working behind the scenes, are "unarticulated."

If I were to chide some of these economists, it would be in their inordinate criticisms of one another, their penchant for overblowing sidelights and word choices. This probably is unavoidable, part of the ambiguous character of the transcendental horizon our work occupies, what Machlup and others call the inherently hypothetical. They're aware of and depend on the ambiguity they face, having struggled with it themselves, yet often don't realize that economic language transcends actuality on purpose. They grasp well the divide between the positive and the interpretive but do a poorer job explaining how they grasp it, are aware of the essentially metaphorical character of their language but often aren't conscious they are.[5]

Of these mentioned for instance, Daniel Klein (100) seems to me the closest to confusing the interpretive with the positive, imagining with Minsky that he can decode empirically what he himself had called deep, demoting it to mere mind and so essentially to biology. Klein gives the feeling he is creating a new thought system rather than interpreting standard language.[6] Schumpeter too, despite his singularly eloquent accounts of an investor's concern for the future (1942, 81–86), often degrades it to lists of specific futural calculations, as though a mechanical process were in action instead of a person facing an uncertain world, which is possibility itself. "Facts and logic" Schumpeter says (1949, 214–218) can indeed dispose of what he calls ideology, but only as interpreted by the decision maker in a particular context, not by us or by Schumpeter

Fritz Machlup on the other hand has distinguished the interpretative from the positive particularly well. Machlup writes, "the fundamental assumptions of economic theory, the economic principle, the postulate of rationality…or whatever they have been called – have been characterized in so many different ways that an enumeration must suffice," and counts at least eighteen beyond those I've been citing, including:

> self-evident propositions, … a priori truths, … rigid laws, rules of procedure, resolutions, working hypotheses, useful fictions, heuristic mental constructs, facts of immediate experience, [and] data of introspective observation.
>
> (1955, 297)

Sufficing they must be, along with the others we've used here, because efforts to pinpoint or define these categories at the level of a given decision are useless. As a particular person's immediate experience, nothing is there for the rest of us to see. We obviously aren't dealing in economics with "a real man," writes Machlup.

Yet efforts are made, I interpret him to say, to help us dwell on their underlying meaning, something that an 'ism' classification will never do.[7]

The Pragmatism of Charles Peirce

Let's move on to a fundamentally different thinker, Charles Peirce, and one of his interpreters J-M Chevalier. To fix the context of Peirce's work, Kant had written in the first paragraph of Kant's Transcendental Deduction that in the absence of intuition, concepts can never relate to objects because they can never have content (B130). He was referring to the question of *how* one knows something. Except for Kant and the phenomenological tradition he initiated, pragmatism has been, it seems to me, the most deliberate in taking up this 'how' task and in that way the rationale for economic modeling. As J-M Chevalier puts it, "there are many good reasons" to regard Charles Peirce as a direct heir to Kant's transcendental philosophy, of the search for the conditions of the possibility of knowledge (114). Chevalier notes however that while Kant saw his work to be directed to the possibility of thought in general, Peirce's "seems to have been more radically oriented toward the possibility of science" (114). As we shall see, Peirce's self-restriction to science came at a price: of ultimately abandoning his search for transcendental possibility as such in favor of a 'transcendental reality' or actuality. To that extent his work would, I argue, be consistent with Lewis and so miss the meaning of contemporary economic theory, which is directed to possibility.

Chevalier's task in "Forms of Reasoning as Conditions of Possibility" is to show how the young Peirce was led by Kant's insight that the pure categories of the understanding are in us innately. With Peirce too, as in Kant, these categories must be deduced as pre-empirical. Chevalier says the question of the categories for Peirce "is properly transcendental in the following sense: whereas in the *Critique of Pure Reason* the *metaphysical* deduction reveals the categories of the understanding, the transcendental deduction justifies their application" (119). In other words, the metaphysical builds a room and the transcendental decides that it will be used, say, as a kitchen. Chevalier amplifies these roles, again paraphrasing Peirce, by arguing that in pragmatism they are related as the normative is to the positive. "While the analysis of the *a priori*...only addresses how we *should* think, the analysis of the mental as relations between signs describes how thought *does* proceed" (119, my italics).

Kant's own, and brief, metaphysical deduction was on the order of a logic, consisting largely of the principles of consistency (non-contradiction) and self-identification, and because they are arguably prior to any other reason, positioned ahead of his *transcendental* deduction of the categories. It thus would partly be consistent with this that Peirce would call his 'transcendental' deduction what were merely logical *devices* like semiotics and which he saw as instances of logic. Transcendence as Kant saw it though, a deduction of the *a priori* categories of the understanding, appears to be missing in Peirce. At least in the mature part of his career Peirce had indeed been operating in the metaphysical dimension, claiming to reach the truth directly as Lewis's empiricism claims.

Noting this confusion in Peirce, Chevalier writes, "the limits of [his] transcendental approach are to be found in his metaphysical project." Peirce was constructing in the metaphysical sense of the word. But as Chevalier asks, "can a philosopher be constructive [metaphysical] and critical [interpretive] at the same time?" (127) Peirce certainly is consistent with himself in claiming laws to be 'innate' in the literal sense of a part of our *nat*ure. Nature and law go hand-in-hand, as physical science ever asserts (119). But laws and the nomological in turn then would be an empirical issue, begging the original issue: how empirical signals are to be recognized and interpreted. The answer is: formally, transcendentally.

Peirce does see this difficulty, noting that the empirics, including psychology, will be a question of gradual experience, particular aspects or skills: a familiarity with the successive links between signs and objects. Chevalier says rightly enough: "Peirce seems to translate Kantian transcendentalism into semiotics," or according to Chevalier, "grammar, logic, and rhetoric [for him] form a complete transcendental theory of representation..." (120). "To sum up, for Peirce," says Chevalier, "the transcendental does not impose a subjective limit on our experience...but rather reveals an objective relation of symbolization" (120–121), the objectivity constituting what Heidegger would call a special or separate metaphysics, and whose possibility Heidegger doubted.

And as Kant and Heidegger would agree, objective relations are no transcendence whatsoever. It rather is for Peirce a question of training oneself in various logical maneuvers, eventually bringing us to what for him is logic's central principle: that it operates by natural steps, one leading to another as nature herself does – the inductive way. In this we have the advantage that nature is orderly. Peirce has returned us to the extensive metaphysics he had started with, essentially – despite his claim – bypassing the formal or transcendental and so assuring he would fall back, from the point of view of economics at least, onto science rather than transcendence in Kant's sense. Chevalier can say then with some force that "few would deny that Peirce was a metaphysician and a realist," not at all inconsistent with his ultimate elimination of the formal or transcendental (127).

How though is it for Peirce that nature just happens to conform to how somebody reasons, or initially failing to conform, bend itself further backward so that it does, as any separate principle of reasoning would behave? Peirce fails to ask, or satisfactorily answer, this 'how' question, which is Hume's question, one that Kant answers with the rigor achieved by combining an outer (empirical) with an inner (pure) intuitive capacity to grasp a situation essential to any subsequent conceptualizations of it, and what I have been arguing utility brings to mainstream economics. Peirce replaces this central insight with various separate kinds of reason, in particular the repetitive logical inference that induction is. But mathematical procedures of such sort are to be distinguished from an epistemological 'how,' and indeed *beg* a 'how' in the sense of how the decision maker does grasp or recognize them *as* procedures. To offer induction in particular for this – in statistics a mere succession of correlations – brings us no closure.

Despite its closure failure, the spirit of correlation certainly has influenced much of recent econometrics, which is on a collision course with economic theory. The "new, empiricist, wave of economic research carries the creeping inductivism…to a new level," William Milberg says, "defined by broader criteria for the generation of new hypotheses, including completely *a posteriori* observation" (366). "Casual empiricism, common sense and introspection – rather than axiomatics – have also motivated the recent research" (367), led by "the sophistication of the measurement of variables and the correlations among them" (357). The implication for Milberg, and I would agree, is that the broadening of *logical* possibilities is narrowing the *statistics* to progressively smaller neighborhoods of interest.

I should qualify this critique of pragmatism. Despite its confusion between metaphysics and transcendence, it has a virtue: of enterprise and questioning. Michael Lawlor (2004) refers to John Dewey's emphasis on the changing character of the world and its implications for how we understand economics. Lawlor paraphrases Dewey as saying in his *Quest for Certainty* that "concepts evolve as the experience in using them to guide investigation evolves" (308), and we are faced with an "ultimate revisability of knowledge, its essential lack of certitude…" (309). Scientific inquiry "results in new knowledge which itself becomes part of [that] world…" (313). This repetitive induction can however easily go too far. As Lawlor writes, Dewey is running against both the empiricist tradition of Hume and Locke *and* the phenomenalist tradition of Kant and even Hegel, all four arguing there to be an immutable reality and in this way unpragmatic.

The Ethical Planning of Allan Gibbard

With immutable reality in mind, let's turn for a moment from the subject of cause to one that frequently touches on it: morality and ethics. Allan Gibbard's work *Thinking How to Live* is of this character, addressed to the tradition of, though questioning, metalogical thought. Gibbard says, "the theory I develop is a form of 'metaethical expressivism.'" While "metaethics asks what ethical questions *are*: [namely] what does it *mean* to call an act wise or foolish, admirable or reprehensible" (6), Gibbard explores "just one aspect of expressivism and normative concepts, what we might call the logical 'workings' of these concepts" (7). Gibbard's workings are, in short, a state of mind in which you stipulate or propose a plan of action to yourself, then ask whether it would be ethical or not. The plan then must be net-satisfying in some fashion. "*Ought* questions and *reason* questions," he says, again contesting the distinction between normative and positive, "are by their very nature questions of what to do" (9). "Thinking what to do amounts to deciding what to do" (17).

Moral decision for Gibbard is a matter of – and this is my own interpretation of him – a bringing of what for Kant are the distinct transcendence (cognition) and metaphysics (moral demand and logic) into a common, co-integrated space. He expresses this conjunction by way of, appropriately enough from Kant's standpoint, a *dis*junction. For instance,

> Either packing now is the thing to do, or by now it's too late to catch the train anyway.
>
> (41)

what Gibbard names a *fac-prac*.[8] By the 'fac' side Gibbard seems to be referring to the transcendental, the locus of our judgment of what the 'facts' are; and by the 'prac' side our moral will, a matter of reconciling conceptual judgment with morality. He calls this synthesis "the maximally specific combination of decisional and factual content" (47), which Hume had said was an empty set – our "rules of morality" not being "conclusions of our own reason" (Hume 547). Instead says Gibbard, "disjunctions and other 'truth-functional' constructions… intertwine fact and plan," namely "how things are with what to do…" (57). "These plan-laden judgments, we can say, are built recursively out of factual judgments and pieces of planning, by combining, rejecting, and generalizing" (58). The 'intertwining' Gibbard is characterizing here is thoroughly Kantian discursivity, the matching of sense with concept and in steps that are discontinuous (discursive) and fallible both intellectually and morally.

In this Gibbard rejects the descriptivist view that a situation's properties are what determine the actions we should take on it. That view Gibbard says, "a naturalistic, scientific theory of good, ought, virtue, and justice, or something of the sort," downplays choice, and, I would interject, overplays certainty. "What makes a normative theory good" to the scientist "is just what makes any other naturalistic theory good – theories of the social sciences, for instance" (160–161), and we would be "defer[ing] to social scientists to tell us the true nature of justice" (161). Following Kant (458, 463) Gibbard writes, "strictly naturalistic concepts are shaped by the demands of causal [as opposed to moral] explanation and understanding" (161), so that "no naturalistic analysis…captures a normative meaning" (237). Here Gibbard is echoing Desmond Hogan, discussed in Chapter I, to the effect that for Kant, human freedom falls outside of any sensation or category because is moral will itself. Or as Kant put it, "I now begin my state as I wish." Indeed because this is so, I argue, Kant's language in his Transcendental Doctrine of the Elements is – especially when related to cause and effect – ultimately symbolic.

Though Gibbard correctly includes the social sciences in this warning about mixing nature with morality, it patently does not apply, as we have just shown, to mainstream economics, which is not scientific or therefore a social science despite sometimes drawing on science for its auxiliary hypotheses. Economics' everyday expressions have a causal sound but finally no causal implication – only implications, as the interactions between Marshallian and Hicksian demands show, for choices. Personal choice in economics is indeed normative in Gibbard's sense, though always one, as Gibbard says, where morality is weighed against judged facts.

In his discussion of judgments without claims to certitude, Gibbard seems to quote virtually directly from what Kant would have said to Hume. "Suppose," writes Gibbard, "that logically, plans needn't be beliefs" with their vindicating sound. We might nevertheless form judgments that constitute full-fledged beliefs…" (258).

> Suppose, though, I came to judge that no such deep vindication exists. I wouldn't then stop making judgments of fact, everyday and scientific. I cannot, after all, lead my life without making judgments. Instead, I would go on making these

> judgments, but *move to a modest assessment of their epistemic status*. I would no longer claim fully to *know* whereof I judged, and so my judgments wouldn't fully be beliefs in this strict sense.
>
> (259, my italics)

Gibbard doesn't once mention Kant in this book. He is addressing analyticist philosophers, not transcendental or phenomenalist ones. But his thought is phenomenological, and so mainstream economic, precisely because, as in our earlier discussion of Hogan and Anderson, it faces the heterogeneity of the transcendental with the metaphysical along with the practical necessity of combining them in a decision. "With a coherent practical faith," a notion that could have been taken from Kant's *Metaphysics of Morals*, Gibbard says: "I have to trust my powers of judgment and investigation, to some degree" (261). In this same vein, Kant writes that the moral command requires "a judgment sharpened by experience" so as to distinguish "in what cases they are applicable…" (5, [6]). Metaphysics, the moral voice, is the seat of the will, not of insight. Given the resultant uncertainties, Gibbard cautions, work back and forth between your sense of an issue (and so your utility) and your moral will for it, between the *fac* and the *prac*.

The Qualified Naturalism of David Armstrong

David Armstrong similarly has been an upstart among naturalist philosophers in ever re-examining their and his claim to the notion of a 'belief,' the necessity and sufficiency of the material dimension of thought. Even in his earlier (1973) work Armstrong saw it is inadequate "simply to assert that mental processes are nothing but certain sorts of physical processes in the brain" (180). There also remains

> the problem of the 'phenomenal' qualities.…Whether these qualities be treated as qualities of *what is perceived*…or of *the perceiving* of what is perceived [empirical intuition], …they are a problem for anybody who tries to give an account of physical phenomena.
>
> (181)

Here the rationale for Kant's philosophy of perception as empirical intuition shows its influence. It is the reduction of sense perception to a psychological or other brain process from which Armstrong particularly steps away. Here he says modern science can be of no direct help. It is revealing that a page later, when asking into what our epistemological foundations might *be*, and especially "how do we determine what it is that we know or what assurance is rational" (182), he asks into what might be "the best *mark* …of knowledge or rational assurance…" (182–183) and which Kant had in 1787 identified as an aspect of the process of schematization that is human judgment.

Armstrong proceeds to characterize a theory of mind in a reductivist manner instead, temporizing however by observing that "logical structures and interrelations of the mental concepts are exceedingly complex." And in noting the variety of major and minor roles certain aspects take in the epistemic structure, concludes that "I am sorry to say that I can do no more than appeal to an intuitive, largely unanalyzed, notion of 'minor role'" (187). And after still further consideration, "I do concede that introspection and/or perception appears to yield some evidence against a materialist view of man" (190), a large step toward Kant and with it toward mainstream economics in inviting-in the phenomenalist, although at this point only the perception end of it.

By 2004, in his "Counterfactualist versus Singularist Theories of Causation," Armstrong has taken deeper steps toward this phenomenalist attitude. After reviewing Lewis's theory of counterfactuality as an 'if-and-only-if' in the subjunctive mood, Armstrong notes it to be a conceptual analysis of causation, in contrast to the singularist theory which is "preferable as conceptual analysis because it yields more intuitive results in difficult and disputed cases" (451), and where by 'singularist' he means, as we have seen in mainstream economics, that each case would finally be different from the others. "Lewis," he says, "stigmatized singular causation as a 'hidden feature,' a phrase [he] well calculated to arouse our Humean reflexes" (452). Yet such negative reflexes should be no obstacle to a theory. Rather, the uniqueness and therefore intrinsic character of a relationship would, in contrast to the extrinsics in Hume and Lewis, appear to be a legitimate aspect of reality and therefore of theory.

Armstrong goes on to quote Evan Fales (1990) to the effect that an essential locus of cause, as humble as it may appear, is "our awareness of pressure on our own body" (454), a uniqueness – emphasized in Kant's notion of an empirical intuition – of a high order because *a* pressure on one's *self*. The phenomenon of pressure therefore should be significant for any personal understanding. Armstrong says furthermore, after Fales, "the phenomenology of the perception of pressure matches properties of a physical vector" (mid 454). This dual character of being both personal and physical, thus empirical and measurable, is interesting for two reasons. First, it implies that a model can well represent or interpret it in quantitative terms, as economic models indeed do. Second, consistent with and indeed more important than this dual character, it is an instance of an empirical signal of 'outer experience' that in Kantian epistemology initiates the allocation or schematization of intuitions to categories constituting the act of judgment.

Peter Menzies (1996) had referred to such empirical signal as "the intrinsic relation that typically holds between two distinct events when one increases the chance of the other" (1010). Though perhaps unaware – if we note that 'intrinsic' here is meant by Kant formally or transcendentally rather than metaphysically – of its Kantian source, Menzies emphasizes its importance for making generalizations. Armstrong says, "for myself, I would favor taking Menzies' 'causal platitude' as fixing the reference of the singular causal relation rather than analyzing the concept," which would be a rationalism (453). Coordinated empirical events, as a bumping against one another, are not yet at the stage of such categories as cause, but phenomenally, transcendentally at the level of empirical intuition in Kant's terms, namely nothing you can yet *say* or *express*.

Armstrong's thinking begins even to merge onto an economic assessment of purposeful decision making. He says, in specifically economic language, "causes characteristically stand to their effects as *means*, or empirically possible means stand to their *ends*" (top mid 455). The lines of this logic proceed by "immanent singular causation" (456), the only combined metaphysico-epistemic principle that would survive application to an individual human person and her understanding. Just as crucially, Armstrong notes that these "theories, I think, require the notion of singular causation to make them work, and so they cannot be the account of what that connection is" (456). Precisely so, as, following Kant, no claim is being made in contemporary economics to know what any situation or context or problem is in *itself*, but only as a model, judgment, and interpretation of it.

In short, Armstrong appears here to be referring to personal judgments of unique situations, schematizations between empirical intuitions like "perception of pressure" and pure, *a priori* intuitions under which categories like cause are judged. The universals Armstrong seeks that is are the *a priori* senses and concepts of Kantian epistemology. As he writes, "…the fundamental laws are, or can fairly be *represented as being* causal laws" (456), which however, being causal laws only in a metaphorical sense, could be nothing but the pure intuition that constitutes utility u in mainstream economics, in particular the intersection of the Marshallian and Hicksian demands in the act of judgment. This distinction between the metaphorical and the literal allows us to side in some respects with both Lewis and Hume and with Kant and Armstrong because causation here, special to *a* person and *a* context, can only be free choice instead, so only metaphorically causative.

The elements of a contemporary economic model, of a particular person in a particular setting and circumstance, testing a particular hypothesis and deriving from it estimates of particular actions, have effectively here been confirmed, much of which Menzies, Fales, and Armstrong, coming *out* of the reductionist school, may not have been aware. At the same time, taking everything literally and so, as ever, extrinsic to the next thing, Hume and Lewis would have been shocked at the gulf between scientific and economic modeling.

The Possibility of Closure

I should say my goal with Charles Peirce here has been the reverse of that with Gibbard and Armstrong. For while with the latter two I've been asking how a philosopher originating from apparently Humean/empiricist roots could ever achieve a sense of the formal or transcendental, in Peirce I've focused on the reverse direction, of arriving at the metalogical and empiricist from an originally formal and transcendental. But the implications have been the same. Our principal theme, sub-rosa perhaps, has been how to recognize when someone – philosopher or economist – is writing symbolically rather than literally. In the world of English-speaking philosophy in particular, words are usually to be taken literally, though they often slip unconsciously into analogy themselves, while economists speak largely, in at least their key categories, analogically while at least subliminally recognizing they do.

And so, we have a basic problem of communication on our hands when comparing the Kantian with the literalist, empiricist attitude.

Is there, in any event, an epistemic conclusion we can draw from the three Neo-Kantian philosophers we have examined here? Recall that it must be epistemological, a matter of transcendence critiquing itself – and metaphysically only in one's moral will. If so, I think our conclusion would be that, in the balance that mainstream economics represents between the intuitive and the conceptual, the intuitive is always the foundational, always the unifier of the two, whether called 'utility,' 'preferences,' or any other such symbolic word. And that while the conceptual is the verbal, the intuitive is the meaning of the verbal, a balance that in any philosophical or economic tendency toward dogma is easily upset.

I conclude that they would have the more accurate, and especially the deeper, sense of mainstream economics who would:

(i) understand its derivation from, its residence in, Kantian reason,
(ii) minimizing therefore the metaphysical (dogmatic) and maximizing the epistemological (critical) dimension,
(iii) thus ultimately the intuitive over the conceptual – to the point that its principal terms are undefinable, only interpretable – more often therefore metaphorical and symbolic than literal,
(iv) integrating concept *with* intuition while noting that the integration itself is an intuitive, discursive (fallible) act,
(v) thereby emphasizing the nonseparability over the separability of economic language, logic, and reason,
(vi) a matter, consequently, of integrating the rational with the empirical,
(vii) so that the uncertain must have our attention over the certain,
(viii) and understanding and judgment our attention over cause-and-effect, 'cause' to be taken, when referring to a person *as* a person, only for expressive purposes,
(ix) that therefore it is easier to claim what economics is *not* than what it is: for instance, that it isn't and can't be science,
(x) that in any event mainstream economics is always two-tiered, the textbooks and professors lecturing about decision makers, who however cannot be reduced to any literal object or event.

Summary Points of Chapter VI

1. The historical contest of the two main competitors for the seat of economics has been remarkable: that while mainstream economists have dwelt little on their philosophical *foundations*, empiricist philosophers have only projected, never realized, their economic *implications*.
2. The economic implications of a logico-empiricist metaphysics will be a set of laws reducible to a set of economic events, so that an empiricist epistemology will be a set of facts about these events.

3. To the extent therefore that empiricist reality is a set of facts, what is not real for it must be a set of counterfacts. A counterfact, that is, could never be anything real. Having fulfilled its task of identifying the conditions for a fact, it must fall away. It is, literally, counter to a fact.
4. In contemporary economics rather, counterfactuals are precisely what do *not* fall away, being to the contrary a model's representation of a decision maker's choices.
5. If the counterfacts of an empiricist economics derive from David Hume, the counterfacts of mainstream economics derive from Immanuel Kant.
6. Counterfacts must then be determinable from a Neo-Kantian philosophy as well. And as it was Kant who bequeathed to economics a balance between intuition and conceptualization, the point of a Neo-Kantian proposal must be to alter this balance in some manner.
7. One such proposal is to consider the dimension of understanding or judgment as an experience of gradual self-learning. 'Self'-learning must be one of nature, which because nature is precisely a matter of one thing following another, is an inductive logic: a statistical correlation.
8. Another proposal, consistent with Kant's ethics and to that extent mainstream economics, is that the understanding (epistemological) and moral (metaphysical) dimensions of a decision respectively constitute a 'wish' and an 'ought,' parallel to and replacing causality.
9. Still another takes up Kant's distinction between an empirical and a pure intuition – noting that the former, being observable, serves as a category's 'marks' that help us distinguish means from ends, drawing us back to mainstream economics and for which pure intuition (utility) is essential.
10. The future of economic thought thus depends on the extent and character of the balance between *empirical* intuition, which is solely observations and measures, and *pure* intuition, which is anticipation and judgment – or in economic language, utility and uncertainty.

Notes

1 Utility's relationship to money income even takes on various functional forms, as we saw for example with expected utility in Chapter IV.

2 I use the term 'empirical' here as Kant does: the immediate sensual 'contact' with one's outer world, what Kant calls subjectivity and largely equivalent to the bumping-against that is much of Hume's theory of causality, but for Kant only the first stage of a judgment process.

3 In a confirmation that empirical intuition is indeed part of transcendence, Allison says that sensibility, empirical intuition and its union with empirical concepts, "makes an autonomous *a priori* contribution to cognition." (16)

4 I leave aside that Kant argued that scientific inference too is formal or transcendental, so even it can lay no claim to much metaphysical ('real) status. That discussion is for another day.

5 Most methodologists do seem implicitly aware that economic inference has an either/or character, either an interpretation or a direct observation. Wicksteed, as cited in Machlup (295), notes matter-of-factly for instance that to appeal to psychological data is to aim at

positivity, while to confine oneself to "economic man" is to be a hypothetical science, an interpretive or heuristic one, with no claim to absolute truth. (142)

6 Mises similarly criticizes an economic theory based on an ideal type, arguing it should confront complexity ("complex phenomena") instead. If by this he means complex possibility, then an ideal type might include it. But Mises doesn't appear to allow for any explicit distinction between possibility and actuality, reducing all of importance to actuality.

7 Consistent with this, Machlup depicts positivism as a claim to derive "*true* deductions from *true* assumptions" – to derive 'truth' in other words – in contrast to the "merely valid deductions from fundamental postulates" that contemporary economics strives for (1978, 295). Machlup's retort to this 'truth' is: if literal truth ('realism') is already contained in the hypotheses, why wouldn't it already be in the conclusions, obviating any further deduction? The only answer he says, is that "while an ideal type is a category of reflection and argumentation," a "real type" must be "a category of observation, classification, … and measurement" only. (1978, 258) Quite so. The depth of Machlup's grasp here of the contrast between mainstream and positivist economic reasoning is remarkable given he doesn't appear to have directly quotedKant, the first thinker to lay it out and to this day the most fully. It does suggest that mainstream economics' Kantian origins, just as positivist economics' Leibnizian and Comtean origins, were both well in the air by the late 18th and early 19th century.

8 Note Gibbard's clever reference here to Lewis's packing-up-on-time story.

References

Allison, Henry E. *Kant's Transcendental Idealism: An Interpretation and Defense.* New Haven: Yale University Press, 1983, 2004.

Anderson, R. Lanier. "The Introduction to the *Critique*: Framing the Question." In: Paul Guyer (ed.), *The Cambridge Companion to Kant's Critique of Pure Reason.* Cambridge: Cambridge University Press, pp. 75–92, 2010.

Armstrong, David M. "Epistemological Foundations for a Materialist Theory of the Mind." *Philosophy of Science* 40, No. 2, pp. 178–193, 1973.

Armstrong David M. "Going Through the Open Door Again: Counterfactual versus Singularist Theories of Causation." In: John Collins, Ned Hall, and L.A. Paul (eds.), *Causation and Counterfactuals.* Cambridge: MIT Press, 2004.

Ayres, C.E. (ed.), *Science and Ceremony.* Austin: University of Texas Press, pp. 163–174, 1976.

Boulding, Kenneth. *A Reconstruction of Economics.* NY: John Wiley, 1950.

Chevalier, Jean-Marie. "Forms of Reasoning as Conditions of Possibility: Peirce's Transcendental Inquiry Concerning Inductive Knowledge." In: Gabriele Gava and Robert Stern (eds.), *Pragmatism, Kant, and Transcendental Philosophy.* London: Routledge, 2016.

Dewey, John. *The Quest for Certainty: A Study of the Relation of Knowledge and Action.* London: Allen and Unwin, 1930.

Fales, Evan. *Causation and Universals.* London: Routledge, 1990.

Gibbard, Allan. *Thinking How to Live.* Cambridge: Harvard University Press, 2003.

Hausman, Daniel M. *The Inexact and Separate Science of Economics.* Cambridge: Cambridge University Press, 1992, 2023.

Hicks, J.R. *Value and Capital.* Oxford: Clarendon Press, 1946.

Houtthaker, Hendrik. "Revealed Preference and the Utility Function." *Economica* 17, pp. 159–174, 1950.

Kant, Immanuel. *Critique of Practical Reason.* Lewis White Beck (Trans.). Chicago: University of Chicago Press, 1949. First published in 1788.

Kant, Immanuel. *Prolegomena to Any Future Metaphysics.* Lewis White Beck (Trans.). New York: Bobbs-Merril, 1950. First published in 1783.

Kant, Immanuel. *Critique of Pure Reason, 1st and 2nd eds.* New York: Random House (Modern Library), 1958. Norman Kemp Smith (Trans.). First published in 1781; revised 1787.

Kirzner, Israel M. *Perception, Opportunity, and Profit: Studies in the Theory of Entrepreneurship.* Chicago: University of Chicago Press, 1979.

Klein, Daniel B. *Knowledge and Coordination: A Liberal Interpretation.* Oxford: Oxford University Press, 2012.

Lawlor, Michael S. "Dewey and Economic Reality." In: Elias L. Khalil (ed.), *Dewey, Pragmatism, and Economic Methodology.* London: Routledge, 2004.

Lewis, David K. *Philosophical Papers, Vol. I.* Oxford: Oxford University Press, 1983.

Machlup, Fritz. *Methodology of Economics and Other Social Sciences.* New York: Academic Press, 1978.

Marshall, Alfred. *Principles of Economics.* New York: Macmillan and Co., 1890, 1920..

Menzies, Peter. "Probabilistic Causation and the Pre-Emption Problem." *Mind* 105, pp. 85–117, 1996.

Merleau-Ponty, Maurice. The Phenomenology of Perception.. Donald Landes (Trans.). London: Routledge, 2023. First published in 1945.

Milberg, William. "After the 'New Economics': Pragmatist Turn?" In: Elias L. Khalil (ed.), *Dewey, Pragmatism, and Economic Methodology.* London: Routledge, 2004.

Peirce, Charles S. *Collected Papers of Charles Sanders Peirce*, Vol. I, Cambridge: Belknap Press, Harvard University, 1960. First delivered in 1903.

Sugden, Robert. "Team Preferences." *Economics and Philosophy* 16, pp. 175–204, 2000.

Schumpeter, Joseph. *Capitalism, Socialism, and Democracy.* New York: Harper and Bros., 1942, 1947, 1950, 81–86.

Schumpeter, Joseph. "Science and Ideology." *American Economic Review* 39, 345–359, 1949.

Postscript

What Have We Concluded about Our Initial Hypotheses?

The philosophy of economics is a troubling affair. It is supposed to be about how economists reason. What however do economists do but reason about how other people reason, who in turn reason how others will? Aren't we in a pickle? Because reason is at the heart of what is human, it also is at the heart of decision making, which involves both the forms of thought (principles, the *a priori*) and the forms of experience (empirics, the synthetic). Unsurprisingly then, there is a tension in philosophy today between these two doctrines, the a priorists saying the way to rationality is powerful concepts or rules, the empiricists saying it is observations. But is either of these, at odds now for at least five centuries, adequate to the situation in economics, where to model decision makers is to model how they model others and so on?

If it is correct to say that every discipline involves a special metaphysics of some kind, then assigning mainstream and any rationalist or empiricist economics theirs would be straightforward. In its conception of reality as a structure of measured objects, metalogical reason is certainly science. It wants to know what is 'actually happening,' a goal consistent with objectification. Although scientists have their own personal worlds that is, their objects do not. Positivist reason, thus a mechanical economics, must then be a worldless one. Let us call a worldless economics technical: a metaphysics of things, whose method would be to render its subjects as objects, mechanical therefore, whether deduced or measured.

We can understand then how so many philosophers have concluded that the key to a methodology of economics is to begin with a methodology of science. Yet this inference – that economic reason must finally be of observables, so finally a science – is forced. It says: (*i*) everything in science is ultimately to be observed; (*ii*) economics is a science; (*iii*) thus, everything in economics must ultimately be observed. Or equivalently, because science projects objectivity onto whatever interests it, and economics is one of its interests, it (economics) must be objective and so measurable. But this is circular reasoning, premise (*ii*) having covertly assumed economics to be a matter of observation, precisely what it had supposed it was proving.

Positive philosophy might wish then to reflect more carefully on its presumptions about the scope of science. For its efforts to discern 'the facts' about 'how people

DOI: 10.4324/9781003514602-9

actually reason' are themselves discursive efforts – the identity of a 'fact' depending, fallibly, on the category under which it is judged. Data for instance aren't what determine that economics is inexact. Judgment is. And judgment involves, as even Hume would say, "going deep."

Reason then, it seems to me, is either a depth or a circularity. We point toward it or we circle around it. To reason circularly is to tautologize. To reason deeply is to judge. Judging effectively involves recognizing that ideas are never directly related to their objects but only by way of intuitions of particular circumstances, which themselves are only tentatively related to 'what really is.' As Kant put it, "judgment is…the mediate knowledge of an object, that is the [intellective] representation of an [empirical] representation" (A68, B93).

Economics cannot in any event, in its view of the world as a structure of persons who have their own worlds, be science. It can only be a *synthetic a priori* grasp of beings who have their own *synthetic a priori* grasps. Because consistency is essential for it, economics is both a priority of thought *and* an *a posteriority* of measure, but which balance rather than countermand one another. This balance is the unity of intuition and conception – the 'getting' of something needed to make a decision about it. Economic theory therefore is an epistemology of a decision maker, metaphysical only insofar as insisting on her personhood over any thinghood, and in that way both a call to moral action and a freedom to accept or reject it. Utility is the intuition behind such decisions, connecting outer with inner sense – outward to one's situation, inward to one's judgments about it. How important is this union of sense with concept where discursive decision-making occurs! Here we economists and philosophers are no better than decision makers are, in no position to treat them and their decisions as things, so that we know, better than they do, what is observable and rational for them and what isn't.

We have arrived then at the epistemic foundations, the transcendentality, of mainstream economics, our hypotheses for which were expressed at the outset of this work. To wit:

(i) Meaning: Empirical observations are *understood* through economic principles but evaluated through the decision maker's pure (*a priori*) intuition, *never in the observations themselves.*
(ii) Inference: Economic principles are *verified* by empirical observation but interpreted through the decision maker's pure intuition, *never in the principles themselves.*
(iii) Point of View: Economic expression is necessarily divided between the professional as professional and the person as person, the former referring symbolically to the latter, the latter mostly silent but each *synthetic a priori.*

Besides the formal dimension furthermore, which in economics is seemingly expressed in cause-and-effect terms, is the metaphysical: logical, aware of the moral call, and free. Logic, as applicable to all of reason, is metaphysical: strictly nonempirical and thus immediately, *a priori*, grasped (47). Moral rules, writes Kant, "cannot be obtained by abstraction from any empirical, and thereby merely contingent, knowledge...." (35). Rather, "all *moral conceptions* have their seat and origin completely *a priori* in the reason" so are entirely certain (35). At the same time the metaphysical's moral element is itself *in*determinate on account of our absolute freedom to obey it or disobey it. So while our knowledge of the metaphysical – logic and the moral law – is certain, the events in it, insofar as free, are not. Here the situation is the reverse of the formal, transcendental dimension, where it is *cognition* (pure intuition, schematization to categories) that is uncertain but empirical *events* (empirical intuition) are not.

And this structure, which presumes the subject to be a person, is via Kant the metaphysico-transcendental, the hylomorphic structure or world comprising mainstream economics. When the subject is presumed to be a thing instead, the dimension of freedom drops away from the metaphysical leaving only noncontradiction, necessity, and sufficiency and their world of caused objects – that is to say, a mechanical economics.

If mainstream economics on the other hand isn't *synthetic a priori*, its modeling and statistical applications – namely its entire point – fall immediately apart. For an econometric error term is nothing but the difference between an observed, empirical variable and a model-estimated, unobservable, formal one. It points, that is, to a judged conformability, a correspondence or unity, between an empirical (*synthetic*) and a pure (*a priori*) sensibility: a human person.

Index

For Product Safety Concerns and Information please contact our
EU representative GPSR@taylorandfrancis.com Taylor & Francis
Verlag GmbH, Kaufingerstraße 24, 80331 München, Germany